SYLLABIC WRITI

AND ITS C'

This volume offers a new and interdisciplinary treatment of syllabic writing in ancient Cyprus. A team of distinguished scholars tackles epigraphic, palaeographic, linguistic, archaeological, historical and terminological problems relating to the island's writing systems in the Late Bronze Age and Iron Age, from the appearance of writing around the fifteenth century down to the end of the first millennium BC. The result is not intended to be a single, unified view of the scripts and their context, but rather a varied collection that demonstrates a range of interpretations of the evidence and challenges some of the longstanding or traditional views of the population of ancient Cyprus and its epigraphic habits. This is the first comprehensive account of the 'Cypro-Minoan' and 'Cypriot syllabic' scripts to appear in a single volume, and forms an invaluable resource for anyone studying Cypriot epigraphy or archaeology.

PHILIPPA M. STEELE is the Lumley Research Fellow in Classics at Magdalene College, Cambridge, and is an affiliated lecturer in the Faculty of Classics. Her publications and research interests cover the scripts and languages of ancient Cyprus, multilingualism in the ancient eastern Mediterranean, the development of the Greek dialects, and the Mycenaean administration and economy. Her doctoral thesis, 'A Linguistic History of Cyprus', was awarded Cambridge University's prestigious Hare Prize for the best Classical thesis.

CAMBRIDGE CLASSICAL STUDIES

SYLLABIC WRITING ON CYPRUS AND ITS CONTEXT

Edited by

PHILIPPA M. STEELE

CAMBRIDGE
UNIVERSITY PRESS

CAMBRIDGE
UNIVERSITY PRESS

University Printing House, Cambridge CB2 8BS, United Kingdom

One Liberty Plaza, 20th Floor, New York, NY 10006, USA

477 Williamstown Road, Port Melbourne, VIC 3207, Australia

4843/24, 2nd Floor, Ansari Road, Daryaganj, Delhi - 110002, India

79 Anson Road, #06-04/06, Singapore 079906

Cambridge University Press is part of the University of Cambridge.

It furthers the University's mission by disseminating knowledge in the pursuit of
education, learning and research at the highest international levels of excellence.

www.cambridge.org
Information on this title: www.cambridge.org/9781108442343

© Faculty of Classics, University of Cambridge 2013

First published 2013
First paperback edition 2017

A catalogue record for this publication is available from the British Library

Library of Congress Cataloging in Publication data
Syllabic writing on Cyprus and its context / edited by Philippa M. Steele.
p. cm. – (Cambridge classical studies)
ISBN 978-1-107-02671-1 (hardback)
1. Writing – Cyprus – History. 2. Cypriot syllabary. I. Steele, Philippa M.,
1983–
P211.3.C9S95 2012
411'.7093937–dc23
2012020516

ISBN 978-1-107-02671-1 Hardback
ISBN 978-1-108-44234-3 Paperback

CONTENTS

CONTENTS

FIGURES

TABLES

CONTRIBUTORS

YVES DUHOUX is Professor Emeritus at the Catholic University of Louvain (Louvain-la-Neuve, Belgium), where he has taught Greek language, Greek epigraphy and the history of the Oriental scripts. He is a member of the Académie des Lettres et Sciences humaines du Canada and of various scholarly associations, and has received the Michael Ventris Memorial Award (Triopian Foundation for Archaeological Research, Chicago, USA) and the Joseph Gantrelle Award (Classical Philology) of the Académie Royale des Sciences, des Lettres et des Beaux-Arts de Belgique. His research interests include the Greek language (from Linear B to the Classical period), Prehellenic languages from Greece and Cyprus, Indo-European linguistics, and Greek, Prehellenic and other scripts.

MARKUS EGETMEYER is Professor of Linguistics at the Greek Department of the Sorbonne. He studied Comparative Indo-European Linguistics and Classics in Würzburg, Munich, Pisa and Paris. His main research interests focus on the Indo-European languages of the Mediterranean area and the Aegean syllabic scripts. He published a grammar of Cypriot Greek in 2010, and is currently working alongside Artemis Karnava and Massimo Perna to compile a corpus of inscriptions in the Cypro-Greek syllabary for the *Inscriptiones Graecae* in Berlin.

SILVIA FERRARA is a research fellow in Aegean Prehistory at Rome 'la Sapienza'. She studied at University College London and at Oxford. After her PhD in Classics in 2005, she became Junior Research Fellow in Archaeology at St John's College, Oxford. She was also granted a Gerda Henkel scholarship at Oxford, Classics Faculty. She taught at University College London, Oxford and Cambridge. Her interests focus on the writing systems of the second millennium BC from the Aegean (Linear A and B), Cyprus

(Cypro-Minoan) and the Near East (alphabetic and syllabic cuneiform, especially from Ugarit in Syria). More broadly, she is interested in reconstructing the sociolinguistic dynamics involved in the creation, development and borrowing of ancient writing systems. Her next monograph seeks to analyse the modes of communication enacted across cultural divides in the eastern Mediterranean during the Bronze Age, and the different writing traditions and scribal practices, especially those observable in multilingual and multicultural environments.

MARIA IACOVOU is Professor of Prehistoric and Protohistoric Archaeology in the Department of History and Archaeology of the University of Cyprus. She received her PhD from the Department of Classics of the University of Cincinnati (1984). She was for ten years (1987–97) Director of the Bank of Cyprus Cultural Foundation, where she had the opportunity to work extensively on the historical cartography of Cyprus and on Cypriot coinage. She was elected Associate Professor in the Department of History and Archaeology in 1998 and Professor in 2009. She was Stanley Seeger Visiting Research Fellow of the Hellenic Studies Programme at Princeton (2006), British Academy Visiting Professor at the Institute of Archaeology, Oxford (2004) and Foreign Research Fellow of the Alexander Onassis Foundation in Greece (2005). In 2011, she was the Onassis Foundation Visiting Scholar in the USA. She is director (since 2006) of the 'Palaepaphos Urban Landscape Project'.

JEAN-PIERRE OLIVIER is Honorary Research Director at the National Fund for Scientific Research in Belgium. He graduated with the Libera docenza in filologia micenea at the University of Rome (Italy) in 1964, the Doctorat en philologie classique at the University of Brussels (Belgium) in 1965 and the Doctorat d'État ès lettres (France) in 1976. His research interests include Cretan and Cypriot syllabic epigraphy of the second and first millennia BC, and he is currently working alongside Louis Godart to publish a comprehensive corpus edition of the Mycenaean texts from Pylos, *Corpus des tablettes en linéaire B de Pylos*.

CONTRIBUTORS

MASSIMO PERNA is Professore a contratto di Archeologia egea at the Università degli Studi 'Suor Orsola Benincasa' di Napoli, where he is a member of the Centro mediterraneo preclassico. His research interests include the Mycenaean economy and the syllabic scripts of the Mediterranean. He is currently working with Markus Egetmeyer and Artemis Karnava to compile a corpus of inscriptions in the Cypro-Greek syllabary for the *Inscriptiones Graecae* in Berlin.

SUSAN SHERRATT is a lecturer in the Department of Archaeology, University of Sheffield. She studied Classics at New Hall, Cambridge, and went on to complete a DPhil on Aegean pottery of the twelfth century BC. Her main research interests are in the Bronze and Early Iron Ages of the Aegean, Cyprus and the wider eastern Mediterranean, particularly in all aspects of trade and interaction within and beyond these regions.

PHILIPPA M. STEELE is the Lumley Research Fellow in Classics at Magdalene College, Cambridge, and is an Affiliated Lecturer in the Faculty of Classics, where she teaches Greek, Latin and Classical Linguistics to undergraduate and graduate students. She also directs studies at Homerton College, where she has built up the Classics department in recent years. Her publications and research interests include work on the scripts and languages of ancient Cyprus, multilingualism in the ancient eastern Mediterranean, the development of the Greek dialects and the Mycenaean administration and economy. Her doctoral thesis, 'A Linguistic History of Cyprus', was awarded Cambridge University's prestigious Hare Prize for the best Classical thesis.

ACKNOWLEDGEMENTS

The editor would like to thank the staff at Cambridge University Press for their kindness and assistance at every turn in the preparation of this book, in particular Michael Sharp, Josephine Lane, Teresa Royle, Gillian Dadd and Thomas O'Reilly, as well as the copy-editor, Christopher Jackson, for his diligence and thoroughness in scrutinising and editing the manuscript. The generosity and guidance of Geoff Horrocks and Robin Osborne, as members of the editorial board of the CUP Cambridge Classical Studies series, were greatly appreciated. Thanks are also owed to everyone who made the conference, from which this book arises, possible: the generous financial contributions of the E Caucus and Chadwick Funds of the Faculty of Classics and the Graduate Exhibition Fund of King's College, Cambridge; and the staff of the Faculty of Classics and the many colleagues who gave up their time to help in various aspects of organising and running the conference. Finally, I must thank my partner, James, especially for his meticulous attention to detail in assisting me on the days of the conference, and my mother, who has endlessly encouraged and supported me through every stage of organising the conference and editing this book.

ABBREVIATIONS

Docs[1]	Ventris, M. G. F. and Chadwick, J. (1956) *Documents in Mycenaean Greek*, 1st edn, Cambridge.
Docs[2]	Ventris, M. G. F. and Chadwick, J. (1973) *Documents in Mycenaean Greek*, 2nd edn, Cambridge.
Docs[3]	Killen, J. T. and Morpurgo Davies, A. (eds.) (in press) *Documents in Mycenaean Greek*, 3rd edn, Cambridge.
GORILA	Godart, L. and Olivier, J.-P. (1976–85) *Recueil des inscriptions en linéaire A*, 5 vols., Paris.
HoChyMin	J.-P. Olivier, with the collaboration of F. Vandenabeele (2007) *Edition holistique des textes chypro-minoens*, Pisa/Rome.
ICS[1], *ICS*[2]	Masson, O. (1961)[1], (1983, reprint with supplement)[2] *Les inscriptions chypriotes syllabiques. Recueil critique et commenté*, Paris.
Kouklia	Masson, O. and Mitford, T. B. (1986) *Les inscriptions syllabiques de Kouklia-Paphos*, Constance.
PM I	Evans, A. J. (1921) *The Palace of Minos at Knossos, volume I*, London.
PM II	Evans, A. J. (1928) *The Palace of Minos at Knossos, volume II*, London.
PM IV	Evans, A. J. (1935) *The Palace of Minos at Knossos, volume IV*, London.
Rantidi	Mitford, T. B. and Masson, O. (1983) *The Syllabic Inscriptions of Rantidi-Paphos*, Constance.
SM I	Evans, A. J. (1909) *Scripta Minoa, I. The Hieroglyphic and Primitive Linear Classes*, Oxford.

CONCORDANCE OF *HOCHYMIN* INSCRIPTIONS CITED

Cypro-Minoan inscriptions are referred to throughout the text by their main numbering in *HoChyMin*. The list below may be consulted for the full reference to each inscription (in numerical order, with encoded information about their place of origin and object type).

##001. ENKO Atab 001
##002. ENKO Abou 001
##003. ENKO Abou 002
##004. ENKO Abou 003
##005. ENKO Abou 004
##006. ENKO Abou 005
##007. ENKO Abou 006
##008. ENKO Abou 007
##009. ENKO Abou 008
##010. ENKO Abou 009
##011. ENKO Abou 010
##012. ENKO Abou 011
##013. ENKO Abou 012
##014. ENKO Abou 013
##015. ENKO Abou 014
##016. ENKO Abou 015
##017. ENKO Abou 015bis
##018. ENKO Abou 016
##019. ENKO Abou 016bis
##020. ENKO Abou 017
##021. ENKO Abou 018
##022. ENKO Abou 019
##023. ENKO Abou 020
##024. ENKO Abou 021
##025. ENKO Abou 022
##026. ENKO Abou 023
##027. ENKO Abou 024
##028. ENKO Abou 025
##029. ENKO Abou 026
##030. ENKO Abou 027

##031. ENKO Abou 028
##032. ENKO Abou 029
##033. ENKO Abou 030
##034. ENKO Abou 031
##035. ENKO Abou 032
##036. ENKO Abou 033
##037. ENKO Abou 034
##038. ENKO Abou 035
##039. ENKO Abou 036
##040. ENKO Abou 037
##041. ENKO Abou 038
##042. ENKO Abou 039
##043. ENKO Abou 040
##044. ENKO Abou 041
##045. ENKO Abou 042
##046. ENKO Abou 043
##047. ENKO Abou 044
##048. ENKO Abou 045
##049. ENKO Abou 046
##050. ENKO Abou 047
##051. ENKO Abou 048
##052. ENKO Abou 049
##053. ENKO Abou 050
##054. ENKO Abou 051
##055. ENKO Abou 052
##056. ENKO Abou 053
##057. ENKO Abou 054
##058. ENKO Abou 055
##059. ENKO Abou 056
##060. ENKO Abou 057

##149. KOUR Avas 001
##150. KOUR Avas 002
##151. KOUR Avas 003
##152. KOUR Avas 004
##153. MAAP Avas 001
##154. MAAP Avas 002
##155. MAAP Avas 003
##156. MAAP Avas 004
##157. MARO Avas 001
##158. MYRT Avas 001
##159. MYRT Avas 002
##160. TOUM Avas 001
##161. KITI Iins 001
##162. KITI Iins 002
##163. KITI Ipla 001
##164. ENKO Mbij 001
##165. KALA Mbij 001
##166. KALA Mbij 002
##167. KITI Mexv 001
##168. ENKO Mins 001
##169. ENKO? Mins 002
##170. PPAP Mins 001
##171. PPAP Mins 002
##172. PPAP Mins 003
##173. PYLA Mins 001
##174. ENKO Mlin 001
##175. ENKO Mlin 002
##176. ENKO Mlin 003
##177. PYLA Mlin 001
##178. CYPR Mvas 001
##179. CYPR Mvas 002
##180. CYPR Mvas 003
##181. CYPR Mvas 004
##182. ENKO Mvas 001
##183. ENKO Mvas 002

##184. MYRT Mvas 001
##185. MYRT Mvas 002
##186. PPAP Mvas 001
##187. ENKO Pblo 001
##188. KITI Pblo 001
##189. PPAP Pblo 001
##190. PPAP Pblo 002
##191. KALA Ppla 001
##192. KALA Ppla 002
##193. CYPR? Psce 001
##194. CYPR? Psce 002
##195. CYPR Psce 003
##196. CYPR? Psce 004
##197. CYPR? Psce 005
##198. CYPR? Psce 006
##199. ENKO Psce 001
##200. ENKO? Psce 002
##201. HALA Psce 001
##202. KOUR Psce 001
##203. PARA Psce 001
##204. PYLA Psce 001
##205. SALA Psce 001
##206. PPAP Vsce 001
##207. ENKO Atab 002
##208. ENKO Atab 003
##209. ENKO Atab 004
##210. RASH Aéti 001
##211. RASH Aéti 002
##212. RASH Atab 001
##213. RASH Atab 002
##214. RASH Atab 003
##215. RASH Atab 004
##216. RASH Mvas 001
##217. SYRI Psce 001

INTRODUCTION: SYLLABIC WRITING
ON CYPRUS AND ITS CONTEXT

PHILIPPA M. STEELE

The papers that comprise this volume focus on the syllabic scripts of ancient Cyprus, which fall into two principal groups: the small number of undeciphered texts mostly dated to the second millennium BC (usually termed 'Cypro-Minoan'); and the somewhat larger number of texts dated to the first millennium BC (traditionally labelled the 'Cypriot Syllabary'), most of which are written in the Greek language, while a few are demonstrably non-Greek, although their language remains unidentified.[1] The contributing authors take a number of different approaches to these scripts, be they epigraphic, linguistic, palaeographic, contextual or archaeological. The result is not intended to be a single, unified view of the scripts and their context, but rather a varied collection that demonstrates a range of interpretations of the evidence and challenges some of the longstanding or traditional views of the population of ancient Cyprus and its epigraphic habits.

The volume was conceived in the wake of a conference of the same name, held in December 2008 with the generous support of the John Chadwick Fund and E Caucus Fund of the Faculty of Classics, and the Graduate Exhibition Fund of King's College, Cambridge; a great many thanks are owed to everyone who made that meeting possible, and especially to the speakers, who kindly agreed to contribute their papers to this volume. It was obvious when the conference was convened that there was some gap to be filled in the published scholarship on Cypriot epigraphy. As far

---

[1] For further comment on the terminology applied to these two groups, see below. At least one first-millennium BC unidentified language can be found in inscriptions from the western part of the island (primarily at Amathus on the south coast) and is usually termed 'Eteocypriot' (see Steele 2011; in press: ch. 2), and there may be a second in the eastern area around Golgoi (see Egetmeyer 2012).

I

back as 1986, a conference entitled 'The History of the Greek Language in Cyprus' took place in Larnaca, bringing together some of the most prominent scholars working at the time on Cypriot Greek in various contexts, with an overwhelming focus on dialectological and similar concerns; its proceedings, edited by Jacqueline Karageorghis and Olivier Masson, appeared two years later.[2] Since then, however, there has been no published single meeting that has concentrated on Cypriot epigraphy or linguistics, even though archaeologically based symposia treating Cyprus during various periods of the second and first millennia BC have been relatively frequent. The published study of ancient Cypriot languages and scripts in the last twenty years has been largely confined to articles appearing in relevant journals and 'Mycenological' colloquia, as well as a few monographs treating particular groups of texts.[3] A meeting focusing on the Cypriot epigraphic material was a clear desideratum, and it was the inter-disciplinary discourse arising from the conference that formed the basic idea for this book.

The structure of this volume

The volume is arranged so that, following an initial chapter whose aim is to present the current state of knowledge of the syllabic Cypriot scripts, a broadly chronological approach is taken, with the writings of the Late Bronze Age tackled before those of the Bronze to Iron Age transition and later the Iron Age itself. However, many of the chapters overlap, and not only chronologically but also in terms of the material treated and sometimes of the approach applied to that material. The reader may wish to peruse the whole volume as a continuous account of the current debates on Cypriot epigraphy and related disciplines, or he or she may dip into one chapter or another as preferred.

The opening chapter, 'The development of Cypriot syllabaries, from Enkomi to Kafizin' by Jean-Pierre Olivier, gives a comprehensive account of the syllabic scripts of ancient Cyprus in the

---

[2] J. Karageorghis and O. Masson 1988.
[3] E.g. Egetmeyer 1992; *HoChyMin*; Egetmeyer 2010a.

second and first millennia BC, detailing the surviving evidence and our current understanding of it. A large part of this chapter was drawn from Olivier's contribution to the as yet unpublished third edition of *Documents in Mycenaean Greek* (*Docs³*), and is reproduced here with the kind permission of Cambridge University Press.

A second chapter by Yves Duhoux follows, 'Non Greek languages of ancient Cyprus and their scripts: Cypro-Minoan 1–3', which highlights some areas of Cypriot epigraphy where there remains some room for dispute, in particular the relations between different categorisations of Cypro-Minoan, approached from an orthographic/linguistic point of view. The emphasis here is shifted to specific methodological concerns, which are of considerable importance when dealing with undeciphered and poorly attested scripts.

Silvia Ferrara's chapter on 'Writing in Cypro-Minoan: one script, too many?' (Chapter 3) then takes a pointedly interdisciplinary approach, looking at palaeography and demonstrating the importance of considering the Cypro-Minoan inscriptions not only as texts but also as objects, with a full archaeological and cultural context. Chapter 4, by Susan Sherratt, on 'Late Cypriot writing in context' follows, presenting an important challenge to common conceptions – potentially misconceptions – about the origins of scripts within a backdrop of the complex political geography of the second millennium BC Aegean and eastern Mediterranean.

Moving on to the first millennium BC, Markus Egetmeyer contributes Chapter 5, 'From the Cypro-Minoan to the Cypro-Greek syllabaries: linguistic remarks on the script reform', which tackles the issue of the elusive 'script reform' that must be assumed to have taken place to account for the transition from Cypro-Minoan to a new script adapted for the Greek language. Maria Iacovou's chapter, on 'The Cypriot syllabary as a royal signature: the political context of the syllabic script in the Iron Age' (Chapter 6), follows, giving an account of the administrative background of the use of this new script in the first millennium BC Cypriot city states. As well as demonstrating the close links between visible writing and political power, this chapter emphasises the importance of considering the political geography of Cyprus over time, since it is clear that the major Cypriot polities known from the Iron Age historical record had their origins in the Late Bronze Age.

The final chapter is contributed by Massimo Perna on 'Rethinking some alphabetic and syllabic Cypriot inscriptions' and provides a thought-provoking postscript to the study of ancient Cypriot scripts, highlighting and correcting some misinterpretations of epigraphic evidence. He also gives some indication of the future prospects of the study of Cypriot epigraphy, reporting on a collaboration that in time will produce the first full and comprehensive corpus edition of Cypriot syllabic inscriptions of the first millennium BC.

A note on terminology

One potentially problematic feature of modern discussions of ancient Cyprus such as those found in this book, owing not least to the complex and multidisciplinary history of the study of the island, is that there will often be some significant variation in terminology used from author to author. The variation is by no means random; indeed, for at least some of the authors in this volume the issue of terminology is important or even central to their argument. However, for the unversed reader who may want to dip into one or another of the chapters, or for a scholar with experience from only one side of the multidisciplinary sphere or the other (an epigraphist with little experience of archaeological scholarship, for example, or vice versa), there follows a brief guide to the terminology that will be encountered in this book.

The syllabic scripts of ancient Cyprus have been divided broadly into two groups. From the earliest appearance of writing on the island around the sixteenth or fifteenth century BC down to the period around 900 BC, a group of rather disparate inscriptions have survived, written in a script that is evidently related in some way to Linear A and B and has traditionally been labelled 'Cypro-Minoan'. Although preserving labels such as CM 1, CM 2 and CM 3 (where CM = 'Cypro-Minoan') for the sake of convenience, Olivier prefers to use a temporal reference to 'second-millennium syllabaries' (in the plural because it seems that multiple similar writing systems are represented).[4] Similarly, Sherratt eschews 'Cypro-Minoan', arguing that, as a biased term emphasising the hypothetical link between this and the Cretan linear scripts, it should be dropped in favour of a term such as 'Bronze Age Cypriot'. However, Duhoux, Ferrara and Egetmeyer continue to use 'Cypro-Minoan', as do many other scholars outside of this volume.

The other group of inscriptions, whose main body dates from the eighth to third centuries BC, has traditionally been referred to as the 'Cypriot Syllabary' (or also 'Cypriot Syllabic', 'Classical Cypriot' or the 'Classical Cypriot Syllabary'), with two sub-divisions of 'Paphian' (usually reading from left to right and found in the south-western area around Paphos) and 'common' (usually reading from right to left and found across the rest of the island) comprising slightly different repertoires of signs. Olivier again prefers a temporal categorisation ('first-millennium syllabaries'; a similar term appears in Perna's chapter), while Egetmeyer introduces 'Cypro-Greek' (abbreviated to CG; in parallel with Cypro-Minoan, and emphasising that the script was adapted specifically to write Greek), and Duhoux uses the more complex 'nCMCs' ('non-Cypro-Minoan Cypriot syllabaries'). Although the reasons for questioning and even overhauling terminology in these areas are obvious, many scholars today continue to use traditional labels, and it is as yet uncertain whether any of the currently proposed replacements will find lasting popularity. For now, however, 'Cypro-Minoan' remains a common choice for the earlier group of texts, and for the later group the publication of Egetmeyer's recent definitive account of the Cypriot Greek dialect, *Le dialecte grec ancien de Chypre* (Egetmeyer 2010a), which uses 'Cypro-Greek' rather than the 'Cypriot Syllabary', will undoubtedly have considerable influence.

Another aspect of terminology that has the potential to cause confusion is in the area of dating. Two types of date will most often be encountered: relative (usually based on ceramic phases, for

---

[4] For varying viewpoints on the issue of multiple writing systems (and potentially languages) present in Cypro-Minoan, see the chapters by Olivier, Duhoux and Ferrara in this volume.

example LC III or CG I, i.e. Late Cypriot III and Cypro-Geometric I respectively) and absolute (for example 'twelfth century BC' or 'c. 1000 BC'). The assignment of absolute dates to ceramic sequences is a matter of some contention, especially when it comes to comparing dating sequences in different areas of the Mediterranean and trying to align stratigraphy in Cyprus with that seen in, for example, Greece or Phoenicia.[5] The following table may be consulted for a rough and generally accepted estimate of the absolute dates to be assigned to the ceramic phases on ancient Cyprus (after Iacovou 2008a: 656):

Late Cypriot I–II	1700–1450
Late Cypriot IIA–B	1450–1300
Late Cypriot IIC	1300–1200
Late Cypriot IIIA	1200–1125/1100
Late Cypriot IIIB	1125/1100–1050
Cypro-Geometric I–III	1050–750
Cypro-Archaic	750–480
Cypro-Classical	480–310
Ptolemaic/Hellenistic	310–30
Roman	30 BC–AD 330

The very fact that the terminology and indeed the categorisations used in the field of Cypriot epigraphy and related disciplines are not straightforward in itself may be taken to demonstrate the importance of the discourse found in this book. The contributors each approach ancient Cyprus from a slightly different point of view, privileging the evidence and methodologies that are most important to their argument. But they also make their approach accessible to scholars of different backgrounds and different viewpoints, and it is through this overarching interdisciplinary dialogue that this volume will, I hope, be of use and of interest to any student of ancient Cyprus and its languages, scripts and material culture.

---

[5] For example, the famous eleventh- or tenth-century BC inscription from Palaepaphos bearing the name *Opheltas* is just one of the important objects whose dating might be called into question based on potential reassessments of alternative chronologies for Cyprus and other areas such as the Levant; see Gilboa and Sharon 2003: 72.

THE DEVELOPMENT OF CYPRIOT SYLLABARIES, FROM ENKOMI TO KAFIZIN

JEAN-PIERRE OLIVIER

This contribution is largely inspired by the section 'The Cypriot syllabaries' which I wrote in 2005 for the chapter on 'Syllabic scripts in the Aegean and Cyprus of the second and first millennia' in the forthcoming third edition of *Documents in Mycenaean Greek*, edited by John Killen and Anna Morpurgo Davies = *Docs*[3].

The parallel and subsequent redaction and publication of the 'holistic' edition of the Cypro-Minoan scripts (*HoChyMin*) allowed me to refine the tables of signs, but my fundamental views about the development of the Cypriot syllabaries remained unchanged: they are the result of fifteen years of work on these still insufficiently studied scripts.

The Cypriot syllabaries of the second millennium

1   The pre-fifteenth-century origins and the syllabaries in general

Evans 1909,[1] on the basis of only fifteen different signs on three inscribed 'balls' and on an engraved ring from Enkomi, already glimpsed the relation between the Cretan writings and what he dubbed 'Cypro-Minoan'. The question of the route by which Linear A arrived in Cyprus is a debatable one, as J. Karageorghis showed;[2] and one can argue about 'eastern' influences on the handwriting, appearance, lay-out and even 'contents' of the first Enkomi tablet (Figure 1.2), as Godart and Sacconi 1979 have done. Their thesis is convincingly refuted by Palaima.[3] Nevertheless, there can be no doubt about the Cretan origin of the Cypriot syllabaries.

---

[1] *SM* I 70–3.   [2] J. Karageorghis 1958: 14–16.   [3] Palaima 1989a: 136–41.

Table 1.1 *Linear B (B) and first-millennium Cypriot (C):
homomorphs and homophones (basically following O. Masson
1956b: 202 and Docs²: 388). Linear A (A) and Cypro-Minoan
(CM) forms are added on the left*

A	CM	B	C	Phonetic value B/C
├ AB 01	├	├	├	*da/ta*
╪ AB 02	╪	╪	╪	*ro/lo*
╪ AB 03	╪	╪	╪	*pa*
╤ AB 05	╪ ╕	╤	⊢ 'common' ∧ Paphian	*to*
╤ AB 06	╤ ╤	╤	╤	*na*
╓ AB 08	╓ ╓	╓	✳	*a*
╜ AB 09	╜	╜	╜	*se*
ʄ AB 10	(	ʄ	∧ Paphian	*u*
╕ AB 11	•	╕	✓	*po*
Y AB 31	V	Ψ	V	*sa*
∧ AB 37	∧	∧	∧	*ti*
⅃ ʟ AB 60	Ɣ	ʟ	∨ ∨	*ra/la*
╦ ╦ AB 67	ʯ	ʯ	╩	*ki*
I AB 75 (= A 319)	I	ʔ	I Z	*we*

The dozen or so homomorphous and homophonous signs in
Linear B and in the Cypriot syllabaries of the first millennium
(Table 1.1) can only have originated both graphically *and* phonetically in a Linear A that was the ancestor of both Linear B and the
syllabaries of the first millennium (via Cypro-Minoan, in the case
of the latter).

One will notice that in the column corresponding to Cypro-Minoan,
to date, no syllabogram equivalent to *po* has been discovered, very
probably due to chance, just as, up until 2005, in Linear A we lacked
the sign ✳ AB 48 = H 006, the existence of which had nevertheless
been predicted in *Docs¹*.[4] And in 2005, it was read on a libation
table found in Kato Symi in 1988 by Lebessi, a complete inscription
(SY Za 4)[5] showing the missing A 48 (Figure 1.1, tenth sign):

---

[4] *Docs¹*: 40.   [5] Cf. Muhly and Olivier 2008: 207–8.

1.1 SY Za 4 with the sign AB 48 (after Muhly and Olivier 2008).

1.2 The first Enkomi tablet (*HoChyMin* ##001).

What we have displayed in Figure 1.2 is no longer Linear A but not yet Cypro-Minoan.[6] E. Masson was wrong to combine the signs of this inscription with those of two other inscriptions,[7] which she dated to the fifteenth century; she described this set as 'archaic' but was relying on an unjustified amalgamation of disparate items.[8] The major differences detectable between the syllabary of this tablet and the signs of *all* the other Cypriot documents of the second millennium (cf. Table 1.2) are hard to explain, even if one supposes there to have been a very rapid evolution. Given that it was found at Enkomi, the writing is, in some way, an ancestor of Cypro-Minoan, but here the mutation is not complete, and the new writing with which we are familiar elsewhere has not yet been created.

The fourth question is destined to remain unanswered until such time as other documentation has been discovered – somewhere between Crete and Syria (but even such a discovery might not be adequate).

---

[6] That is why I dubbed it 'CM 0' in *HoChyMin* in order to avoid any confusion.
[7] *HoChyMin* ##129 and ##095.
[8] E. Masson 1974: 11–12; nonetheless the date itself, though questionable, is not impossible.

Table 1.2 *The second-millennium* BC *Cypriot syllabaries (CM 1, CM 2, CM 3) compared with Linear A (A) at left and the first-millennium Cypriot syllabaries (CC) at right*

Three decades after Evans, Daniel began to individualise and classify the signs of Cypro-Minoan on the basis of the main evidence at his disposal, namely the marks on vases.[9] Olivier Masson 1957c drew up a list of the inscriptions, and Emilia Masson published most of the documents and then compiled tables of the signs (in 1974 and 1985).

She distinguished three syllabaries:[10]

Cypro-Minoan 1 (CM 1)   from the fifteenth century to the eleventh, used throughout the island, on all kinds of objects; 206 documents with *c.* 1,300 signs

Cypro-Minoan 2 (CM 2)   from the twelfth century, at Enkomi, on 3 large fragmentary clay tablets bearing *c.* 2,000 signs

---

[9] Daniel 1941: 249–82.   [10] E. Masson 1974: 11–17.

Cypro-Minoan 3 (CM 3)   from the thirteenth century, at Ras Shamra (Ugarit) on the Syro-Palestinian coast, on tablets and other types of material; 8 documents bearing *c.* 350 signs

Palaima's critique,[11] according to which all three groups feature the *same* writing, should be rejected. Table 1.2 shows that CM 2 (sixty-one signs) includes seventeen signs that are new as compared with the forty-three signs that it shares with CM 1 (seventy-two signs). In other words, 39 per cent of its signs are new. In comparison, Linear B includes twenty-three signs that are new in relation to the sixty-four signs that it shares in common with Linear A; in other words, only 35 per cent of its signs are new. Of course, CM 1 does not constitute a homogeneous whole – any more than Linear A does! – but CM 2, for its part, represents the most coherent and most extensive palaeographic group of all the Cretan and Cypriot writings. As for CM 3 (fifty signs), the six signs that are to be found neither in CM 1 nor in CM 2 likewise might indicate a quite separate script. CM 1 and CM 2 thus constitute *two* scripts, used to record *two* languages; as for CM 3, it may have been used for several of the other languages spoken in Ugarit in the thirteenth century (not only the language noted by CM 1, but Ugaritic, Babylonian, Hurrian, Hittite, Egyptian, etc.). With insufficient documentation, we cannot be sure. (It should be noted that, along with Hiller,[12] by CM 3 I mean all attestations of Cypro-Minoan writing at Ras Shamra. It would be more correct to follow E. Masson and try to distinguish between CM 1 and CM 3 on the Syrian coast, but at the moment this turns out to be almost impossible).

Furthermore, contrary to what Palaima suggests,[13] the *c.* 1,500 legible syllabograms of CM 2, as well as the *c.* 1,300 signs of CM 1, guarantee that the syllabaries that they represent are more or less complete (while CM 3, with its *c.* 350 signs only, does not reach that level). The Idalion tablet,[14] which, with its 1,010 syllabograms, provides 51 of the 55 signs of the theoretical syllabary of the first millennium, in itself points to the above conclusions, without it being necessary to resort to a statistical analysis.

---

[11] Palaima 1989a: 155–61.   [12] Hiller 1985: 72–3.
[13] Palaima 1989a: 124–5 and 157–8.   [14] *ICS* 217.

2   CM 1 *(fifteenth–eleventh centuries)*

The 206 CM 1 inscriptions, with *c.* 1,300 signs, are found on many kinds of materials and objects throughout the island. The explanation for why over half come from Enkomi is the intensive nature of the excavations carried out there.

– clay:	• 1 tablet: *HoChyMin* ##001
	• 90 'balls' (spheres, *c.* 2 cm. in diameter, bearing an average of 5 signs): ##002–091
	• 1 terracotta disk: ##092
	• 2 ostraca: ##093–094
	• 1 'loomweight': ##095
	• 1 wall plaque (?): ##096
	• 6 'cylinders' (of *c.* 2 to 4 cm. in diameter and *c.* 3 to 6 cm. high, the 2 intact specimens of which bear respectively 27 lines with 217 signs and 18 lines with 141 signs): ##097–102
	• 1 statuette: ##103
	• 57 vases (engraved or painted, either before or after firing): ##104–160
– ivory:	• 1 pipe: ##161
	• 1 rod: ##162
	• 1 decorated plaque: ##163
– metal:	• 14 objects of different types (bronze votive ingots, instruments, gold and silver jewellery, etc.): ##164–177
	• 9 vases (1 silver, 8 bronze): ##178–186
– stone:	• 4 blocks: ##187–190
	• 2 lids: ##191–192
	• 13 cylinder seals: ##193–205
– vitreous paste:	• 1 seal: ##206.

The writing runs from left to right (with two or three right-to-left exceptions); all the texts, except those on the 'cylinders', are very short (between two and fifteen signs), and most must have carried no more than the name of a person or a dedication. Some word-dividers are attested (*c.* 140), but they are not employed systematically (even on the 'cylinders'). Only two *logograms* have been recognized, on the engraved ostracon from Enkomi, where they are followed by numbers.[15] Numbers, too, are rare: they appear

---

[15] *HoChyMin* ##093.

definitely on only four documents, the above-cited ostracon, a fragmentary 'cylinder' from Kalavassos (##101), the silver bowl from Enkomi (##182) and the ivory rod from Kition (##162).[16] This rarity of non-syllabograms is linked with the *nature* of the documents that have survived, none of which belongs to an accounting archive. The same applies to CM 2 and to most of CM 3;[17] the situation remains similar in the first millennium. We should not allow our view of what a script is to be distorted by the Cretan 'logogrammatical' examples, for they are not representative: the notation of the language's sounds is of primary interest; all the rest is of secondary importance even if, in certain domains of human activity, accessories may become essential (like the numbers and logograms in accounting archives).

The outlook for decipherment is not promising:

- The dozen homophones-homomorphs in the Cypriot syllabaries of the first millennium and Linear B that derive from Linear A, in the first case via CM 1, in the second directly (Table 1.1), constitute no more than one-sixth of the CM 1 signs; the homomorphisms between CM 1 and the syllabaries of the first millennium that may be suspected in at least twenty pairs of signs do not, for their part, necessarily concern homophones,[18] and over thirty signs remain without any morphological equivalent.
- We have no inkling about the contents of the longer texts, those on the 'cylinders'.
- 'Reading' a personal name here in Greek, there in Ugaritic – or even Hurrian – in the best cases 'confirms' the phonetic values of homomorphs with the first-millennium syllabaries. However, with texts that are so short, this may simply be a matter of a vicious circle.

3   CM 2 (late twelfth century)

The three large, fragmentary clay tablets bearing *c.* 2,000 signs come from different quarters of the town of Enkomi.[19] They were discovered, without their context, amid rubble; moreover, one is the result of joining together a fragment from the north of the town

---

[16] On these, see Palaima 1989b: 43–50.
[17] With the possible exceptions of *HoChyMin* ##213 and ##214.
[18] It is exactly the same situation between Linear A and Linear B, *pace* all the would-be decipherers.
[19] *HoChyMin* ##207, ##208 and ##209.

with another from its southern centre.[20] This is reminiscent of the fills that contained archival documents in 'hieroglyphic', in Linear A and in Linear B in the palace of Knossos and in 'hieroglyphic' and in Linear A in the palace of Mallia. The date of the writing on these tablets could thus be a little earlier than that attributed to them by archaeology, but their similarities suggest that they are probably contemporary.

The format of the tablets is reminiscent of the rather more 'cushion-like' Near Eastern format than that of the Aegean 'page', and the direction of rotation for inscribing the reverse side, along the horizontal axis, although not unknown in Linear A and B, is far from being the most common. Originally, they measured c. 20 × 16 × 2–4 cm, and the text was generally presented on each face in two columns of about 45 lines; with an average of 20 signs a line, each tablet contained approximately 3,600 signs. The direction of the writing runs from left to right. Dividers between words are regularly employed. Whereas no such dividers were to be found in the earliest (and only) CM 0 tablet, here we find c. 340. On at least two of the documents, a heavy dot is positioned at the end of every ten lines. It no doubt serves as a line-count indicator. The reduced height of the signs (from c. 0.25 to 0.5 cm.) explains why certain drawings are more perfunctory than in CM 1 (for the 42 signs shared in common), but graphically the engraving of the characters produces very similar results in both writings.

We have no inkling of the contents of these tablets, although we do know for certain that they are not inventories, lists or letters, but rather long continuous texts that are very carefully composed; ##209 side A, which is the only face to be divided into 'squares' by horizontal rules after groups of two, three or four lines, shows the repetition of an identical group of three signs (in two different sequences) that we find at the end of the eleven 'squares' that are still complete, and thus offers a different kind of content whose meaning escapes us.

In view of the length and apparent coherence of the texts, the possibility of decipherment is not ruled out, provided that they are written in a known language. However, any attempt at deciphering

---

[20] Michaelidou-Nicolaou 1980: 10.

them should first involve a meticulous analysis of the signs, words and phrases and of the tablets themselves – an analysis that has already been largely undertaken, it must be said, by E. Masson, who first published these texts.

4   CM 3 (thirteenth century)

With only 8 documents with c. 350 signs, this 'script' (which, for the moment, constitutes no more than a convenient geographical grouping of disparate pieces originating mostly in Ras Shamra (Ugarit) on the Syrian-Palestinian coast) cannot, strictly speaking, be said to be one at all. It should therefore be treated with circumspection:

- in CM 1 (?): 2 fragments of *tablets* of 13 and 33 signs[21]
- in CM 3 *stricto sensu*: 2 tablets, one of 78 signs,[22] the other of 211 signs[23]
- of uncertain status: 2 'labels' bearing a seal impression, of 2 and 5 signs,[24] the second of which has not yet been published
- of debatable status: a cylinder seal of 4 signs[25] and a silver cup of 4 signs.[26]

The writing runs from left to right, except on one tablet,[27] on which it is boustrophedon, and on the silver cup,[28] on which it may be from right to left. Word-dividers are well attested. Both logograms and numbers are present on two tablets.[29]

Attempts to decipher the script have concentrated principally on the longest tablet,[30] upon which it has seemed possible to detect the formula 'X ₩ ⟨ Y', 'so-and-so, *son of* so-and-so', which is repeated eleven times in nineteen lines.[31] However, the identification of the language is not convincing.

For an overview of the attempts to decipher CM 1, CM 2 and CM 3, see Hiller 1985.[32] For a judgement of their value, we should side with Palaima, who declares: 'all past and current schemes of decipherment of Cypro-Minoan are improbable', adding only that nothing has changed since then.[33]

---

[21] *HoChyMin* ##213 and ##214.   [22] *HoChyMin* ##212.   [23] *HoChyMin* ##215.
[24] *HoChyMin* ##210 and ##211.   [25] *HoChyMin* ##217.   [26] *HoChyMin* ##216.
[27] *HoChyMin* ##212.   [28] *HoChyMin* ##216.   [29] *HoChyMin* ##213 and ##214.
[30] *HoChyMin* ##215.   [31] E. Masson 1974: 39.   [32] Hiller 1985: 79–92.
[33] Palaima 1989b: 121 (developed in 122–6 and *passim*).

The Cypriot syllabaries of the first millennium

1   The transition

In Greece, between the disappearance of Linear B at the end of the thirteenth century (when the Mycenaean palaces were destroyed) and the appearance of an alphabet in the eighth century, four centuries were to elapse *without writing*. In Cyprus, there is one period, the tenth and possibly the ninth centuries, *in which syllabic writing is not attested*. However, this must be due to a gap in documentation rather than to an illiterate hiatus, since the syllabic writings of the first millennium are the heirs of those of the second millennium, and there can have been no interruption in the written tradition.

At this point it should be noted that the Phoenician alphabet appeared in Cyprus as early as the ninth century,[34] whereas the Greek alphabet was not, to our knowledge, used there until the sixth century[35] (although the arrival of the earliest Greek-speaking peoples in Cyprus probably dates back to the late fifteenth century and was to be followed by successive waves of them, the last of which, the one that was to implant the Arcado-Cypriot dialect, arrived after the collapse of the Mycenaean kingdoms, in the twelfth century).

The largely accepted picture of a succession of syllabic writings between the second and the first millennia that E. and O. Masson have painted is misleading.[36] The inscription of five signs engraved on a bronze obelos found in 1979 by V. Karageorghis in a tomb in the Palaepaphos region (Figure 1.3, top),[37] along with vases from the period 1050–950, does *not* in truth represent 'a perfect example of a transitory phase in between Cypro-Minoan 1 and Old Paphian script',[38] for it *still is* Cypro-Minoan. This error of interpretation resulted from the fact that, in the 1980s, the second sign ʃ and the fifth ◀ were not recognized as belonging to CM 1; they were accordingly identified as 'Old Paphian' (sixth century), and the first

---

[34] O. Masson and M. Sznycer 1972: 13–20.   [35] Jeffery 1990: 346, 352.
[36] Together: E. Masson and O. Masson 1983; separately: O. Masson 1994.
[37] V. Karageorghis 1983: 60, 75; *HoChyMin* ##170.
[38] E. Masson and O. Masson 1983: 411.

1.3 The *Opheltas* obelos (*c*. 1050–950 BC) at top, 'Cypro-Minoan I version' (fifteenth–eleventh centuries) at centre, 'Old Paphian version' (sixth century) at bottom.

sign ẉ was also declared to be 'Paphian', although it really corresponds to a 'non-Paphian' *o* (the form of a Paphian *o* is ⊥, not Ɏ). In the present century, however:

1 A sign Ƨ (*011*: four times in CM 2) can be read at least twice (perhaps four times) on the clay cylinder from Enkomi[39] and once in an inscription[40] that E. Masson[41] left out of her table of CM I on the grounds that it was 'archaic' (sixteenth to fifteenth century).[42]

2 A ᛀ sign (*012*) 'opening toward the left' is attested several times in Cypro-Minoan, but only the ᚡ 'opening toward the right' was recognized by E. Masson, who, moreover, did not accept the equivalence between 'left-facing' and 'right-facing' forms such as ⊣ and ⊢ *004*, ᚴ and ᛏ *019*, ᛟ and ᛞ *044*, ᚢ and ᚤ *087*, the first, third and fourth pairs of which exist in Linear A (⊣ and ⊢ AB *01*, ᛀ and ᛁ AB *09* and ₂⌋ and |ₛ AB *60*). In Linear A, ᛀ and ᚡ AB *10* is also to be found and is probably the ancestor of CM ᛀ and ᚡ *012*.

This means that the five signs on the obelos do not constitute 'the most ancient syllabic Cypriot inscription [of the first millennium]' as O. Masson asserts in the title of his 1994 article, but they are in truth *the most recent inscription in CM I*. CM I, which is well attested in the eleventh century, contains all the signs on the obelos, so it is not necessary to invent, on the basis of sixth-century forms, writing that would be a kind of 'proto-Paphian' (Figure 1.3, bottom), which would furthermore contain a non-Paphian *o* (ẉ): CM I already provides the exact form ɏ, as it does all the other signs in the inscription (Figure 1.3, centre).

When one applies to these obelos signs the values of the homomorphic signs of the syllabic systems of the first millennium, the

---

[39] *HoChyMin* ##097.06, sign 2 and .12, sign 4.   [40] *HoChyMin* ##095.
[41] E. Masson 1974: 12 fig. 1 no. *I*.
[42] On the conflation of disparate items in this table, see above, p. 9.

Table 1.3 o-pe-le-ta-u = Ophéltau

CM 1	⚜	⟩	(ⁱ)	⊢	/\
new Paphian	⊥	⟩	/ĩ	⊢	人
'common'	⋙	⟩	8	⊢	Υ
phonetic values	o	pe	le	ta	u
= Greek	Ophéltau				

inscription is 'readable' through Greek (*o-pe-le-ta-u* = *Ophéltau*, the genitive of *Ophéltās*, Table 1.3), just as one of the inscriptions on the Enkomi clay balls is, perhaps, 'readable' in Ugaritic[43] (*i-li-pa-li* = *ilb'l*).[44] In both cases, all the signs may be found *in both scripts*, and whatever is noted with the signs of the first may be read with the phonetic values of the second. If the reading has any meaning in Greek (or in Ugaritic?), that is because we are dealing with an identifiable Greek (or Ugaritic?) personal name.

Evans proceeded in exactly the same way when he 'read' (or, to be more precise, refused to 'read', because the '*Minoan Cretans*' in his view could not speak Greek) the group of Linear B signs ⟋ ┼ '*po-lo*' = πῶλος 'foal' by attributing to it the phonetic values of the homomorphic Cypriot syllabic signs of the first millennium ⟩ and ┼.[45]

But one must be well aware that, even if the 'reading' is *not o-pe-le-ta-u*, the script is, and will remain, Cypro-Minoan. O. and E. Masson were misguided about the script, first, because they were looking, at all costs, for the 'missing link' between the syllabaries of Cypro-Minoan and the syllabaries of the first millennium and, second, because they had insufficient knowledge, at the time, of the CM I syllabary.

To be sure, this reassessment once again raises the question of the date of the creation of the first-millennium syllabary, but it does

[43] *HoChyMin* ##080. [44] E. Masson 1974: 40. [45] *PM* IV, 799, n. 3.

not affect the hiatus of the tenth and ninth centuries, which still remains in our documentation.

2 The tenth and ninth centuries

The bronze obelos of Palaepaphos, examined above, was found in a tomb containing several burials, along with vases from the period 1050–950. It might date from the eleventh century; to place it in the tenth century would simply lower the date at which CM 1 is attested.

It will not be possible to speak of a 'first-millennium syllabary' (I prefer this expression to 'Syllabic Cypriot' or 'Classical Cypriot', both of which lead to confusion) until such time as we can identify in some inscription one feature at least that is not known in Cypro-Minoan and therefore constitutes an innovation. And we cannot speak of 'Greek' until such time as the language is identified as such.

In the tenth century, we find *nothing* of the kind. In the ninth century, we do *perhaps* have the inscription that was painted, before firing, on a jug dating from the Cypro-Geometric III period (900–750), found in a tomb in the Palaepaphos region; the inscription probably runs from left to right, and two of the five signs (which are identical) can be identified as the 'Paphian' *to*, ᛡ.[46] However, that is insufficient evidence for us to be certain of the existence of a Paphian variety of the syllabary in the ninth century, particularly given that the other signs display forms that may be described either as 'Cypro-Minoan' or, more simply, as 'archaic', and the word that we read in this inscription, although complete, cannot be transcribed as Greek.

The first scholar to publish this inscription described its language as 'Eteocypriot',[47] a word modelled on 'Eteocretan', which is commonly used to describe the pre-Greek language spoken by the first-millennium inhabitants of Crete. This 'Eteocypriot' is used above all in inscriptions from Amathous dating from the fourth century, but also, by extension, in any inscription in the Cypriot syllabary of the first millennium that is not comprehensible as

---

[46] *ICS²* 18c.   [47] J. Karageorghis in V. and J. Karageorghis 1956: 357.

Greek.[48] The fact is that, as in the second millennium, several languages were both spoken and written, although only sporadic traces of them are to be found (inscriptions in 'Eteocypriot' are estimated to number about seventy; they display fewer than 10 per cent of the signs of all first-millennium syllabic inscriptions). Perhaps it is acceptable to speak of an 'Eteocypriot' of Amathous, of Golgoi and, in this instance, of Paphos, provided one is aware that the word probably covers a number of different languages. However, the expression 'non-Greek languages' is preferable.

The transition from the one syllabary to the other may have taken place during this period that covers the tenth and ninth centuries, but it is likewise possible that the Cypro-Minoan writing continued to be used principally to record one or several non-Greek languages but also, here and there, the odd word of Greek (or indeed of any other language).

3   The eighth century

For the history of the syllabary of the first millennium in Cyprus to be plausibly explained, it would have to:

- have been created in Paphos: over half of the most ancient evidence comes from this region, although some has been found outside the island (so may have been exported; the places of origin of these documents are of course hard to pin down)
- have originated in the eighth century (or slightly earlier): certainly, none of the evidence in our possession is earlier, and among the earliest documents testifying to the new writing, roughly half do not record Greek; so this script (invented for the writing of Greek, as, in its time, was Linear B) was soon being used to write at least one other of the island's languages
- have spread within circles that wrote from right to left (Phoenician writing: as early as the second half of the ninth century, traces of a Phoenician presence are detectable at Kition), where the writing was to adopt that direction and make radical changes to at least three signs (Ɣ *u*, Ȣ *le* and Ɜ *ri*): this was to become the 'common' syllabary

---

[48] See Egetmeyer 2010b.

- have continued to be written in its place of origin, Paphos (hence the name 'Paphian' syllabary). Here, it was to retain its left-to-right direction and also three signs that it alone was to preserve from its ancestor, Cypro-Minoan (ʌ *u*, ⸂ *le* and ⸕ *ri*, whereas these were to change wherever the script spread), although it was soon to modify the form of three other signs (⊥ *o*, ⊥ *so* and ⼋ *to*): the first and third of these were to be found in Paphos in the eighth century, and the second, which is quite rare, is morphologically linked to the first). The latter three signs were to be preserved in their form derived from Cypro-Minoan (⿻ *o*, ⿻ *so* and ⼗ *to*) in the 'common' syllabary once the script spread.

NB In both scripts other changes in the form of the signs were to take place more gradually and develop independently up until their disappearance in the Hellenistic period.

In 1961,[49] O. Masson had no evidence for the eighth century, except possibly the inscription on the jug from Palaepaphos cited above.[50]

Today, we possess five documents. Two of them (which were not found in Cyprus) are written in Greek, two others (from Paphos and Kition) are probably in another language. Of these documents, two are written from right to left, and two may be written from left to right. As for the fifth, it is impossible to say, except that its two syllabograms are no longer Cypro-Minoan.

All the above data are set out in Table 1.4.

Even if we add to this collection two other documents from Kition, which might likewise date from the eighth century (although this is less certain), we still find identical features: the direction of the writing runs from left to right in some cases, from right to left in others; both features characteristic of the Paphian syllabary *and* others characteristic of the 'common' syllabary are detectable; the language may be either Greek *or* non-Greek. The only overall impression is that the inscriptions seem 'archaic', and the period to which they belong seems to be one in which different languages co-existed and different directions of writing were being tried out, as were new forms for some signs. However, it also seems that the Paphian syllabary and the 'common' syllabary both existed

---

[49] *ICS*[1].   [50] *ICS*[1] 174 = *ICS*[2] 18c.

Table 1.4 *Eighth-century Cypriot inscriptions*

	Origin	Object	Material	Syllabary	Language	Direction of writing	Syllabograms	Date
1	Paphos	sieve	bronze	archaic	?	?	2	750–700
2	Paphos	bowl	bronze	Paphian o	non-Greek	left to right?	4	750–700
3	Kition	jug	clay	archaic	non-Greek	left to right?	5	725–700
4	Mende (Chalcidice)	Attic amphora	clay	archaic	Greek	right to left	5	725–700
5	Adana region (Cilicia)	seal	agate	'common' to	Greek	right to left (on imprint)	10	750–700

[1] *ICS²* 18d.
[2] O. Masson in Karageorghis 1987: 96.
[3] *ICS²* 258a.
[4] Vokotopoulou and Christidis 1995.
[5] Egetmeyer 2001 and 2002.

already and that those who used the 'common' syllabary were expanding geographically during this period.

It is sometimes said that the Paphian syllabary is the more 'conservative', the 'common' syllabary the more 'progressive'. But that makes very little sense given that features of both types appear in both syllabaries in roughly the same proportions in each.

The division of the Cypriot syllabaries into two branches, attested as early as the eighth century, was to persist throughout their existence: around 385, for example, mercenaries of the Pharaoh Akhoris, natives of Paphos, wrote their names and ethnics on the walls of a temple in Karnak; the writing runs from left to right and is in the Paphian syllabary; meanwhile, mercenaries from Ledra and Salamis were doing likewise, but writing from right to left in the 'common' syllabary.[51] Only Paphian coins (from the sixth to the fourth centuries) were to be inscribed with the 'common' syllabary (except for the very latest coins, c. 350–325, produced at a time of political and graphic reaction); but this is understandable, as these coins were made to be used (and thus read) outside the realm of Paphos. The latest attestation of the Paphian syllabary, still written from left to right, was found in the coin-hoard at Gülnar (Cilicia, c. 250–240), along with ten or so graffiti in the 'common' syllabary and running from right to left. The latest attestation of Cypriot syllabic writing was found in the Kafizin sanctuary (close to Nicosia), where there were sixty-eight inscriptions on ceramics dating from c. 225–218, bearing writing in the 'common' syllabary. (On the twenty or so sealings of c. 150–30, from an office in Nea Paphos, all that we have is residual traces of writing, stamped with old seals inscribed in the 'common' syllabary, which probably nobody could read any more at the time.)

The two syllabaries were to influence each other in every period. About 10 per cent of the inscriptions with writing running from right to left have been found in places using the Paphian syllabary, and almost as many running from left to right have been found in places using the 'common' syllabary; and 'Paphian' forms are often to be found in 'common' areas, just as 'common' ones are

[51] *ICS*[2] 421–453*h*.

found in 'Paphian' places. So, ascription to a specific syllabary must always depend on several criteria, especially when small fragments of unknown provenance are concerned.

4 From the seventh to the third centuries

We possess thirty or so inscriptions from the seventh century (although some may go back to the eighth century, and others may be as late as the sixth century, or even later). They divide equally between, on the one hand, the Paphian syllabary (always written from left to right, except in the three examples from Kourion and Marion, frontier regions of Paphos) and, on the other, the 'common' syllabary (which nearly always runs from right to left). Only four of these are not (or may not be) in Greek; 'archaic' features appear in fewer than half of them. So the two syllabaries reached a state of equilibrium that was to be maintained in the centuries that followed.

Both syllabaries are widely attested in the sixth century, and, up until the end of the third century, they are to be found on all kinds of materials, using all kinds of techniques and employed for all kinds of purposes: on stone and metal, baked and unbaked clay; engraved or painted, stamped or chiselled; on ceramics, coins, seals, jewellery or tablets, in mural graffiti and in official inscriptions, in sanctuary dedications and on ostraca from offices – in short, on every kind of material capable of being inscribed that has come down to us. And since those who used the syllabaries travelled, as did many of the objects that they inscribed (seals, coins, vases . . .), traces of the syllabaries have been found from Egypt to Italy, and from Syria to Cyrenaica. Given this wide diffusion of writing, the situation is definitely different from that of second-millennium Crete and mainland Greece. But faced with this specific situation (in which no coherent body of objects, such as archives, has survived), any study of the script is complicated by this atomisation of the writers, the times and places where they lived, the objects upon which they wrote (14,000 signs from 6 centuries, found in over 100 places, written by more than 1,200 persons, as opposed to 70,000 signs (five times more) from two centuries (three times less), discovered in no more than 10 places (10 times less), written

Table 1.5 *The Cypriot syllabaries of the first millennium* BC *(after O. Masson, T. B. Mitford and others)*

	Old Paphian c.600-500	New Paphian 325-309	Common c.500-300	Kafizin 225-218		Old Paphian c.600-500	New Paphian 325-309	Common c.500-300	Kafizin 225-218
a	(sign)	(sign)	(sign)	(sign)	pe	(sign)	(sign)	(sign)	(sign)
e	(sign)	(sign)	(sign)	(sign)	pi	(sign)	(sign)	(sign)	(sign)
i	(sign)	(sign)	(sign)	(sign)	po	(sign)	(sign)	(sign)	(sign)
ja	•	•	(sign)	•	pu	(sign)	•	(sign)	•
je	?	(sign)	•	•	ra	(sign)	(sign)	(sign)	(sign)
jo	(sign)	(sign)	(sign)	(sign)	re	(sign)	(sign)	(sign)	(sign)
ka	(sign)	(sign)	(sign)	(sign)	ri	(sign)	•	(sign)	(sign)
ke	(sign)	(sign)	(sign)	(sign)	ro	(sign)	(sign)	(sign)	(sign)
ki	(sign)	(sign)	(sign)	(sign)	ru	(sign)	•	(sign)	•
ko	(sign)	(sign)	(sign)	(sign)	sa	(sign)	(sign)	(sign)	(sign)
ku	(sign)	•	(sign)	•	se	(sign)	(sign)	(sign)	(sign)
la	(sign)	(sign)	(sign)	(sign)	si	(sign)	(sign)	(sign)	•
le	(sign)	(sign)	(sign)	(sign)	so	(sign)	(sign)	(sign)	(sign)
li	(sign)	•	(sign)	(sign)	su	(sign)	•	(sign)	•
lo	(sign)	(sign)	(sign)	(sign)	ta	(sign)	(sign)	(sign)	(sign)
lu	•	(sign)	(sign)	•	te	(sign)	(sign)	(sign)	(sign)
ma	(sign)	(sign)	(sign)	(sign)	ti	(sign)	(sign)	(sign)	(sign)
me	(sign)	(sign)	(sign)	(sign)	to	(sign)	(sign)	(sign)	(sign)
mi	(sign)	(sign)	(sign)	•	tu	(sign)	(sign)	(sign)	(sign)
mo	(sign)	(sign)	(sign)	(sign)	u	(sign)	(sign)	(sign)	(sign)
mu	(sign)	•	(sign)	(sign)	wa	(sign)	(sign)	(sign)	(sign)
na	(sign)	(sign)	(sign)	(sign)	we	(sign)	(sign)	(sign)	(sign)
ne	(sign)	(sign)	(sign)	(sign)	wi	•	(sign)	(sign)	(sign)
ni	(sign)	(sign)	(sign)	(sign)	wo	(sign)	(sign)	(sign)	(sign)
no	(sign)	•	(sign)	(sign)	xa	•	•	(sign)	•
nu	(sign)	(sign)	(sign)	(sign)	xe	•	•	(sign)	(sign)
o	(sign)	(sign)	(sign)	(sign)	za?	(sign) ?	•	(sign)	(sign)
pa	(sign)	(sign)	(sign)	(sign)	zo	(sign)	•	(sign)	•

by probably a little more than 100 persons (certainly more than 10 times less) in the case of Linear B: these are not real statistics, but the palaeographic 'dilution' of the Cypriot scripts of the first millennium viz. Linear B is in a proportion of about 1 : 1,500, and, if it is far from being 'homeopathic', strictly speaking, it certainly does not facilitate our studies). This explains the very real difficulties that arise in producing tools for research (study of hands, tables of signs, not to mention the 'corpus' about which we have been speaking since the nineteenth century).

The 'common' syllabary in its best-known state dates from the first half of the fifth century; it is principally represented by the inscription on the bronze tablet from Idalion:[52] 31 lines and 1,262 signs (i.e. syllabograms, logograms, figures and word-dividers), dated about 450. This document, together with legends on coins, is the one that enabled the Duc de Luynes, in 1852, to present Cypriot syllabic writing to the public. The script, partially deciphered by G. Smith in 1871, has fifty-five signs. We know of over 1,300 inscriptions (65 per cent in the 'common' syllabary, 35 per cent in the Paphian syllabary), comprising roughly 14,000 signs, as already mentioned. The majority contain the local Arcado-Cypriot dialect of Greek (whose affinities with the dialect of the Mycenaean tablets are well established), but never the *koine*. It is not a surprising fact that Cyprus, part of which was occupied by the Phoenicians from at least the ninth century, was the area in which non-alphabetic writing of Greek survived longest. Table 1.5 shows four stages of the syllabaries: Old Paphian (sixth century), New Paphian (used during the reign of King Nikokles, from 325 to 309), the 'common' syllabary of the fifth to fourth centuries, and the later stage of this, at Kafizin (between 225 and 218).

Considering the situation, this table of signs constitutes an elementary working tool, nothing else. What would be really useful would be tables of signs, place by place, epoch by epoch, kind of support by kind of support, but that will require years of labour.

---

[52] *ICS* 217.

2

NON-GREEK LANGUAGES OF ANCIENT CYPRUS
AND THEIR SCRIPTS: CYPRO-MINOAN 1–3

YVES DUHOUX

This chapter studies several features of the languages and scripts of the three most important Cypro-Minoan writing systems, CM 1, 2 and 3.[1]

CM 1

1   CM 1's main features

Name: CM 1.

Number of texts: 204[2] records found exclusively in Cyprus (whole island, including Enkomi).

Total number of phonograms:[3] 1,079[4] (i.e. 39.6 per cent of the whole corpus of all CM phonograms).

---

[1] On the archaeological and historical context of these writing systems, see Panayotou-Triantaphyllopoulou 2006. I shall of course use the new edition of the CM texts in *HoChyMin*. This book may be rightly considered as a major advance and an invaluable tool in the CM field, although it is unfortunately marred by too many inaccuracies – several of which will be reported below. It is not a corpus, as Olivier (2008: 607) explicitly agrees, but it will make such a corpus much easier to achieve – a 'Cypro-Minoan Corpus' is planned by Joanna S. Smith and Nicolle Hirschfeld (Smith 2002a: 29–30). Unless otherwise stated, all the CM data reproduced here are taken from *HoChyMin*, corrected when necessary.

[2] *HoChyMin*: 25, 63–280. The famous Opheltas bronze spit has been excluded from my count, since I try to show in Duhoux (in press) that it is not written in the CM 1 script, as *HoChyMin*: 243 submits, but in one of the non-Cypro-Minoan Cypriot syllabaries (= nCMCs). On this name, see the note on abbreviations at the end of this chapter.

[3] A 'phonogram' contrasts with an ideogram. I call an 'ideogram' any sign having an intrinsic meaning (for instance, in English script, the sign *1*, which expresses in itself the 'unit one'). A 'phonogram' has no intrinsic meaning but expresses a meaningless sound. Phonograms may render phonemes (or the like; these signs are called 'letters', like the English sign *w*) or syllables (these signs are called 'syllabograms', like the 'common' nCMCs signs ⚹ and ⅋, rendering *e* and *ro* respectively).

[4] Personal count of all the CM 1 identified phonograms (even if deliberately erased by an ancient writer) as edited in *HoChyMin*: 63–280. The five phonograms of the Opheltas bronze spit have been excluded, however: see above. Reconstructed examples and unidentified ones have not been considered. Olivier 2008: 607 estimates the number of all CM 1 *signs* at

---

Actual number of different phonograms: 72.[5]
Number of different phonograms as estimated by the Mackay formula:[6] $c.$ 77.
Proportion of reduplicated phonograms:[7] 1.1 per cent (12/1,079). Most of the six relevant words are probably anthroponyms,[8] probably characterised by a meaningful reduplication.[9]
Use of word-dividers: yes.

$c.$ 1,500. The list of the CM 1 sequences of phonograms given in *HoChyMin*: 419–25 is useful but unfortunately incomplete: about fifty identified phonograms are lacking. Moreover, several forms quoted in this list are different from those in the edition proper. *HoChyMin* does not handle the erased text in *HoChyMin* ##098. On this palimpsest, see Smith 2002a: 24: the cylinder 'preserves three different inscriptions. The final inscription is fifteen lines long, its beginning marked by a horizontal line. Two other parts of horizontal lines, however, are also preserved, one in the middle of the seventh line of text and the other at the end of the last inscription. Parts of both earlier inscriptions survive.' Smith 2003: 283 publishes full (but barely legible) facsimiles of *HoChyMin* ##098.

[5] *HoChyMin*: 413–14. This list has a total of seventy-two phonograms but has: (a) forgotten *078* (*hapax* in *HoChyMin* ##064); (b) mistakenly included *083* and *084* that do not occur in the texts – both signs appear only in the apparatus criticus of *HoChyMin* ##071, while a reading *061* has been preferred to *083* and *084* in the edition; the same apparatus criticus wrongly quotes an example of *084* in *HoChyMin* ##163 (in this same text there is no *084* at all, and the relevant sign is read as *064* or, in the apparatus criticus, as *061*); (c) analysed as an ideogram ('stiktogram') the sign &, which I consider a phonogram – in another passage of his book, Olivier has a view similar to mine ('je pencherais plutôt pour un syllabogramme': *HoChyMin*: 123). Thus, 72 + 1 − 2 + 1 = 72.

[6] The formula devised by Mackay (1965) is useful for estimating the approximate total number of signs used in a script whose complete signary is unknown. Here is its calculation for the CM 1 script: ((1,079 x 1,079) : (1,079–72)) − 1,079 = 77.15. I have checked the accuracy of the Mackay formula on samples of *c.* 240 phonograms of signaries whose actual number of phonograms is larger than 50 (Duhoux 1998: 4). The result is that the formula has a strong tendency to underestimate the length of the signaries. If applied to samples of *c.* 1,000 phonograms, like the CM 1 corpus, the underestimation depends on the length of the relevant signary. An excellent result appears with the 'common' nCMCs (theoretically fifty-five different syllabograms). The longest nCMCs inscription, the Idalion bronze table (*ICS* 217), is 1,024 syllabograms long (personal count of the *ICS*[1] 236–7 edition; '1010 syllabogrammes différents', as in Olivier 2008: 607, is doubly wrong). This text uses fifty-one different syllabograms; the Mackay formula supposes that its signary has *c.* fifty-four syllabograms: an underestimation of *c.* 2 per cent only. With the Linear B signary of theoretically eighty-eight syllabograms, the result is not so good. A corpus of 1,124 Linear B syllabograms of Knossos uses 67 different syllabograms. The Mackay formula supposes that its signary has *c.* seventy-one syllabograms: an underestimation of *c.* 19 per cent. The number of *c.* seventy-seven CM 1 signs is thus probably underestimated.

[7] Six occurrences of pairs of reduplicated phonograms: # *004–004–097* # (*HoChyMin* ##179) – # *006–006–004–099–046* # (*HoChyMin* ##086) – *025–025* (*HoChyMin* ##122 – two superposed signs engraved on a jug handle) – *041–041–068* (*HoChyMin* ##123) – # *041–041–097- &* (*HoChyMin* ##097.10–11) – *038–087–087–004–009–069–023* (*HoChyMin* ##106).

[8] Four out of the six examples of words with reduplicated phonograms are written on vases, and such inscriptions regularly express the owner's name. The same seems true for a fifth one, written on a clay ball. These five forms are, then, probably men's names.

[9] Since the CM 1 phonograms are in fact syllabograms (see below), we have here six examples of reduplicated syllabograms. Their concentration in presumed anthroponyms suggests that they probably render a *meaningful* reduplication (e.g. Linear B *de-de-me-na*, *dedemena*, 'bound', with the root of the verb, *de-*, preceded by its own reduplication:

Date:[10] theoretically 1600/1575–850;[11] probably fifteenth/fourteenth century–950.[12]

Deciphered: no[13] (but see Annex I below for some tentative phonetic readings).

Decipherment theoretically possible according to the length of the corpus ('unicity distance' of Shannon):[14] yes.[15]

---

de-de-mena) rather than a *meaningless* one caused by the accidental juxtaposition of two examples of one and the same syllabogram (e.g. Cypriot *ta-ta-la-to-ne*, *tan dalton*, 'the plate'). A meaningful reduplication may convey grammatical or expressive features.

[10] The absolute dates of Vandenabeele 2007 are unfortunately puzzling – it regularly happens that many (up to nine!) completely different durations are given to one and the same relative period. The 'Concordance générale' of *HoChyMin*: 39–55 should be supposed to reproduce these absolute dates, but it regularly introduces other new ones. *HoChyMin*'s use of absolute dates 'semblera une aberration à la plupart des archéologues: qu'ils sachent que pour tous les autres ... leurs sigles ésotériques ... ne représentent rien, sinon une suite abstraite de lettres et de chiffres' (*HoChyMin*: 23 n. 1). In fact, what is really absurd is not the presence of absolute dates, but their inconsistency. The conclusion is then clear: a coherent set of absolute dates should be substituted for those of Vandenabeele and Olivier. I have thus conventionally adopted here the absolute dates of Aström 1972a: LC IA: 1600/1575–1525/1500; LC IB: 1525/1500–1425/1415; LC IIA: 1425/1415–1375/1360; LC IIB: 1375/1360–1320; LC IIC: 1320–1190; LC IIIA: 1190–1125/1100; LC IIIB: 1125/1100–1050. One should add CG I: 1050–950; CG II: 950–850; CG III: 850–750. All these dates are of course approximate.

[11] The two possibly oldest inscriptions are dated LC IA–B: 1600/1575–1425/1415 (*HoChyMin* ##095; relative date: Vandenabeele 2007: 34, 'bien qu'il n'y ait pas de contexte ni de vrai parallèle') and LC I – II: 1600/1575–1190 (*HoChyMin* ##193; relative date: Vandenabeele 2007: 37). The next-oldest inscriptions are *HoChyMin* ##165 and 002, dated LC IIA: 1425/1415–1375/1360 (relative date: Vandenabeele 2007: 36 – these items are wrongly referred to as *HoChyMin* ##166 and 003 (*sic*)). The latest inscriptions are dated CG I: 1050–950 and (*HoChyMin* ##190), CG I–II: 1050–850 (relative date: Vandenabeele 2007: 37).

[12] Vandenabeele 2007: 38 dates the whole CM 1 corpus 'du quatorzième siècle jusque vers 950 avant notre ère' (*sic*).

[13] This means that several phonetic readings of the signary and/or identifications of the relevant language have been proposed, but that none of them has thus far gained general approval. Twenty years after its publication, the negative appreciation of Palaima 1989a is unfortunately still valid.

[14] The 'unicity distance' of C. E. Shannon gives a useful estimation of the minimal length that a text written in an undeciphered script should have to be in order to be successfully deciphered – a 'successful decipherment' means that the solution discovered can be proved to be the *only possible one*. Let us take an extreme example. If an English text written in an undeciphered script has only three signs, for instance Xyz, several decipherments can be submitted, and it proves impossible to choose between them – in this case, Xyz could perfectly well be read as e.g. *are* or *one* or *the* or *you* etc. The same is true of a text of four signs like Xyza, which could be read as *hare* or *ones* or *they* or *your* etc. If we want to be sure that only one decipherment is possible, a longer text is needed, and the 'unicity distance' allows us to estimate this length. In fact, the actual length of the text must be several times greater than the 'unicity distance' to ensure a trustworthy result. More about the 'unicity distance' in Duhoux 2009: §13.

[15] In this case, it is *c.* eighty or *c.* eighty-six phonograms (calculated on the actual (seventy-two) or estimated (*c.* seventy-seven) number of phonograms). The 1,079 phonograms of the corpus are much larger and thus make a decipherment theoretically possible.

This script has provided by now the largest bulk of CM documents, but not of CM phonograms: CM I (39.6 per cent) comes after CM 2 (50.3 per cent). Its number of different phonograms, actual and estimated, shows that it cannot but be a syllabary. The CM I phonograms are thus in fact syllabograms.

2   What is the relationship between the CM 0 and CM 1 scripts?

The CM 0 script seems older than that of CM I (the unique short CM 0 inscription cannot be later than 1525/1500–1425/1415 BC).[16] Here are the clearest characteristics of both scripts:

> Actual number of different syllabograms: 20 or 21 (CM 0) ~ 72 (CM 1).
> Number of different syllabograms as estimated by the Mackay formula: difficult to estimate (CM 0) ~ c. 77 (CM 1).
> CM 0 syllabograms present in CM 1: about 40 per cent.[17]
> CM 0 syllabograms absent in CM 1: about 60 per cent.[18]
> CM 1 syllabograms absent in CM 0: 88.9 per cent (64/72).
> Use of word-dividers: CM 0: no ~ CM 1: yes.

About 60 per cent of the twenty or twenty-one CM 0 syllabograms are unknown in CM 1. Since the CM 1 corpus of syllabograms is more than forty times (!) larger than its forerunner, this absence is probably significant. This means that several CM 0 signs were lacking in the CM 1 branch, or disappeared, or perhaps changed in an unpredictable way.

All the CM 0 syllabograms absent in CM 1 seem also to be unknown in CM 2 or 3. This suggests that the CM 0 script was not the ancestor of the other known later CM syllabaries.[19]

Why was CM 1 created? No sure answer is at hand, but one of the possibilities is that CM 0 and CM 1 were devised to write different languages. For some features of the language of CM 1, see section 3 under CM 2 below.

---

[16] LC IB (relative date: Vandenabeele 2007: 33). On the CM 0 script, see Duhoux 2010.

[17] 8/20 (40 per cent) or 8/21 (38.1 per cent). Here are the eight reasonably likely formal identities that I find between the CM 0 ~ CM 1 signs: *02* (🕮) = *102* (Ⴘ); *03* (Ⴡ) = *004* (Ⴑ); *04* (Ⴕ) = *008* (Ⴕ Ⴟ Ⴣ); *07* (✛) = *005* (✛ Ⴕ); *08* (Ⴒ) = *069* (Ⴒ Ⴒ); *14* (Ⴑ) = *044* (Ⴑ); *15* (Ⴥ) = *023* (Ⴥ); *21* (Ⴤ) = *104* (Ⴤ Ⴤ).

[18] 12/20 (60 per cent) or 13/21 (61.9 per cent).

[19] As Olivier (*HoChyMin*: 21) correctly writes.

CM 2

1 CM 2's main features

Name: CM 2.

Number of texts: three clay tablets found in Enkomi (Cyprus).[20]

Total number of phonograms: 1,369[21] (i.e. 50.3 per cent of the whole corpus of all CM phonograms).

Actual number of different phonograms: 61.[22]

Number of different phonograms as estimated by the Mackay formula: *c.* 64.[23]

Proportion of reduplicated phonograms:[24] 3.4 per cent (46/1,369).
About seven of the relevant words are likely anthroponyms with a meaningful reduplication (see under CM 2 section 3d below).

Use of word-dividers: yes.

Date: not later than 1190–1125/1100[25] and 1125/1100–1050.[26]

Deciphered: no (but see Annex I below for some tentative phonetic readings).

---

[20] *HoChyMin*: 25, 281–383.

[21] Personal count of all the CM 2, identified phonograms as edited in *HoChyMin*: 281–383. Reconstructed examples and unidentified ones have not been considered. Olivier (2008: 607) evaluates the number of all CM 2 *signs* at *c.* 1,300 – an obviously impossible number, since it includes not only the 1,369 phonograms but also no fewer than 347 ideograms (personal count of the stiktograms in *HoChyMin*: 480). *HoChyMin*'s 427–479 concordance (not an index, contrary to its title!) of the CM 2 sequences of phonograms is extremely useful, but unfortunately not fully reliable: thirteen identified phonograms are lacking; about sixty others are printed twice; several forms differ from those of the edition proper.

[22] *HoChyMin*: 413, 415.   [23] In fact, *c.* 63.8.

[24] 23 occurrences of pairs of reduplicated phonograms. # *006–006* # (*HoChyMin* ##209.B.09) – # *006–006–010–051–•* [(*HoChyMin* ##207.A.I.28) – # *006–006–078*[(*HoChyMin* ##209. B.03) – *006–006–082* # (3 ex.; *HoChyMin* ##209.B.02, B.03, B.06) – *107–006–006–090–013* # (*HoChyMin* ##209.B.13) – *102–013–013* # (*HoChyMin* ##209.B.11) – # *030–017–017* # (*HoChyMin* ##207.B.I.07) – # *038–017–017* # (*HoChyMin* ##207.B.I.03) – # *102–029–017–017* # (*HoChyMin* ##208.A.02) – *025–025* # (*HoChyMin* ##209.B.09) – # *027–027* # and # *027–027*[(3 ex.; *HoChyMin* ##207.B.I.12, B.I.24, *HoChyMin* ##209.A.I.2.01) – # *079–030–030–005* (*HoChyMin* ##207.A.I.31) – # *047–047–060–059* # (*HoChyMin* ##209.B.07) – # *75–087–059–059* # (*HoChyMin* ##207.A.I.31) – *078–075–075* # (*HoChyMin* ##208. B.26) – # *107–075–075* # (*HoChyMin* ##208.A.18) – *107–082–082* # (*HoChyMin* ##208. A.20) – *038–087–087–027* # (*HoChyMin* ##207.B.I.23) – •-*097–097* # (*HoChyMin* ##208. A.09). The pair (-)*006–006*(-) (to be possibly read as [-]*pa²-pa²*[-]: see below) is the most frequent (7/23) of all the reduplicated phonograms – the next most frequent are -*017–017* and *027–027* (thrice each).

[25] LC IIIA (*HoChyMin* ##208, ##209; relative date: Vandenabeele 2007: 37).

[26] LC IIIB (*HoChyMin* ##207; relative date: Vandenabeele 2007: 37).

Decipherment theoretically possible according to the length of the corpus ('unicity distance' of Shannon): yes.[27]

The number of different CM 2 phonograms, actual and estimated, shows that the script cannot but be a syllabary. The CM 2 phonograms are thus in fact syllabograms.

2 What is the relationship between the CM 1 and CM 2 scripts?

Here are the main data:

> Actual number of different syllabograms: 72 (CM 1) ~ 61 (CM 2).
> Number of different syllabograms as estimated by the Mackay formula: *c.* 77 (CM 1) ~ *c.* 64 (CM 2).
> CM 1 syllabograms present in CM 2: 62.5 per cent (45/72).[28]
> CM 1 syllabograms absent in CM 2: 37.5 per cent (27/72).
> CM 2 syllabograms absent in CM 1: 26.2 per cent (16/61).[29]
> Use of word-dividers: regularly used in CM 2, as in CM 1.

The differences between CM 1 and CM 2 are impressive. They give distinctive proof of creativity and cannot be understood without supposing either systematic and important reform(s) or autonomous developments. Why did such an evolution occur? Was it prompted or stimulated by linguistic diversity? To answer this question, we must try to discover some data about the languages written in both scripts (see section 3 below).

3 Are the languages of CM 1 and CM 2 apparently similar?

3a Method used

Trying to explore the CM 1 and CM 2 languages sounds like an impossible task. We can nevertheless venture it. Indeed, even if a syllabically written text is not deciphered, it may teach us several things about the grammar of its language and the spelling of its

---

[27] In this case, the unicity distance (see under CM 1 section 1) is *c.* sixty-seven or *c.* seventy-one phonograms (calculated on the actual (sixty-one) or estimated (*c.* sixty-four) number of phonograms). The 1,369 phonograms of the corpus are much larger and thus make a decipherment theoretically possible.

[28] See the table of *HoChyMin*: 413 corrected as indicated under CM 1 section 1. Olivier 2008: 607 estimates that there are forty-two syllabograms common to CM 1 and CM 2.

[29] Olivier 2008: 607 estimates that eighteen CM 2 syllabograms are lacking in CM 1.

32

script. Let us remember A. Kober's wonderful analysis of some Linear B texts well before the decipherment, when she succeeded in showing *inter alia* that there was probably a declension in the language of these tablets.[30] I shall apply this kind of procedure to the CM 1 and CM 2 corpora. My aim will be to find what I shall conventionally call 'nuclei': these are groups of consecutive syllabograms that may receive 'additions'. These 'additions' are made up of one or more syllabograms put before and/or after a 'nucleus'. They may teach us interesting characteristics of the corpus' language and orthography. I illustrate this method with a few Linear B words:

1 *a-mi-ni-so* ~ *a-mi-ni-si-ja* ~ *a-mi-ni-si-jo* ('Amnisos' ~ 'Amnisian' (nominative feminine ~ masculine)) may be conventionally analysed as a 'nucleus' (*a-mi-ni-*) and three posterior 'additions' (*-so* ~ *-si-ja* ~ *-si-jo*).
2 *do-e-ro* ~ *do-e-ro-i* ~ *do-e-ro-jo* ('slave', nominative singular ~ dative plural ~ genitive singular) may be conventionally analysed as a 'nucleus' (*do-e-ro*[-]) and three posterior 'additions' (*-Ø* ~ *-i* ~ *-jo*).

With only two groups of words, as here, we can just observe that the 'additions' are always posterior ones and that they are one or two syllabograms long. If more groups like these were examined, however, we would get a fairly good picture of some Linear B grammatical and/or orthographical apparent features.

This method will be applied to CM corpora whose scripts are undeciphered and languages unknown. I shall make a context-free analysis which identifies 'nuclei' through their form only, with neither any knowledge of their meaning nor attention paid to their contexts. I have tested this kind of examination in four reasonably large Linear B corpora.[31] Here are the results. 'Nuclei' of two syllabograms must be excluded because their forms are too frequently irrelevant.[32] Those of four syllabograms and more offer excellent results, with 99 per cent correct matches.[33] Those of three syllabograms are in between: their range of success

---

[30] Pope 2008: 3–4.
[31] About 2,390 syllabograms each, totalling more than 9,500 syllabograms.
[32] For example, the Linear B sequences *ta-ra-nu* and *ta-ra-si-ja* would be wrongly supposed to share a 'nucleus' **ta-ra*-, when they are in fact two completely different words: *thrānus* 'footstool' and *talasia* lit. 'weighed quantity (of items to be processed)'.
[33] All together, they have only 1 error out of 104 forms.

goes from 74 to 88 per cent (average: 81 per cent).[34] The method is thus certainly far from perfect, but its results are not too exceedingly awful. Several other examinations should be conducted to go beyond the sole apparent features: I hope to be able to do so elsewhere. Anyway, a further caveat is necessary: in too many cases, the word-division is not indicated in the inscriptions, and we rely on our own interpretation.[35]

3b   CM 1: 'additions' to the 'nuclei' of at least three syllabograms

The complete list of all the forms is given in Annex II section 2 below. Total occurrences of the 'nuclei': twenty-nine (fifteen occurrences of seven different 'nuclei' of three syllabograms; twelve occurrences of four different 'nuclei' of four; two occurrences of one 'nucleus' of five). For the tentative phonetic values, see Annex I. The 'additions' found in 'nuclei' of more than three syllabograms are put in **bold**.

Initial 'additions' (4 occurrences; 4 different 'additions'; total number of the syllabograms used in the 4 occurrences: 7):
006- (= # *pa*²-; 1 ex. (102b), 3 signs 'nucleus')
027–005- (= *027-l/ro*²-; 1 ex. (101b), 3 signs 'nucleus')
044- (= # *se*²-; 1 ex. (107b), 3 signs 'nucleus')
102–082–069- (= *a*²-*082–069-;* 1 ex. (107a), 3 signs 'nucleus').
Final 'additions' (14 occurrences; 13 different 'additions'; total number of the syllabograms used in the 14 occurrences: 25):
-& (2 ex. (103b, 106b), 5 and 4 signs 'nuclei')
-005–102–087–078 # (= *-l/ro*²-*a*²-*087–078* #; 1 ex. (104b), 3 signs 'nucleus')
-007 # (1 ex. (101a), 3 signs 'nucleus')
-008–023 # (= *-to*²-*ti*² #; 1 ex. (111a), 3 signs 'nucleus')

---

[34] Duhoux 1978: 93–5. In this examination, I considered 'nuclei' of three syllabograms *only if* their 'additions' appeared in 'nuclei' of four syllabograms or more. This restriction was intended to minimise the number of false matches. In the CM examination, the restricted number of data prevented the use of this procedure. It is, then, probable that the proportion of errors in the CM 'nuclei' of three syllabograms will be higher than in my original research. Several CM 'nuclei' of three signs seem rather trustworthy, however. In CM 1 (see Annex II section 2), the pair 101 is found in the same text; the pairs 102, 104 and 105 have been found in the same place and are written on similar clay balls; moreover, the pair 105 is written by the same Hand; the pair 111 is found on two bronze bowls. In CM 2 (see Annex III), the pairs 201, 207, 208 and 209 are found in the same texts. In CM 3 (see Annex IV), the two pairs are found in the same text.

[35] *HoChyMin*: 419–25 gives a useful list of such interpretations for the whole CM 1 corpus and comments (484–85) on the divisions that it has adopted for *HoChyMin* ##097.

-*011–006* # (= -*pe*$^{??}$-*pa*$^?$ #; I ex. (102a), 3 signs 'nucleus')
-*013–023* # (= -*013-ti*$^?$ #; I ex. (111b), 3 signs 'nucleus')
-*015* # (1 ex. (108b), 4 signs 'nucleus')
-*019–110* # (1 ex. (105b), 3 signs 'nucleus')
-*021–023* # (= -*021-ti*$^?$ #; I ex. (112b), 3 signs 'nucleus')
-*023* # (= -*ti*$^?$ #; 1 ex. (109b), 4 signs 'nucleus')
-*082–008* # (= -*082-to*$^?$ #; 1 ex. (110b), 4 signs 'nucleus')
-*096–023* (= -*096-ti*$^?$; I ex. (101b), 3 signs 'nucleus')
-*110–073* # (1 ex. (109c), 4 signs 'nucleus').

A remarkable feature is provided by the sign *023/ti*$^?$ which appears in no fewer than five posterior 'additions' (five occurrences), always as last syllabogram (either on its own (once) or preceded by another one). Here are its alternations in the groups of 'nuclei':

-Ø # ~ -*021–023* #   =   -Ø # ~ -*021-ti*$^?$ # (112)
-Ø # ~ -*023* # ~ -*110–073* #   =   **-Ø # ~ -*ti*$^?$ # ~ -*110–073* # (109)**
-*007* # ~ -*096–023*   =   -*007* # ~ -*096-ti*$^?$ (101)
-*008–023* # ~ -*013–023* #   =   -*to*$^?$-*ti*$^?$ # ~ -*013-ti*$^?$ # (111).

Observe the apparent complex alternation in pair 111: -*023*/-*ti*$^?$ is the last sign, but is preceded by two different syllabograms, -*008*-/-*to*$^?$- and -*013*-.

3c   CM 2: 'additions' to the 'nuclei' of at least three syllabograms

The complete list of all the forms is given in Annex III. Total occurrences of the 'nuclei': thirty (twelve different 'nuclei' of three syllabograms). For the tentative phonetic values, see Annex I.

Initial 'additions' (9 occurrences; 9 different 'additions'; total number of the syllabograms used in the 9 occurrences: 12):
    # *017*- (1 ex. (203a), 3 signs 'nucleus')
    # *023*- (= # *ti*$^?$-; 1 ex. (203b), 3 signs 'nucleus')
    # *025–054*- (1 ex. (208a), 3 signs 'nucleus')
    # *030*- (1 ex. (204b), 3 signs 'nucleus')
    # *047*- (1 ex. (208b), 3 signs 'nucleus')
    # *070–027*- (1 ex. (202a), 3 signs 'nucleus')
    # *078*- (1 ex. (205b), 3 signs 'nucleus')
    # *079*- (1 ex. (202b), 3 signs 'nucleus')
    # *104–092*- (1 ex. (203c), 3 signs 'nucleus').
Final 'additions' (11 occurrences; 7 or 8 different 'additions'; total number of the syllabograms used in the 11 occurrences: at least 11):

-013 # (2 ex. (207b, 209b), 3 signs 'nuclei')
-017 # (2 ex. (206b, 210b), 3 signs 'nuclei')
-054 ([#]) (2 ex. (201a, 212b), 3 signs 'nuclei')
-064 # (= -*o*$^{??}$ #; 1 ex. (204b), 3 signs 'nucleus')
-075 # (1 ex. (203a), 3 signs 'nucleus')
-095 # (1 ex. (201b), 3 signs 'nucleus')
-096 ⟨#⟩ (1 ex. (211b), 3 signs 'nucleus')
-•[(1 ex. (203b), 3 signs 'nucleus').

3d   Comparison of the main apparent linguistic/orthographic features of CM 1 and CM 2

There is no statistically significant difference between the features of the 'nuclei' and the 'additions' of CM 1 ~ CM 2 (see sections 3b and 3c above). For instance, the proportion of the occurrences of 'nuclei' with posterior 'additions' only is 14/29 (CM 1) ~ 8/30 (CM 2). Fisher's exact test[36] reveals that it has an 11.02 per cent chance of being accidental, which is not significant. In interpreting this result a warning is necessary, however. When a statistical test gets no significant difference, it never proves that no difference exists. It simply shows that there is no statistical evidence for it. In this case, a difference could either really not exist or exist but become detectable only under another examination (for instance, if further data were added). The absence of statistically significant difference between the 'nuclei' and the 'additions' of CM 1 ~ CM 2 thus does not prove anything about their languages and/or orthographies.

Some other features are or could be significant, however:

1 *Proportion of reduplicated signs*: significantly less frequent in CM 1 than in CM 2 (1.1–3.4 per cent).[37]
2 *'Addition' used differently*: *023/ti*$^?$ has a quite different use in CM 1 and CM 2. It appears five times as *posterior* 'addition' (*-023/-ti*$^?$ – once in a four-syllabogram 'nucleus') in CM 1, but never so in CM 2. Conversely, *023-/ti*$^?$- is used once as *anterior* 'addition' in a three-syllabogram CM 2 'nucleus', but never so in CM 1. More details about the use of *-023* in CM 1 are discussed above under CM 2 section 3b.

---

[36] On this test, see e.g. Agresti 1990: 60–6, 70. Fisher's exact test is a classic of statistical comparison of very small-sized samples.
[37] See under CM 1 section 1 and CM 2 section 1. Fisher's exact test estimates that the difference between CM 1 and CM 2 has 0.02 per cent chance of being accidental, which is highly significant.

3 There are ten different forms (twelve examples) with the same signs reduplicated in the two scripts (see references in section 1 under CM 1 and section 1 under CM 2 above):

- # 006–006–004–099–046 # (CM 1) ~ # 006–006 # – # 006–006–010–051-•[– # 006–006–078[– 006–006–082 # (3 ex.) – 107–006–006–090–013 # (CM 2)
- 025–025 (CM 1) ~ 025–025 # (CM 2)
- 038–087–087–004–009–069–023 (CM 1) ~ 038–087–087–027 # (CM 2).

The three CM 1 words are probably anthroponyms characterised by a meaningful reduplication (see under CM 1 section 1 above). They have several features in common with the relevant CM 2 forms: (a) the CM 1 form # 006–006–004–099–046 # begins with 006–006- just like four of the five CM 2 words; (b) 025–025 (CM 1) and 025–025 # (CM 2) are, strictly, identical; (c) 038–087–087–004–009–069–023 (CM 1) and 038–087–087–027 # (CM 2) begin with the three same first syllabograms (including the reduplicated ones). It is then tempting to consider that most (if not all) of the seven different CM 2 words are also probably anthroponyms character-ised by a meaningful reduplication.

4 *Possible identical words*: four identical sequences of three consecutive signs appear in both CM 1 and CM 2: 038–087–087–004–009–069–023[38] (CM 1) ~ # 021–009–069–023 #[39] (CM 2); 038–087–087–004–009–069–023[40] (CM 1) ~ 038–087–087–027 #[41] (CM 2); # 104–011–024–006–012–023-&[42] (CM 1) ~]104–011–024 #[43] (CM 2); 023–092–097 #[44] (CM 1) ~]•-029–023–092–097 #[45] (CM 2). None of these forms appears in the CM 1 or CM 2 'nuclei'. Unless due to pure chance, some of these sequences could perhaps be proper names (this is probably the case with the pair beginning with 038–087–087-: see point 3 above).

There is no doubt that several of these data must be considered not secure. We do not know: (a) the readings, the functions and/or the meanings of the 'nuclei' and 'additions'; (b) whether the same signs render identical or different sounds; (c) whether we are right in considering several reduplications meaningful; (d) whether the identical sequences of three consecutive signs cover identical or different words. Our results are thus highly hypothetical. On the whole, however, feature 1 is the less ambiguous and suggests that

---

[38] *HoChyMin* ##106. [39] *HoChyMin* ##208.B.19. [40] *HoChyMin* ##106.
[41] *HoChyMin* ##207.B.I.23. [42] *HoChyMin* ##097.06.
[43] *HoChyMin* ##207.B.I.01. [44] *HoChyMin* ##162c. [45] *HoChyMin* ##207.B.I.02.

different languages in CM 1 and CM 2 seem more likely than identical ones. Feature 2 goes in the same direction, although one of its 'additions' has a 'nucleus' of three syllabograms only. Features 3 and 4 are ambiguous, but, if right, would just imply that both CM 1 and CM 2 shared a common onomastic stock. One or possibly two features thus suggest a linguistic difference between CM 1 and CM 2, and this is not contradicted by the two others. If so, the creation of these two scripts could have been prompted or at least stimulated by this supposed difference.

CM 3

1   Is CM 3 a distinct script?

Olivier's answer to this question is negative. He considers that CM 3 'ne constitue pas une "écriture" à proprement parler ... il s'agit d'une désignation *géographique* (les documents trouvés à Ras Shamra/Ougarit) qui peuvent [*sic*] recouvrir du CM 1 et une (ou même plusieurs écritures) [*sic*] propre(s) à la côte syro-palestinienne'.[46] Hence his use of quotation marks in 'CM 3'.

Nine CM 3 phonograms are absent from CM 1,[47] while sixteen are lacking in CM 2.[48] Since the CM 1 and 2 corpora are four and five times larger than that of CM 3, these absences are highly significant. It is especially impressive that no fewer than seven CM 3 phonograms are totally unknown in both CM 1 and 2.[49] It is true that the actual CM 1 and 2 signaries could lack *c*. five and *c*. three signs, and that these numbers could be underestimated (see under CM 1 section 1 above), as suggested by the Mackay formula. But even so, some of these CM 3 signs could be lacking in the theoretical CM 1 and CM 2 signaries.

We shall see (next section) that there are actually fifty different syllabograms used in CM 3. This number differs distinctly from those of CM 1 and CM 2: seventy-two (CM 1) ~ sixty-one (CM 2).

---

[46]   *HoChyMin*: 21 (author's italics).
[47]   *040, 051, 058, 071, 074, 094, 098, 100, 105*. See the table at *HoChyMin*: 413 corrected as indicated under CM 1 section 1.
[48]   *002, 007, 019, 040, 050, 053, 055, 058, 071, 073, 094, 098, 099, 100, 103, 105*. See the table at *HoChyMin*: 413.
[49]   *040, 058, 071, 094, 098, 100, 105*.

The same is partly true for the number of different syllabograms as estimated by the Mackay formula: *c.* seventy-seven (CM 1) ~ *c.* sixty-four (CM 2) ~ *c.* sixty-two (CM 3).

These differences suggest, then, that CM 3 is more probably an autonomous script than a part of CM 1 or CM 2. More data are needed, however, in order to be sure.

Two other differences are interesting, although their weight should not be overestimated:

- The CM 3 inscriptions have a distinct local flavour because 'the method of inscription mimics the cuneiform method of punching, but with a rounded stylus. Further, the shapes of the tablets and the arrangement of the signs on the tablet surfaces mimic Ugaritic texts ... particularly in the wide spacing of signs and occasional use of ruling lines.'[50]
- A few CM 1 signs seem to differ from their CM 3 correspondents: compare *007* (♣ ~ ♣) or *073* (🀫 🀫🀫 ~ 🀫 🀫).[51] Since no photograph of the main CM 3 texts has been published, a check of the facsimiles is impossible for the present.

2   CM 3's main features

Name: CM 3.
Number of texts: 8[52] (all found in Ugarit, modern Ras Shamra, Syria).
Total number of phonograms: 253[53] (i.e. 9.3 per cent of the whole corpus of all CM phonograms).
Actual number of different phonograms: 50.[54]

---

[50] Smith 2003: 284.   [51] *HoChyMin*: 413–14, 416.

[52] *HoChyMin*: 25. The clay label *HoChyMin* ##211 is not edited, however (*HoChyMin*: 386).

[53] Personal count of all the CM 3-identified phonograms (even if deliberately erased by an ancient writer) as edited in *HoChyMin*: 385–409. Reconstructed examples and unidentified ones have not been considered. Olivier gives two totally different evaluations of the number of all the CM 3 *signs*: fewer than 250 (an obviously impossible number: *HoChyMin*: 21) and *c.* 350 (Olivier 2008: 607). *HoChyMin*'s list (481–482) of the CM 3 sequences of phonograms is useful but unfortunately incomplete: about twenty identified phonograms are lacking; several forms differ from those of the edition proper.

[54] The tables of *HoChyMin*: 413, 416 rightly list fifty different CM 3 phonograms. However, the edition proper and the index of the sequences wrongly edit two further ones, *022* and *072*. (a) The sequences **022–082–075–051* and **102–075–051–055–082–022–009* are supposed to be read in *HoChyMin* ##215.B.13 and B.16 (405–6, 481–2, 498). In these two texts, **022* must be corrected to *021*. (b) A sequence **019–087–072–096* is supposed to be read in *HoChyMin* ##215.B.12 (405, 481, 498), but **072* must be corrected to *073*.

39

Number of different phonograms as estimated by the Mackay formula: *c.* 62.[55]

Proportion of reduplicated phonograms:[56] 0.8 per cent (2/253).

Use of word-dividers: yes.

Date: 1320–1190 and 1190–1125/1100.[57]

Deciphered: no (but see Annex I for some tentative phonetic readings).

Decipherment theoretically possible according to the length of the corpus ('unicity distance' of Shannon): yes.[58]

The number of different CM 3 phonograms, actual and estimated, shows that the script cannot but be a syllabary. The CM 3 phonograms are thus in fact syllabograms.

3   Is the language of CM 3 apparently similar to those of CM 1 and/or CM 2?

If we do the same examination of the 'nuclei' and their 'additions' as above for CM 1 and CM 2, we get a very restricted number of alternating forms, which are given in Annex IV.

Total occurrences of the 'nuclei': four (two different 'nuclei' of three syllabograms). The results are meagre, it must be admitted – but so are the 253 syllabograms of CM 3 compared with the 1,079 and 1,369 of CM 1 and CM 2. Here are the main data:

Initial 'additions' of 'nuclei' of at least three syllabograms in CM 3
(2 occurrences; 2 different 'additions'; total numbers of the syllabograms used in the 2 occurrences: 4):
082–058- (1 ex. (301a), 3 signs 'nucleus')
104–009- (1 ex. (301b), 3 signs 'nucleus').

Final 'additions' of 'nuclei' of at least three syllabograms in CM 3
(1 occurrence; 1 'addition'; total number of the syllabograms used in the occurrence: 1):
-051 # (1 ex. [302b], 3 signs 'nucleus').

---

[55] In fact, *c.* 62.3.

[56] One occurrence of a pair of reduplicated phonograms: # *102–004–004–096* # (*HoChyMin* ##215.A.05).

[57] Maybe LC IIC and LC IIIA (relative date: Vandenabeele 2007: 38).

[58] In this case, the unicity distance (see under CM 1 section 1) is *c.* fifty-four or *c.* sixty-eight phonograms (calculated on the actual (fifty) or estimated (*c.* sixty-two) number of phonograms). The 253 phonograms of the corpus are more than three times larger and thus make a decipherment theoretically possible.

3a   Comparison of the main apparent linguistic/orthographic features of CM 3, CM 1 and CM 2

The very few CM 3 data make any conclusion highly hypothetical. Here are some possible hints:

1   *CM 3 proportion of reduplicated syllabograms*: significantly different from the CM 2 score (0.8–3.4 per cent).[59] The difference between CM 3 and CM 1 is not significant.
2   Another common feature between CM 3 and CM 1 is one sequence of two reduplicated *004* syllabograms (# *102–004–004–096* # [CM 3] ~ # *004–004–097* # [CM 1]). We are, unfortunately, unable to know whether this identity is accidental or not.

These results show one or two possible common points between the languages of CM 3 and CM 1 – but are they not an illusion?

Annex I: Tentative phonetic reading of some CM 1–3 syllabograms

We have seen that the CM 1–3 scripts are still undeciphered. However, some tentative readings are possible. The range of the proposed identifications is large,[60] but I shall limit myself to the few which seem to me reasonably likely.

1   Some CM 1–3 syllabograms resemble perfectly or closely signs of at least two or even three other Mediterranean scripts: (1) the later non-Cypro-Minoan Cypriot syllabaries (nCMCs); (2) the Mycenaean Linear B (= LB) syllabary; (3) the Minoan Linear A (= LA) syllabary.[61] Moreover, the nCMCs and LB syllabograms share identical or very similar phonetic values. These correspondences suggest that the CM signs could *probably* have similar phonetic values. These values will be followed below by *one* question mark (e.g. *pa²*).
2   Some CM 1–3 syllabograms resemble perfectly or closely signs of the later nCMCs. The correspondence with the shapes of only one script

---

[59] Fisher's exact test estimates that the difference between CM 3 and CM 2 has a 2.5 per cent chance of being accidental, which is significant.
[60] See for example the methodological discussion by Nahm 1981: 52–9.
[61] The nCMCs and Linear B signs printed here are standardised ones, unless stated otherwise. All the Linear A syllabograms are facsimiles of *GORILA*: XXVIII–XLII.

(but a Cypriot one) suggests that the CM signs could *possibly* have similar phonetic values. These values will be followed below by *two* question marks (e.g. *we*$^{??}$).

CM 1–3 *001* (**I, I, I**) = *we*$^{??}$ – cf. ncMCs *we*: Ⲭ;

CM 1–3 *004* (**⊢, ⊢, ⊢**) = *d/ta*$^?$ – cf. ncMCs *ta*: ⊢; LB *da*: ⊢; LA: ⊢;

CM 1–3 *005* (**✚ ┼, ✚, ✚**) = *l/ro*$^?$ – cf. ncMCs *lo*: ✚; LB *ro*:✚; LA: ✚;

CM 1–3 *006* (**✦, ✦, ✦ ✦**) = *pa*$^?$ – cf. ncMCs *pa*: ✦; LB *pa*: ✦; LA: ⊥;

CM 1–3 *008* (**Ŧ Ŧ ⅄, Ŧ, Ŧ**) = *to*$^?$ – cf. ncMCs *to*: Ŧ; LB *to*: Ŧ; LA: Ŧ;

CM 1–3 *011* (**∫, ∫, ∫**) = *pe*$^{??}$ – cf. ncMCs *pe*: ∫;

CM 1–3 *012* (**Λ ˥ ∫, ∫**, missing) = *u*$^{??}$ – cf. ncMCs (ancient Paphian) *u*: Λ;[62]

CM 1–3 *023* (**Λ, Λ Λ, Λ**) = *ti*$^?$ – cf. ncMCs *ti*:∏; LB *ti*: ∏; LA: Λ;

CM 1–3 *024* (**Λ, Λ**, missing) = *le*$^{??}$ – cf. ncMCs (ancient Paphian) *le*: Λ;[63]

CM 1–3 *033* (**Λ Λ, Ŗ**, missing) = *re*$^{??}$ – cf. ncMCs (ancient Paphian) *re*: Λ Λ;[64]

CM 1–3 *035* (**∭,**[65] **∭, ∭**) = *ne*$^{??}$ – cf. ncMCs *ne*: ∫;

CM 1–3 *044* (**Ш, Ш, Ш**) = *se*$^?$ – cf. ncMCs *se*: Ш; LB *se*: Ш; LA: Ш;

CM 1–3 *064* (**Ψ, Ψ**, missing) = *o*$^{??}$ – cf. ncMCs *o*: ✕;

CM 1–3 *102* (**Ж Ж, Ж, Ж**) = *a*$^?$ – cf. ncMCs *a*: ✳; LB *a*: Ϯ; LA: Ж.

Annex II: 'Nuclei' and 'additions' found in CM 1

1   A problem of reading

There is a problem with the edition of a sequence in *HoChyMin* ##*097.02*, *09* and *26*. The book reads either (#) *082–095–088–023-* or (#) *082–096–088–023-*, with one and the same sign rendered as either *095* or *096*, as shown in Table 2.1.[66]

The three relevant signs are identical, occur in the same text and appear in identical sequences of four signs: # *082-Ŧ-088–023-&-*,

---

[62] *ICS* 66.   [63] O. Masson and Mitford 1986: 13.   [64] *Ibid.*

[65] The facsimiles (∭ ∭) of the CM 1 syllabogram *035* are inaccurate in *HoChyMin*: 414 and *passim*. I give here the photograph of the example of Kalavassos, clay cylinder *HoChyMin* ##*098.12* as shown by E. Masson (1983: pl. XVIII). Olivier (*HoChyMin*: 134) wrongly writes that 'il n'existe pas de vue cavalière des cylindres de Kalavassos'. In fact, E. Masson (1983: 132 and pl. XVIII) has published the isometric projection of *HoChyMin* ##*098* (photograph of the mould) plus a facsimile of the isometric projection.

[66] The shapes of *095* and *096* in columns 3–5 are those shown in the CM 1 table of signs at *HoChyMin*: 414.

Table 2.1 *Different readings of the signs* 𐙇 / 𐙇ʿ / 𐙇ʿ *in* HoChyMin.

The signs actually in the texts	References for the inscriptions	Readings in *HoChyMin*: 123, 126, 132, 485	Readings in *HoChyMin*: 231	Readings in *HoChyMin*: 423
(α) 𐙇	ENKO Arou 001.02	*096*: 𐙇 𐙇	*095*: 𐙇	*096*: 𐙇 𐙇
(β) 𐙇ʿ	ENKO Arou 001.09	*096*: 𐙇 𐙇	*095*: 𐙇	*096*: 𐙇 𐙇
(γ) 𐙇ʿ	ENKO Arou 001.26	*096*: 𐙇 𐙇	*095*: 𐙇	*095*: 𐙇

082-𐙇ʿ-088–023-&- and *082-𐙇ʿ-088–023-*. It is then perfectly clear that one and the same syllabogram is used here. How should it be read?

Let us begin with a correction of *HoChyMin*'s standardised form of *095*:[67] 𐙇 does not accurately show the unique (!) CM 1 example of the sign presented as certain, and its real form is 𐙇.[68]

There are, then, eight CM 1 examples of *096* presented as certain in *HoChyMin*: (a) 𐙇,[69] (b) 𐙇,[70] (c) 𐙇,[71] (d) 𐙇 and 𐙇,[72] (e) 𐙇,[73] (f) 𐙇,[74] (g) 𐙇,[75] (h) 𐙇.[76]

Here are the main differences between *095* and *096*:

---

[67] As published in *HoChyMin*: 80, 413–14.
[68] *HoChyMin* ##034 (clay ball: *HoChyMin*: 80). The other (possible) example appears in *HoChyMin* ##161 (ivory pipe: *HoChyMin*: 231).
[69] *HoChyMin* ##008 (clay ball: *HoChyMin*: 67).
[70] *HoChyMin* ##014 (clay ball, Hand Zaza?: *HoChyMin*: 70).
[71] *HoChyMin* ##028 (clay ball: *HoChyMin*: 77, with the comment '-*096*-: deux petits traits verticaux de chaque côté').
[72] *HoChyMin* ##102.05 (clay cylinder: *HoChyMin*: 168; first facsimile by E. Masson, second one by Olivier).
[73] *HoChyMin* ##102.05 *lat. dex.* (clay cylinder: *HoChyMin*: 168).
[74] *HoChyMin* ##105 (clay pithos: *HoChyMin*: 172).
[75] *HoChyMin* ##165 (golden ring: *HoChyMin*: 238).
[76] *HoChyMin* ##166 (golden ring: *HoChyMin*: 239).

- *The upper part* of sign *096* has six or seven strokes, while the unique certain example of sign *095* has only four upper strokes (〒′).

  Examples (a), (c), (d), (e), (f), (g) and (h) of *096* have six strokes: two horizontal lines in the middle; in the exterior part, four vertical or oblique strokes added to the horizontal lines – a fine example is (g) 帀.

  Example (b) 帋 of *096* has a seventh vertical line dividing in two the upper part of the sign. This supplementary line is missing in sign *095* (〒′).

- *The lower part* of sign *096* has one or two strokes (帀: (a), (b), (c), (d), (e), (f) ~ 帀: (g), (h)), while the lower part of sign *095* has one stroke (〒′).

We may now come back to the signs (α) 帀, (β) 帀′ and (γ) 帀′: we must decide whether they should be read as *095* or *096*. They share the vertical line dividing the superior part[77] that *096* shows in (b) 帋 but that *095* 〒′ lacks. Moreover, the superior left part of (α) 帀 has *two* strokes,[78] just like all the examples of *096*; a similar feature is shown in (β) 帀′ (right side)[79] and (γ) 帀′ (left side)[80] – while *095* 〒′ uses only *one* stroke in both sides. There can thus be no reasonable doubt: (α) 帀, (β) 帀′ and (γ) 帀′ are examples of *096*.

2   List of the 'nuclei' and 'additions' found in CM I[81]

The forms with 'nuclei' of more than three syllabograms are put in **bold**.

101:   **025–004–099–007** #[82] ~ 027–005–025–004–099–096–023[83]
102:   # 025–082–097–011–006 #[84] ~ # 006–025–082–097 #[85]

---

[77] Visible on *HoChyMin*'s photographs and facsimiles.

[78] On *HoChyMin*'s photograph and facsimile.

[79] On *HoChyMin*'s photograph and facsimile.

[80] On *HoChyMin*'s photograph and facsimile.

[81] These 'nuclei' and 'additions' have been collected from the CM I edition in *HoChyMin*: 63–280 – not from the *HoChyMin*: 419–25 list of the CM I forms (see under CM I section 1). The following sequences have not been listed as alternations, since the reading of the sign • is unknown: # •–087–104–097 # (*HoChyMin* ##163; clay ball: *HoChyMin*: 95) ~ # 102–087–104–097 # (*HoChyMin* ##045 (Hand Zazie), ##072; clay balls: *HoChyMin*: 85, 99).

[82] *HoChyMin* ##097.24 (clay cylinder: *HoChyMin*: 131, 484–485).

[83] *HoChyMin* ##097.22 (clay cylinder: *HoChyMin*: 130, 484–485).

[84] *HoChyMin* ##057 (clay ball: *HoChyMin*: 92).

[85] *HoChyMin* ##058 (clay ball: *HoChyMin*: 92).

44

103: # *027–013–110–097–023* #[86] ~ # *027–013–110–097–023-&*[87]

104: # *027–050–012* #[88] ~ # *027–050–012–005–102–087–078* #[89]

105: # *044–061–097* #[90] ~ # *044–061–097–019–110* #[91]

106: *082–096–088–023*[92] ~ (#) *082–096–088–023-&*[93]

107: *102–082–069–088–097–023*[94] ~ # *044–088–097–023*[95]

108: # *102–009–082–085* #[96] ~ # *102–009–082–085–015* #[97]

109: # *102–073–004–097* #[98]/# *102–073–004–097* #[99]/# *102–073–004–097* #[100] ~ # *102–073–004–097–023* #[101] ~ # *102–073–004–097–110–073* #[102]

110: #*102–087–107–097* #[103] ~ # *102–087–107–097–082–008* #[104]

111: # *102–109–004–008–023* #[105] ~ # *102–109–004–013–023* #[106]

112: # *110–023–059* #[107] ~ # *110–023–059–021–023* #[108]

---

[86] *HoChyMin* ##202 (hematite cylinder seal: *HoChyMin*: 276 ('sens de lecture arbitraire')).

[87] *HoChyMin* ##097.04–05 (clay cylinder: *HoChyMin*: 124, 484–5).

[88] *HoChyMin* ##044 (clay ball: *HoChyMin*: 86).

[89] *HoChyMin* ##064 (clay ball: *HoChyMin*: 95).

[90] 2 ex. *HoChyMin* ##020 (clay ball: *HoChyMin*: 73); *HoChyMin* ##051 (clay ball, Hand Zozo: *HoChyMin*: 89).

[91] *HoChyMin* ##047 (clay ball, Hand Zozo: *HoChyMin*: 87).

[92] *HoChyMin* ##097.26 (clay cylinder: *HoChyMin*: 132, 484–485 and see Annex II section 1).

[93] *HoChyMin* ##097.02, 09 (2 ex.; clay cylinder: *HoChyMin*: 123, 126, 484–485 and see Annex II section 1).

[94] *HoChyMin* ##112 (clay amphora: *HoChyMin*: 179).

[95] *HoChyMin* ##097.23 (clay cylinder: *HoChyMin*: 131, 484–5).

[96] *HoChyMin* ##085 (clay ball: *HoChyMin*: 106).

[97] *HoChyMin* ##054 (clay ball: *HoChyMin*: 90).

[98] *HoChyMin* ##016 (clay ball: *HoChyMin*: 71).

[99] *HoChyMin* ##048 (clay ball: *HoChyMin*: 87).

[100] *HoChyMin* ##109 (clay pithos: *HoChyMin*: 176).

[101] *HoChyMin* ##163v (ivory plate with a representation of the god Bes: *HoChyMin*: 236).

[102] *HoChyMin* ##024 (clay ball: *HoChyMin*: 75).

[103] *HoChyMin* ##055 (clay ball: *HoChyMin*: 91).

[104] *HoChyMin* ##088 (clay ball: *HoChyMin*: 108).

[105] *HoChyMin* ##183 (bronze bowl: *HoChyMin*: 256).

[106] *HoChyMin* ##179 (bronze bowl: *HoChyMin*: 252).

[107] *HoChyMin* ##065 (clay ball: *HoChyMin*: 96).

[108] *HoChyMin* ##161.02 (ivory pipe: *HoChyMin*: 231).

Annex III: 'Nuclei' and 'additions' found in CM 2[109]

201: # 004–025–074–054[110] ~ 004–025–074–095 #[111]

202: # 070–027–005–061–095[112] ~ # 079–005–061–095[113]

203: # 017–009–060–059–075 #[114] ~ # 023–009–060–059-•[[115]
~ #104–092–009–060–059 (#)[116]

204: 021–005–075 #[117] ~ # 030–021–005–075–064 #[118]

205: # 025–004–075 #[119] ~ # 078–025–004–075 #[120]

206: # 038–012–097 #[121] ~ # 038–012–097–017 #[122]

207: # 038–033–051 #[123] ~ # 038–033–051–013 #[124]

208: # 025–054–047–060–059 #[125] ~ # 047–047–060–059 #[126]

209: # 052–030–021 #[127] ~ # 052–030–021–013 #[128]

210: 068–025–097 #[129] ~ # 068–025–097–017 #[130]

211: # 102–025–075 #[131]/# 102–025–075 #[132] ~ 102–025–075–
096 <#>[133]

212: # 102–075–004 #[134] ~ 102–075–004–054 [#][135]

---

[109] These 'nuclei' and 'additions' have been collected from the concordance of the CM 2 syllabograms published in *HoChyMin*: 427–79, with the corrections needed (see under CM 2 section 1).

[110] *HoChyMin* ##208.A.12 (clay tablet: *HoChyMin*: 327, 491–3).

[111] *HoChyMin* ##208.A.14 (clay tablet: *HoChyMin*: 326, 491–3).

[112] *HoChyMin* ##208.A.17 (clay tablet: *HoChyMin*: 329, 491–3).

[113] *HoChyMin* ##207.A.I.43 (clay tablet: *HoChyMin*: 295, 487–8).

[114] *HoChyMin* ##207.A.I.30 (clay tablet: *HoChyMin*: 289, 487–8).

[115] *HoChyMin* ##208.B.12 (clay tablet: *HoChyMin*: 337, 491–3).

[116] *HoChyMin* ##209.B.04, B.05 (2 ex.; clay tablet: *HoChyMin*: 374–5, 497).

[117] *HoChyMin* ##207.A.I.31 (clay tablet: *HoChyMin*: 288, 487–8).

[118] *HoChyMin* ##208.A.04 (clay tablet: *HoChyMin*: 322–3, 491–3).

[119] *HoChyMin* ##208.B.16 (clay tablet: *HoChyMin*: 338–9, 491–3).

[120] *HoChyMin* ##207.B.I.10 (clay tablet: *HoChyMin*: 307, 489–90).

[121] *HoChyMin* ##209.B.14 (clay tablet: *HoChyMin*: 379, 497).

[122] *HoChyMin* ##207.B.I.13 (clay tablet: *HoChyMin*: 308–9, 489–90).

[123] *HoChyMin* ##208.A.05, A.08, A.11 (3 ex.; clay tablet: *HoChyMin*: 322, 324, 326, 491–493). Notice that # 038–033–051 # is directly followed by # 038–033 # in *HoChyMin* ##208.A.05.

[124] *HoChyMin* ##208.A.19 (clay tablet: *HoChyMin*: 328–9, 491–3).

[125] *HoChyMin* ##209.B.22 (clay tablet: *HoChyMin*: 383, 497).

[126] *HoChyMin* ##209.B.07 (clay tablet: *HoChyMin*: 374, 497).

[127] *HoChyMin* ##208.A.01 (clay tablet: *HoChyMin*: 322, 491–3).

[128] *HoChyMin* ##208.B.18 (clay tablet: *HoChyMin*: 338, 491–3).

[129] *HoChyMin* ##209.B.10 (clay tablet: *HoChyMin*: 376, 497).

[130] *HoChyMin* ##208.A.15 (clay tablet: *HoChyMin*: 327, 491–3).

[131] *HoChyMin* ##208.A.15 (clay tablet: *HoChyMin*: 326, 491–3).

[132] *HoChyMin* ##207.B.I.22 (clay tablet: *HoChyMin*: 313, 489–90).

[133] *HoChyMin* ##209.B.08 (clay tablet: *HoChyMin*: 376, 497).

[134] *HoChyMin* ##208.A.11, A.14 (2 ex.; clay tablet: *HoChyMin*: 327, 491–3).

[135] *HoChyMin* ## 208.A.I.30 (clay tablet: *HoChyMin*: 288, 487–8).

Annex IV: 'Nuclei' and 'additions' found in CM 3[136]

301: # *082–058–055–009–070* #[137] ~ # *104–009–055–009–070*
      #[138]

302: # *102–025–087* #[139] ~ # *102–025–087–051* #[140]

Abbreviations and sigla

nCMCs	non-Cypro-Minoan Cypriot syllabaries[141]
~	versus
#	sequences' division considered as clear
*	reconstructed form
**	form considered as unacceptable
001	not securely identified sign
[ ]	deliberately erased text.

---

[136] These 'nuclei' and 'additions' have been collected from the CM 3 edition in *HoChyMin*: 385–409 – not from *HoChyMin*: 481–2 list of the CM 3 forms (see under CM 3 section 2). I have therefore not taken into consideration **004–013–036-[023] (*sic*; *HoChyMin* ##212.A.03: 481). If correct, this sequence should be compared with *004–013–036* (*HoChyMin* ##215.A.04) and would yield a 'nucleus' **004–013–036(-). In fact, **004–013–036-[023] does not exist: it is a mistake for *104–036-[023]*.

[137] *HoChyMin* ##215.B.19 (clay tablet: *HoChyMin*: 407).

[138] *HoChyMin* ##215.B.14 (clay tablet: *HoChyMin*: 405).

[139] *HoChyMin* ##215.A.01 (clay tablet: *HoChyMin*: 400).

[140] *HoChyMin* ##215.B.15 (clay tablet: *HoChyMin*: 406).

[141] The denominations currently given to the syllabic scripts of Cyprus that are not members of the Cypro-Minoan group are troublesome (and the regular use of quotation marks – e.g. 'Classical' Cypriot syllabaries – do not solve the problem). (a) 'Classical syllabaries' or such like is difficult, since these scripts appear already in the *archaic* period. (b) 'Cypro-syllabic scripts' 'Cypriot syllabary', 'Linear C' or the like are not better, since these labels theoretically match *the whole range of the Cypriot syllabic scripts, second and first millennium included*. (c) 'Cypriot Greek syllabaries' or such like is not appropriate either, since these scripts were used to write not only Greek but also a *non-Hellenic* language (Eteocypriot). (d) I had wondered whether 'first-millennium Cypriot syllabaries' would not be a good label. It cannot be properly used, however, because some CM inscriptions could be ascribed to the first millennium (e.g. *HoChyMin* ##190, dated CG I–II, 1050–850; relative date: Vandenabeele 2007: 37). Moreover, a Cypriot syllabic inscription securely dated to the *second millennium* BC and not written in a CM script could perhaps be discovered. Hence my (admittedly complicated) 'non-Cypro-Minoan Cypriot syllabaries'.

3

WRITING IN CYPRO-MINOAN: ONE SCRIPT, TOO MANY?

SILVIA FERRARA

From a general perspective, this contribution focuses on the palaeography of the Cypro-Minoan script and, more in particular, it will examine the long-debated question of whether Cypro-Minoan constitutes one homogeneous script, or whether it rightfully denotes subgroups of the same writing system. This question, and the possibility of reaching a balanced, if perhaps not definitive, answer to it, is not idle. It bears more than one implication, as it calls for further arguments and the assessment of their validity on fields other than pure palaeography. It of course branches into the nature of the relationship between writing and language on Cyprus at the end of the Late Bronze Age, specifically the possibility of positing multiliteracy and multilingualism, and it will need to be measured against the dissonances and contradictions emerging from a complementary examination of the archaeological record.

Palaeography and beyond

Most of the less recent studies on Cypro-Minoan have concentrated on the possible nature of the language behind the script,[1] and as such they have focused on questions of sign morphology and to drawing graphic and phonetic parallels with the other, better-known, linear systems. While such a direction assumes, in a rather

I am very grateful to Philippa Steele for having invited me to the conference from which this volume arises. I am also grateful to Dr S. Sherratt and Prof. J. Bennet for their comments and suggestions, and to Dr M. Egeler and A. Rigolio for reading earlier drafts of this chapter.
[1] E. Masson in her publications spanning two decades is the principal contributor to the study of this subject, while several other scholars have advanced a number of interpretations that aim to shed light on the language(s) registered in Cypro-Minoan.

49

mechanical and uncritical manner, that Cypro-Minoan is to be accepted as filially rooted in the Aegean writing tradition without fully or cogently explaining how and why (See Sherratt, Chapter 4 in this volume), it has altogether been taken at the virtually complete expense of an analysis of the epigraphy of the script, and almost always betrays an underlying bias towards linguistic interpretation.

A study that focuses on matters of sign morphology, that identifies shape variants based on the recognisable master signs, that looks for scratches, ornaments and traits, cannot be decoupled from a study of the physical characteristics of the inscribed objects, of the writing implements used, of the individual hands, and the assessment of whether or not they betray a membership of a certain style or 'scribal tradition' (Driessen 2000). Such a study cannot shy away from an evaluation of what can be described, paraphrasing A. Bataille (between 1954 and 1959–60), as the struggle between medium, stylus and the hand that produces writing.

Even from a superficial consultation of the repertoire of signs attested in the syllabary, as compiled by E. Masson (E. Masson 1974), the palaeography of the Cypro-Minoan script appears rich in graphic oddities and segmental minutiae: given the impossibility of discerning sign variants from separate signs, these were not appraised for the sake of elaborating a normalised repertoire but simply compiled in lists. Clearly, at that point, the syllabary had yet to be perfectly defined in its graphic structure.

Here lies the problem: in the absence of an immediate graphic homogeneity, the relationship between the signs' renditions and the material supports that carry them becomes an essential trajectory of analysis. So how does the range of inscribed objects, which in the case of Cypro-Minoan is particularly wide, influence the manner of inscription? And can we recognise a level of homogeneity in the allegedly pervasive graphic variation?

The Cypro-Minoan script stands today divided into four different subsystems: Archaic CM (or CM 0, see *HoChyMin*), CM 1, CM 2 and CM 3 (E. Masson 1972; 1976). This classification, established predominantly by E. Masson, with the input of Olivier Masson (O. Masson 1968), in the late 1960s has thrived in the last few decades, and every publication on the script accepts it *de facto*, without any radical or even superficial questioning of its validity. In the 1980s, some level of pressure was exercised on dismantling it, first by A.B. Knapp and A. Marchant (Knapp and Marchant 1982) and then, more forcefully and exhaustively, by T.G. Palaima (Palaima 1989a). Such prompting seems to have fallen into oblivion, because since then all publications that mention Cypro-Minoan have bypassed the issue, and, oddly, even those written by the scholars who firstly purported the invalidity of the classification (Palaima 2005) reiterate it, taking it for granted, without openly disowning their previous stance.

This puzzling state of affairs deserves a further and closer look, one that will not limit its scope to the minutiae of palaeography and sign-shapes, but that will embrace a more contextual approach, drawing in archaeological as well as historical factors in considering the implications of Masson's classification. Before analysing the classification in detail, it must be noted that the grounds upon which the subsystems are devised are uniquely palaeographic, deriving from the peculiarities shown in each purported class and the divergences seen between classes in the graphic manifestations of the script. It will be stressed below that the contextual ramifications of such a construction are far-reaching and pervasive, and it will be pointed out that the palaeographic picture that emerges does not mirror in any close way the archaeological situation.

Let us now turn to a description of the three subgroups, from a perspective that considers typological, chronological and geographical factors. In this analysis I shall list Palaima's concerns (1989a), and stress my own, by extending the picture further into linguistic and historical considerations. The so-called Archaic CM will be treated last, because it deserves particular attention, as it presents insurmountable problems, both from a palaeographic and from an archaeological perspective. CM 1 is supposed to denote the original, principal foundation of the script, allegedly used to record the indigenous language of the Late Bronze Age Cypriot population, and from it CM 2 and CM 3 are thought to have originated (E. Masson 1972). The subgroups will need to be analysed individually with respect to the material range in which they are inscribed, and consequently their contextual details will need to be discussed. In surveying this first aspect, I shall detail some considerations that have to do with the manner in which the objects reviewed are inscribed and the difficulties that ensue in identifying correctly the varieties of Cypro-Minoan signs. This survey is significant because it highlights, visually, the relationship between epigraphy (broadly, how medium or writing support affects graphemes) and palaeography (the resulting manner of inscription), and brings to life the particular difficulty of addressing this issue where Cypro-Minoan is concerned.

CM 1 is recorded on a wide range of epigraphic supports. It was inscribed on clay, painted, incised on hard metals, ivory and stone, and was also impressed. The variety in media and the resulting different styles of inscription (*ductus*) are technical aspects that will, naturally and to a wide-ranging degree, affect and dictate the appearance of the graphemes and influence the overall graphic effect. Indeed, the result is more varied and diverse than the number of different media used. When painted, the inscription seems to be created by rounded punches, with a blot-like effect produced by the ink (Smith 2003). On the clay balls the writing implement seems to be tapered in triangular or even rectangular section and gives a wedge-like quality to the impressions, but sometimes the effect is more drawn and linear. When inscribed on already fired clay, as on the pottery fragment no. 4025 (Dikaios 1967: 84–5 pl. vi b, b; E. Masson : 22 fig. 8), the signs seem incised rather than inscribed, dragged along on the clay and yielding more angular, almost scratched shapes. A similar result is also achieved on the miniature bronze ingots (O. Masson 1952: 451–4), albeit with deeper incisions into the metal. Given the diversity observable, it is worth considering the material classes inscribed in CM 1 to give an idea of how remarkably varied and complex the epigraphic picture is. This analysis allows us, at times, not only to reconstruct and re-enact the activity of inscribing objects but also to ascertain the identification of signs and the frequent uncertainties that riddle the 'reading' process.

On Cyprus there are five examples of small clay cylinders from Kalavassos-*Ayios Dhimitrios* (E. Masson 1983) and one larger example from Enkomi, inv. no. 19.10 (E. Masson 1971a: figs. 1–7). The five cylinders from Kalavassos were originally thought by Masson to have functioned as ritual foundation deposits, given the alleged formulaic contents of the texts. This theory was later reassessed and the cylinders reinterpreted as administrative texts concerning the industrial activities run in the building (Smith 2002b: 20–5). In the course of this re-examination, two specimens were identified as palimpsests, carrying two or more texts superimposed which, together with the identification of numerical notations on one item (K.A-D 338), led to the conclusion that these documents may have had an economic function.

Despite the poor preservation and very damaged state of the Kalavassos cylinders, during another autopsy on these pieces I became convinced that two more specimens bear numerical notations (K.A-D 405 and K.A-D 545, see Ferrara 2012b). This conclusion can only be advanced while at the same time admitting that most of the signs on these objects are identifiable only tentatively even by the sharpest of eyes, and that, contrary to E. Masson's claim, no sequences seem, except with a deal of imagination, to be repeated. As to the possible purpose, the context in which the cylinders were found can hardly support the theory that they were tied to religious practices. On the other hand, even though the repeated attestations of numerals should give a strong hint, one must be circumspect in guessing their function, because palimpsests are not a prerogative of administrative texts only: we find plenty of evidence for that in practice texts in the Near East too. But even more significantly, it must be conceded that the shape of the objects cannot be seen as practically conducive to easy consultation, a prerequisite for accounting records to be conveniently read at a glance.[2]

Some of the most problematic cases of sign identification are due to the rendering of the script on metal. Of the thirty inscriptions on metal objects, more than two-thirds present signs that are not immediately recognisable. Even within the same class of object, technical variation is observable. An example of such variation is seen on the three copper miniature ingots from Enkomi[3]

---

[2] Also, as a corollary, it remains to be seen how the Kalavassos pieces relate to the larger Enkomi cylinder, whose subject matter appears not to be linked to an administrative function (since no numerals are recorded): although this piece appears to fall into the same typological category, its ultimate purpose need not be related.

[3] Inv. nos. 53.2, 53.3 and 1936/VI-19/1.

(O. Masson 1952; Ferrara 2012b) Two specimens are incised in hardened metal, and their signs are sharp, thin and shallow; the incision on the third (no. 1936/VI-19/1) is thick, deep and rather similar to an inscription applied on a soft material, produced, it seems, through the lost-wax technique (Catling 1964: 268 pl. 49h).[4] So, even within the small number of incised Cypro-Minoan signs on metals, a great variety of technical expertise can be observed, and the competence in craftsmanship does not necessarily go hand in hand with knowledge of the script and its intricacies. Such often-inferable inaccuracy is nothing but a parasitic element and a further interpretational impediment. And when it comes to examples of inscribed stone, the difficulty of identifying sign-shapes is even more frustrating: the incisions are always tentative and hesitant, and some of the signs seem to have been incised and then incised again over the original design, to re-affirm their shape (Ferrara 2012a).

Even more fitting is the graphic variety seen on the clay balls. There are ninety examples of such objects: size-wise, the majority of the balls lies within an average diameter of 2 cm. Small size and spherical shape are not theoretically conducive to regular writing, and inscribing on items such as these requires a high level of dexterity in maintaining the inscription on a regular horizontal plane while turning the ball round its vertical axis, and equally avoiding the smudging of already inscribed signs. This class of object offers remarkable insight into the techniques of inscription, since its graphic idiosyncrasies are a striking feature. The characteristics of the signs vary to a remarkable extent: the discrete strokes that compose the syllabograms can be deep and thin, thin and shallow, and deep and thick. What is more intriguing is that the repertoire of signs presents some oddities, despite the already mentioned differences resulting from different writing procedures. These oddities point to what has been defined as 'a certain deformation of the signs' (E. Masson 1971b: 479–504), since more than one sign is unidentified and apparently unattested outside this class of objects (see below).

---

[4] It should be noted that the photograph of this ingot is upside-down in Catling's publication.

To conclude this brief survey, according to Masson's classification CM 1, in all its epigraphic and palaeographic diversity, is attested in all the primary urban centres of Cyprus and in some of the secondary inland ones across the whole of the Late Bronze Age. It spans at least 300 years, is represented in a very broad range of classes of object and is quantifiable on the basis of more than 200 inscriptions, most of them very short, but some relatively long.

CM 2, however, is geographically concentrated, synchronic and typologically homogeneous. It is represented by four fragments of tablets found at Enkomi,[5] two of which were joined together in 1980 (Michaelidou-Nicolaou 1980). The sign repertoire is unparalleled in its uniformity, and this has been the motivating factor for grouping the four tablet fragments into this separate CM 2 set. Its homogeneity does not stop at the manner of inscription, or at the assumed completeness of its signary.[6] The fragments are also more or less concentrated chronologically (Dikaios 1967), share a similar format (E. Masson 1970, 1973, 1978) and, more importantly from an interpretative perspective, present a high number of repeated word-sequences in their continuous writing.

Again according to Masson, two tablets found at Ugarit,[7] in coastal Syria, and a cylinder seal from Lattakia,[8] located north of Ugarit, represent the third subgroup CM 3 (E. Masson). Often in the past literature, and also in very recent publications on the subject, it has been noted that the third subgroup forms the *entirety* of the material found at Ugarit, singled out, it seems, on the basis of a handier, but inaccurate, geographical principle. The material consists altogether of nine inscriptions, one of which, a pithos rim, is missing, and another of which, a label from the residence of Urtenu, is still awaiting publication.

Now let us concentrate on some implications deriving from the founding of this classification. First, it is necessary to reiterate that Masson's three subgroups are not evinced on the basis of a geographical principle, nor is the typological criterion the discriminating factor, since not all three subgroups are consistently

---

[5] Inv. nos. 1687, 53.3, 1193 and 20.01. The latter two are the ones joined together.
[6] With fifty-nine distinct signs, the syllabary of the Enkomi tablets is thought to be relatively 'perfectionné', cf. E. Masson : 49 and fig. 3.1.
[7] Inv. nos. RS 20.025 and RS 17.006.   [8] Inv. no. RS 358.

homogeneous in relation to the typological class of material support inscribed (with the exception of CM 2), nor are they chronologically consistently and dependably coherent. The sole criterion upon which Emilia Masson observed and established the classification is purely and uniquely palaeographic: it is assumed that a number of signs in the three subgroups are not shared and differ to the extent whereby the Cypro-Minoan script can, and rightfully should, be fragmented and divided.

Micro-contexts: the classification reassessed

One can wonder, at least in theory, whether such a principle, even though indispensable and urgent, may suffice in isolation to definitively settle the matter and validate the classification as it is. Specifically in one case, such a criterion cannot be deemed sufficiently cogent, and this case is represented by Archaic CM or CM 0. The corpus of inscriptions constituting this subgroup is represented by two jars from Katydata,[9] a 'weight'[10] and a clay tablet from Enkomi[11] (E. Masson 1974). The criterion Masson used for collecting this material together and gathering it under the definition of Archaic is, evidently, chronological, given the name of the subset, as well as palaeographic. She gathers together disparate material: what she calls a 'weight', which allegedly dates to the middle of the sixteenth century BC, and two jars, which she assumes are roughly coeval. The supposed 'weight' may not even be such, as it is unlikely that it was meant to be suspended, since the inscription would have had to be read upside-down; most probably it is a label of the flat, oblong type, pointed at one end, that is sometimes found on Crete as well (*GORILA*: pl. vi, 3, pl. vii, 6 (which preserves a numeral: 7000) and 7).[12] The date of this piece is not beyond dispute, since the circumstances of its recovery are, at best, extremely vague. As to the jars, Masson's chronological

---

[9] Inv. nos. A1493 and A1496.   [10] Inv. no. 19.13.   [11] Inv. no. 1885.

[12] Comparative evidence from the Cretan Hieroglyphic deposits at Knossos and Mallia shows that labels fall into the same typological sphere as our 'weight'. They are flat, oblong pieces of clay, pointed at one end, where they are also pierced, and usually inscribed on one or both sides. Only one example of a label inscribed in Linear A, from Phaestos, with a logogram 412^{vas} and the numeral 1, is attested (PH 9, in *GORILA*, vol. 1: 298).

details are incorrect, since they are quite reliably dated by Aström 1989 to the Late Cypriot IIB and the Late Cypriot IIC–IIIA phases, therefore a century later at the earliest. Even palaeographically, the collection of this material is not coherent: the repertoire of signs on the jars fully mirrors the later graphic development of Cypro-Minoan, and parallels with this 'subsystem' can be clearly drawn. Somehow it seems completely discordant to find it here.

I would be tempted to conclude that this corpus of inscriptions cannot be singled out to constitute a separate subsystem, and, if we accept that the dates for the weight and the jars are not reliable, the Archaic repertoire, even if we wish to call it that, is therefore represented only by the Enkomi tablet (*HoChyMin*: 25, 30, 60–1; and also Olivier, Chapter 1 in this volume). The contextual details surrounding this fragment are less vague, if still not completely sound, and thus we may concede that this is indeed the first attestation of formal Cypro-Minoan we have.

In quantitative terms, the number of individual signs here, twenty-one in total, cannot be accepted as a 'writing system', even if we saw it in terms of a subset. If anything, this is a subset of an early form of Cypro-Minoan that we cannot see in its completeness because we have no further evidence for it. Whether it is an abandoned branch of the script, which is the view that Olivier favours (Chapter 1 in this volume), or whether it is an already modified stage of the newly developed writing system borrowed from Minoan Linear A, it is impossible to ascertain, but, quite simply, it cannot be accepted as a formally attested, quantifiable, scientifically observable subgroup.

In listing the quantitative deficiencies inherent in all the subsystems, by the same line of reasoning CM 3, too, raises doubts. The notion that the two tablets from Ugarit and the cylinder seal from Lattakia can constitute a self-standing branch of Cypro-Minoan is hardly tenable. The number of attested signs in the repertoire of CM 3 *stricto sensu* is fewer than 300. In addition, it remains to be explained why the remainder of the inscriptions found at Ugarit were not grouped with the real CM 3. Masson never gives grounds for her classification from a perspective other than the palaeographic, and naturally this is a scenario that requires to be delved into more thoroughly than the extant literature allows; this is only achieved if different viewpoints are adopted in order to make sense of the oddities and graphic divergences observable in the morphology of the CM 3 sign-shapes. In other words, it is not enough to state that CM 3 is a convenient geographic subgroup. Palaeographically, it is nothing but a disparate material collation of CM 3, represented by the two tablets and a cylinder seal (inv. nos. RS 20.025, RS 17.006 and RS 358, respectively), together with some inscriptions ascribed to CM 1 (two tablet fragments: inv. nos. RS19.001 and RS19.002, and the published label RS 94.2328, Yon 1999: fig. 4), and a silver bowl (RS 3.289, E. Masson : 19), which Masson does not ascribe to any subgroup. Why is this? Can we go beyond stating that at Ugarit at least two different branches of Cypro-Minoan are attested and make sense of this geographical overlap between CM 1 and CM 3?

A possible explanation for finding Cypro-Minoan inscriptions at Ugarit which appear, to a degree, divergent in their graphic renditions, may be that the two tablets written in CM 3 were written in situ at Ugarit, probably by Ugarit agents, whereas the other two tablet fragments, and most probably the labels too, may have been sent from Cyprus. This is not a recondite assumption if one looks at the pinacology of the CM 3 tablets: in their cushion shape and minute dimensions, and in the punched manner of their inscription, they both fit remarkably well into the cuneiform writing tradition. Also, from a micro-contextual perspective, they are embedded in the highly organised archival system of Ugarit, found in association with epigraphically similar Akkadian syllabic cuneiform tablets (Courtois 1990). This would justify their apparent oddities in the sign-shapes as simple scribal variations from the CM 1 found on Cyprus, probably resulting from the fact that the scribes responsible for their compilation were not particularly versed in the art of writing with the original Cypro-Minoan script attested on the island. This conclusion, if at all correct, prompts another question of a linguistic nature and points to a reconsideration of past views: is there a specific reason why the Ugarit scribes would use the Cypro-Minoan script to register their indigenous language, Ugaritic, as Masson proposes in her monograph on the script (E. Masson 1974)?

Therefore, if this brief survey has any value as fitting historical explanation, it will regrettably not solve the difficulty raised when we turn to the sign repertoire of this subset, with its forty-nine individual signs: this is, just like the Archaic CM, not a complete, formally 'workable' writing system. If we reasoned *per absurdum* and chose to claim that the three subsystems indeed record three different languages, and even if we were fully capable of reading Cypro-Minoan (i.e. of identifying and recognising the values of all its signs), we would still not fully be able to read CM 3, simply because we cannot see all the graphemes in the syllabary, since we only possess incomplete attestations.

But the imbalances do not cease here. They are also observable when we look at the other subgroups, CM 1 and CM 2. Fewer than 250 inscriptions altogether (Ferrara 2012a and 2012b; *HoChyMin*, which catalogues only 217 inscriptions), the corpus is in itself so small that seeking ways of fragmenting it appears impractical and counterproductive (Knapp and Marchant 1982). And just by way of viewing the corpus from angles other than the analysis of its signs, on chronological, geographical and typological grounds, the subgroups are somewhat imbalanced (Palaima 1989a). Conversely, however, one may wonder whether, at least theoretically, the con-textual imbalances one sees at a macro level should be rightfully considered a problematic feature: if the script is so graphically varied, it has to be classified through division into subgroups. But one should not stop at claiming that this is indeed the case without providing further and fuller explanation as to why this is. And even if the imbalances emerge from a superficial snap-shot of the evi-dence, even if they are but a collateral feature, a contingency that does not impinge on evaluating the nature of the script, they still need to be explained by means of the same instrument that engen-ders them: context. Just as the imbalance observable in the dispa-rate material collation that constitutes CM 3 can be explained through context, by the same token we should aim to unravel the oddities we see between CM 1 and CM 2. And this is where further problems surface.

CM 1 is distributed all around Cyprus but, with more than 120 inscriptions, the evidence from Enkomi is overwhelming. This is of course partially due to the fact that the number of clay balls attested there (86) accounts for the vast majority of the inscribed material in CM 1 (Ferrara 2012a). However, Enkomi is also where we find the four tablet fragments that constitute the second subgroup, CM 2 (see note 5). This overlap is not only geographical but also chronological. A good portion of the balls and the tablet fragments are approximately contemporary. So, if it is true that CM 1 and CM 2 record two different languages, how do we explain their cohabitation in the same place at the same time? Are we to suspect that at least two different language (or fully bilingual) groups were incorporated at Enkomi towards the end of the Late Bronze Age? If this is so, can we claim that they appropriated different ways of recording information, one dedicated to the tablet format, and another, articulated in a more varied fashion, that comprised the manufacture of the clay balls? And again, how do we reconcile the fact that clay balls are also attested at Kition (Karageorghis and Demas 1985: 104, 281–2 and 114, 282)[13] and Hala Sultan Tekke (Walters 1897:–8; Obrink 1979 5),[14] therefore possibly being part of an island-wide material *koine*? If these objects are indeed firmly integrated in the indigenous Cypriot material culture, what do we make of the tablets, which are only attested on the island at Enkomi and nowhere else? In other words, are the tablets an extraneous feature both linguistically and typologically, and do they mark the passage of a new people group, in the same way that Linear A was appropriated by the Mycenaeans to create Linear B and record their own language?

In an effort to answer these questions, it does not help that the archaeological contexts for the tablets representing CM 2 are less than clear. We can say they are definitively not in primary deposition (Dikaios 1963). Had they been found in a concentration or assemblage, in a unique location that would represent or approximate an archive of sorts, we would be tempted to make sense of their coherence and accept them as a self-standing group, *a fortiori* and because of their contextual isolation. But such an inference is impossible. It would be pointless to relate again the associations in which these pieces were found, as Dikaios has already done this (1963), and in the present analysis they would confuse the picture further. Let it suffice to say that tablet inv. no. 1687 was found discarded in the filling of a hearth, and tablet inv. no. 1193 was used with other fragments of pottery as part of the building material in

[13] Inv. nos. 4215 and 4959.   [14] Inv. nos. 98.12–1.204 and N6035.

north Enkomi (Ferrara 2012a). By the time these pieces were re-used they had clearly lost their significance as writing supports. It is equally impossible to assume, archaeologically, the presence of a different population with a different material culture: though reliance on obvious material indications of such a kind is in theory problematic, there is, in any case, no trace of an abrupt discontinuity in the archaeological record, and there seems to be no considerable migration influx and, clearly, no 'invasion'.

Altogether, the picture is complicated and partial: Cypro-Minoan as a writing system is a variegated affair that engenders, inherently, problems of classification. And even if we are to accept Masson's idea, the issue is whether we should accept her subsets as they are presented, because, as we have seen, the Archaic one at least is not at all justified or justifiable on chronological or palaeographic grounds, and CM 3 does not represent a self-sufficient system that can be defined as a 'system of writing' in the sense of a formal script.

In whichever way we evaluate the details of her contribution, with the due caveats and the due exemptions, what is crucial is that when we look at the inscriptions as part of a material record that is well integrated in terms of chronology, geography and typology, the overall picture that we gain is at times disharmonious or plainly reticent. Palaeography tells us a story that archaeology does not particularly reflect or agree with. And even if we accept the idea that there is no such thing as a single homogeneous Cypro-Minoan, if we conclude that we are dealing with a substantially fragmented reality of different writing systems, then we still have to explain why this is by means other than a mere palaeographic analysis, albeit an accurate and detailed one. The idea is that even if we do have more than one Cypro-Minoan, we need not stop at palaeography to make sense of the contextual imbalances and the problematic overlaps, and that although palaeography may explain *how* the scripts differ from each other it cannot explain *why*. Clearly, these questions should bear equal weight, and the answer can only be found when both disciplines work in synergy.

Now that we have surveyed the classification from the viewpoint of the epigraphy and the range of material records, and have evaluated the ramifications that such a classification engenders from the viewpoint of archaeology and contexts, we need to consider in more detail the fundamental points that highlight the differences between CM 1, CM 2 and CM 3 in their essence as 'syllabaries'. In an effort to see the big picture, we should not lose sight of the minute details. To these we shall turn, but not before we have mentioned the observant researchers that have contributed to the palaeography of Cypro-Minoan and detail their views in the light of our reassessment.

Micro-structures: the syllabaries

Studies of Cypro-Minoan began in 1900 when Arthur Evans analysed three clay balls and a gold ring from Hala Sultan Tekke (Evans 1900). With as many as fifteen distinct signs in the repertoire at his disposal, Evans identified patterns of similarity with the Aegean linear scripts and set out parameters for cross-comparisons that may be questionable today but that, at the time, gave an insightful account of the origin of writing on Cyprus. What he thought was the 'absolute conformity' of the Cypriot prototypes with Aegean specimens was the basis for naming the writing system Cypro-Minoan. Later, Evans added the evidence provided by another clay ball, and a pottery fragment (*PM* IV). The points of comparison with the other Aegean scripts that he noticed led him to postulate, with surprising foresight, a repertoire of about a hundred potential signs for the Cypro-Minoan signary. Despite this, he never formalised it.

Daniel, after him, produced the first repertoire of signs (Daniel 1941). Although his collection lacks all the formal inscriptions, such as the tablets, which were to be discovered at a later date, he applied some rational principles for classifying the available material and for extracting a comprehensive repertoire of distinct signs. More importantly, Daniel was the first scholar to draw attention to the sensitivity of *ductus* and the process of writing signs onto a variable range of supports. This makes him the pioneer of Cypro-Minoan palaeography, and his signary is the basis on which all later works have relied. More than half the signs added to his repertoire were to be preserved in the signary established in the 1970s by Emilia Masson.

But we need to fast-forward thirty years, before her work was published and before we find in her the principal contributor to the analysis of the Cypro-Minoan script. Masson's publications are scattered, but they have greatly enlarged our knowledge of the peculiarities of the signary. Her work, though remarkably influential on account of the accurate publication of the transcription of the texts and insightful on account of the painstaking observations on the peculiarities of sign-variations, falls short of establishing a standardised syllabary in full form. The principal problem is that what she produced was an essential list of the sign repertoire, but she falls into the same trap that lured Daniel, despite having much more material at her disposal: her signary is a collation of all the attested distinct signs (gathered under her tripartite classification) as they appear on the inscriptions, in all their graphic variations, but presented in an undigested fashion.

Palaima's reaction to her division into subgroups was to declare it invalid (Palaima 1989a). He sought to review and dissolve the classification on account of two principles: the first is that Masson did not see the intertwined relationship between the shapes of signs and the objects that received them, and she failed to see the graphic expression of a script as influenced by its physical transposition onto one or several media. The act of writing is both at the mercy of the object to be inscribed, and also at the mercy of the hand of the individual who produces it – a correlation that, Palaima claims, Masson failed to see. The second principle was that progress in the study of the script had to be directed towards a re-classification of the objects in the light of the different techniques by which inscriptions are created, and the evidence ought to be analysed in accordance with each class of inscription separately: pottery, clay balls, tablets, etc. Consequent to this goal is an assessment of the level of stability and fluctuation in the morphology of the signs depending on the influence that the physical characteristics of a medium exercise on them and frame the degree of variation within the same typological class of object from a synchronic perspective. His methodology is as pragmatic and sound as can be. A contextual epigraphic analysis was indeed necessary. But would this lead to the complete dissolution of Masson's classification?

Jean-Pierre Olivier thinks not. In the signaries he produced for his *Édition holistique des textes chypro-minoens*, affectionately and characteristically acronymised *HoChyMin*, he revises

63

Masson's list on the basis of the methodological stance urged by Palaima. Each class of inscribed object was studied separately, and the different hands responsible for the different variations in the sign-shapes were analysed in relation to the inscribed objects; we, however, only get to see the end-result: Olivier revises Masson's CM 1 signary and produces the first standardised syllabary for this subgroup, in which some idiosyncratic signs (thirteen in total),[15] which Masson singled out in her list, are assimilated, merged together with others and deemed to be nothing but slightly divergent graphic variants of the same sign, (e.g. mirror images of an already attested sign) or to present minute variations (cf., for instance, the three variants of sign 82, isolated by Masson (E. Masson : 15), but incorporated by Olivier (*HoChyMin*: 414)).

Conversely, signs that might be deemed very similar ought not to be confused as being the same if they appear on the same document and are therefore written by the same hand (cf. signs 23 and 24, *HoChyMin*; *ibid*.). The figures relative to CM 1 are, therefore, as follows: 1,300 attested signs that create a repertoire of 72 distinct signs (and not the total of 85 which Masson produced in 1974). Out of this pool of data, nineteen signs are particular to this subgroup, which means that they are not attested in the other subgroups. When we move to the repertoire in CM 2, the syllabary elaborated by Masson is not greatly modified by Olivier's intervention, with the exception of three signs.[16] Again the details and figures relative to the CM 2 subcategory: although it appears only on the four tablet

---

[15]
1   sign 14 in Masson is disposed of
2   sign 16 is assimilated to 82 Y
3   sign 18 is assimilated to 19 𝄚
4   sign 31 is assimilated to 41 𝈀
5   sign 32 is assimilated to 30 𝈁
6   sign 42 is assimilated to 39)(
7   sign 43 is assimilated to 55 '𝈂'
8   sign 45 is a mirror of 44 𝈃
9   sign 48 is assimilated to 82 Y
10   sign 57 is assimilated to 82 Y
11   sign 77 is assimilated to 75 ⊞
12   sign 106 is disposed of
13   sign 111 is disposed of.

[16] sign 13 in the shape 𝈄 does not feature in Masson; sign 57 𝈅 is actually sign 82 Y for Olivier, and sign 91 𝈆 is introduced by Olivier, since it does not feature in Masson.

fragments from Enkomi, we have more signs attested here, just short of 2000, than in the entirety of CM 1. The signs in the repertoire are fewer, only sixty-one, and the signs attested only in this subgroup are fifteen. And lastly, comparing the signary for CM 3 in Masson and Olivier, it is clear that Olivier introduced three more signs to the repertoire, and assimilated the mirror image of sign 19.[17] Figures for CM 3 are limited: as we saw above, it comprises, strictly speaking, only two tablets and a cylinder seal, and the number of attested signs in these three documents does not reach quite a total of 300. As mentioned, the repertoire of individual signs is not fully represented, but out of the signs that are attested, seven are peculiar and found are only in this subgroup.

If we try to find some level of common ground and some shared features in the three subgroups as drawn by Masson and rectified by Olivier, we see that what we define as Cypro-Minoan, what makes the essence of this script recognisable and ascribable to the same tradition and the same family, is this: a mere thirty-two signs. This is exactly one-third of the total of ninety-six signs that form the three repertoires of CM 1, CM 2 and CM 3 that we find in Olivier's index. This is far too small to represent a complete syllabary, and even if we exclude from this analysis the third, only partially represented, subgroup, CM 3, we can see that the common ground between CM 1 and CM 2 is only forty-two signs. The same conclusion applies.

The shared repertoire cannot trump and compensate for another overarching reality, namely what is *not* common to the three subgroups: the signs not shared, the signs peculiar to each of the subsets, represent the one piece of evidence that will trigger logical implications of a nature other than the palaeographic: how do we explain the fact that CM 1 differs from the other subgroups in no fewer than nineteen signs, and that CM 2 differs in no fewer than fifteen? Conversely from the situation observable in the shared repertoire, this unshared portion of the script is remarkably large and considerable, and such a conclusion seems to undermine, at first sight, the argument that at least the CM 1 and CM 2 syllabaries may be viewed as a single writing system: provided that the signs have been

---

[17] Olivier introduced sign 53 **W**, sign 69 **B** and sign 99 **Ψ**.

correctly singled out, one would be hard-pressed to see them as the same thing. But again, we need to venture further and see exactly *where*, in what contexts, these particular signs are found.

The nineteen signs attested only in CM 1 are the result of Olivier's intervention in Masson's list. This subgroup is the one that manifests the quirkiest, most idiosyncratic variation and substantial diversion in the sign-shapes. Oddly enough, most of these graphic idiosyncrasies are observable primarily in the inscriptions found on the clay balls, and the frequency and occurrence of some of these signs are often very low, if not occurring only as *hapax legomena*. One may conclude that these syllabograms are special to this subgroup; alternatively, one may decide to object and claim that these are mere diversions, that they represent simple irregularities due to hands either uninterested or not trained sufficiently to adhere closely to a palaeographic template, or that the adherence to the regular template was to an extent physically hindered by the impracticality of inscribing on a small spherical object.

The same applies to the corpus of CM 2 inscriptions. The relevant signs here number fifteen: the majority of these recurs quite frequently. Out of the repertoire of individual signs, therefore, the ratio is 1:4, meaning that one sign out of four is peculiar to this group. This compares well with the ratio in CM 1, which is approximately the same. For CM 3, the figures are surprising: the seven signs attested only in this subgroup do not seem a considerable number, or at least they are fewer in relation to the other subgroups, but these signs represent 12 per cent of the entire CM 3 repertoire and, even more importantly, the ratio is 1:8, which means that one sign out of eight is uniquely attested here: half the ratio we have in the other groups, but quite high.

What do we make of all of this? At this point we need to take stock and see the broader implications. Even though we may be facing syllabaries that are incomplete even as we have them attested, we still need to frame what these graphic variations mean in practical terms. Clearly, the signs peculiar to each subgroup are the crux of the problem. Again, if we assume that they are correctly identified and singled out, then each subgroup will have, independently of the others, introduced different signs in its repertoire, and those signs may be signifiers of different sounds or further phonological refiners. This means that, if we assume that the graphic variations, that the peculiar signs, are meaningful, they may be meaningful phonologically, representing sounds not recorded in the other subgroup. Theoretically, however, we could postulate some phonographic reshuffling too: namely, the sounds in question may be recorded in the other subgroups as well, by means of signs unrelated in terms of graphic structure.

Implications: script and language

Let us turn to the consequences arising from such reflections. If we exclude CM 3 from the analysis (because it is clearly the least complete of all three and therefore an unknown quantity hiding an unknown quality), the easiest deduction is that CM 1 and CM 2 record two different languages, and this is simply because the number of signs that one group, or the other, introduces into the repertoire is too large to justify the presence of such innovations otherwise.

Graphically, too, CM 2 seems keen to slightly modify the basic trait of signs attested in CM 1 by adding a small oblique stroke to the right of the sign, which Masson defines as *épine* (E. Masson 1985). It would be tempting to see this as a graphic modifier, marking a phonological differentiation, or functioning as a diacritic, and it is no coincidence that the signs that show this feature are for the most part attested only in CM 2. But does this actually mean that they record a different language? One may wonder whether perhaps the subject matters between, say, the clay balls and the Enkomi tablets may be so dissimilar as to require the use of different vocabulary items that could blur the pattern and greatly enlarge the disparities we see in the signs which are not common. But this can be a warranted conclusion only if we assume that CM 1 and CM 2 are incomplete syllabaries. We cannot be certain, of course, although the attested signs in each subgroup seem sufficiently numerous to suppose that the respective syllabaries are more or less complete, that, in other words, we see virtually all (if not quite all) the syllabograms that form each graphic repertoire.

For clarity's sake and in support of an exhaustive account, it may be productive to weigh a couple of theoretical stances, to see which possibilities we may be facing and which we need to rule out.

Let us reintroduce our excluded CM 3 again into the analysis of all three subgroups together and postulate theoretically that we are dealing with one script *only*, that records one language *only*. Contextually, it would be indicative of a cultural and linguistic *koine* across the island and beyond. Graphically, it simply does not explain the differences across the subgroups.

We have one script and many (by 'many' one means more than one) languages recorded. On the one hand, we are back to the conundrum raised by possibility no. 1, whereby the number of graphic divergences is not explained. On the other, even if the script were uniform in terms of signary, this possibility would not be easy to spot, given that the script is undeciphered and a sylla-bary. The Roman alphabet records several different languages, whose sign repertoires are roughly the same (diacritics being the distinguishing feature) regardless of the language: we could not distinguish Italian from French as two different languages if they were recorded syllabically (especially in CV patterns), and if we were not able to read the script that records them.

We have many scripts that record the same language. Conceivably we could assume that the signs that CM 2 introdu-ces into its system may be phonologically significant, namely they record new sounds, but this does not necessarily mean that the sounds introduced are sounds that CM 1 does not have in its own language. These innovations could be complex signs, a plethora of CVC sounds that may enlarge the phonological repertoire of CM 1, or else they could even indicate homophony, introducing the same sounds with different sign morphology. In either case, we need not seek to explain this through language differentiation.

There is a problematic corollary to this hypothesis. If this were the case, this change in phonotactic strategies ought to have been transmitted to the Cypriot Syllabary of the first millennium, and, as a result, we should see a number of complex signs, comparable to those in CM 2, in the Cypriot Syllabary as well. But with its fifty-five distinct syllables, this syllabary does not have any complex signs, and the problematic feature remains unsolved, unless we postulate that its streamlined repertoire may be the result of a selective process that borrows only what is absolutely necessary.

This could be a tantalising explanation, but more investigation needs to be done on the matter.

We have three scripts that record three different languages.[18] This would explain the palaeographic differences, but it raises a lot of questions for the archaeologist. First, if this were the case, it would be apparent that more than one linguistic group was not only present on Cyprus in the course of the Late Bronze Age (more specifically towards the end of it) but was also in the position to acquire, master and perfect the technology of writing to make its own language a physically permanent manifestation of its own culture. This is not an inconceivable possibility, but we would need to justify a linguistic *koine* across the island in the course of the Late Bronze Age, represented by CM 1, coalescing with another linguistic reality written down at Enkomi only, at the hands of a portion of the population well integrated into the culture of Enkomi at that time. In this way CM 2 would not mark the passage of a different group of people that come to inhabit, let alone invade, Enkomi. It marks the established presence of such a group.

The latter possibility requires a fuller, fresh investigation, since it seems to be subsumed in all the past literature on the subject, as a result of the general acceptance of the tripartite classification. More importantly, the historical and linguistic repercussions it brings about have not been explained or questioned anywhere else, and the problematic features raised by archaeological analysis deserve to be examined in full detail for the first time.

That Cyprus may have been a multilingual society in the second millennium BC is not a far-fetched idea. Cypriot onomastica recorded in the Amarna and Ugarit texts sees a mixture of uncertain Hurrian elements and more certain Semitic elements (Knapp 1996) but, notoriously, personal names are the least reliable ingredient to use in reconstructing linguistic make-up. Comparatively, that Cyprus was multilingual in the first millennium is to be taken for granted, given that we have good evidence for Phoenician and (admittedly, less good) evidence for Eteocypriot (whatever its

---

[18] Or even more than three: with CM 3 being an incomplete system, it is not impossible that the two tablets from Ugarit (RS 17.006 and RS 20.025) may have been written in two different languages.

language) coexisting with a Greek dialect. Three languages are therefore attested. When we relate this to the scripts they used, however, we find that Phoenician was always recorded in its own script: no other system of writing is ever borrowed, and the long-standing tradition of this script certainly played a part in such graphic conservatism.

It is often the case that script and language are bound to show some very strong links, even though they encompass two completely separate realms, but in certain cases such links are more fluid: an example of such flexibility is the case of Eteocypriot, a language that appears to have borrowed a script, the Cypriot Syllabic, which had been specifically adapted to record the Greek language. There is little point in stretching the evidence further, given the sometimes strict, but sometimes lax, relationship between language and writing, but it is worth stressing firmly that if CM 2 was introduced to record a language that was not that of CM 1, we cannot leave this borrowing process undetected and we need to try to understand what prompted it from a historical, if not fully archaeological, perspective. If we accept the multiple-script/multiple-language option for the second millennium, and assume that CM 1 and CM 2 represent two different languages, then we need to postulate that whoever adapted CM 1 to create CM 2 did not have a script of their own to use, and that they were fully integrated into the society of Enkomi, because they left no trace of a differentiated material culture. But on looking more closely into the scenario, we find some problems. We see two writing traditions, whose agents are people living in the same quarters, seemingly using two different scripts for two seemingly different languages, written on different media: CM 2 used only for tablets, and CM 1 for all the other supports.

This is an odd state of affairs: is there a parallel or similar situation elsewhere? In the Proto Palatial period, on Crete, in the palaces of Mallia and Knossos, we find deposits that contain documents in both Linear A and in the Cretan Hieroglyphic script. We see here the coexistence of the two writing systems in what has been defined as a healthy symbiosis, not an intrusion (Karnava 2007, 2009, *pers. comm.*). But there is a differentiation, of an epigraphic nature. Half of the inscriptions in Cretan Hieroglyphic are engraved on stone seals, whereas seals are never engraved with Linear A. It has been suggested that they could represent two parallel traditions, one 'glyptic' and one 'linear', of the same script (Bennet 2008), but we do not have enough identical word-sequences in the two systems to corroborate this. If we did, we could prove that the language may be the same. However, no viable explanation has been offered as to the motivating factors behind the parallel usage of Cretan Hieroglyphic and Linear A, apart from two different languages being noted. Similarly to the situation at Enkomi, the contextual implications that such a conclusion engenders have not been contemplated. We seem to be back at square one: if we see two scripts, do we need to see two languages?

Perhaps documents we can actually read are, in fact, a more suitable comparandum to turn to, in order to shed some light on the relationship between multiliteracy and multilingualism. The archives at Ugarit, with their literate diversity and scribal exper-tise, may provide a profitable ground for expanding our search. If the idea that Ugarit may have been a veritable babel of scripts and language is a rough overstatement, it is nevertheless true that seven languages in five different scripts are attested for the end of the Late Bronze Age. But only Akkadian and Ugaritic were written and currently spoken, with Hurrian being widely used as a third established language. In order to record their indigenous West Semitic language, the scribes of Ugarit created a unique alphabet, written in the cuneiform fashion, whose function was, mostly, to register the domestic activities of their kingdom.

In the same cultural environment and in the same writing tradition and spirit, Akkadian cuneiform was used for the great majority of documents that dealt with international affairs. Akkadian, being the *lingua franca* of the Late Bronze Age, had a wider intelligibility than local Ugaritic. Nonetheless, cuneiform syllabic or alphabetic were not used in an inextricable relationship of dependence on the languages they were devised to record. Boundaries there are at times less clean-cut than one may expect: we find Akkadian texts written in alphabetic and Ugaritic texts written in syllabic cuneiform (albeit more rarely), and this provides us with an example not only of biliteracy and bilingualism but also of a natural ease with script-switching.

When it comes to the third spoken and written language at Ugarit, Hurrian, script confines are non-existent: alphabetic and syllabic cuneiform systems were employed almost in equal measure and were, often and quite seamlessly, interchangeable. Two scripts were harmoniously and efficiently used to record one language. And two possible explanations can be sought for this state of affairs: one is that the Hurrian association with writing was so symbiotic with Ugaritan *mores* that the scribes responsible, if Hurrian speakers, did not choose to create their own script to mark their linguistic distinction. Without wishing to call it an intrinsic Hurrian laziness, the possible political, social and cultural dynamics behind this naturally go beyond linguistic factors. Or else, Ugaritan scribes, versed in either script, recorded a non-indigenous native language for the benefit of the Hurrian section of that society: in this case, the use of the Ugaritic alphabet would reveal simply a local script preference. Whichever the explanation, biliteracy is functioning and efficient, and the issue of *who* wrote *in what script* acquires a new significance still not fully explored.

If we transpose the same question to the situation on Cyprus, at exactly the same time, we need to take in the unknown element, namely the linguistic make-up of the population. If CM 1 and CM 2 were to represent two different scripts, we would need to justify how they could co-habit in the same place at the same time. We would also need to seek clues as to the possible agency behind the creation of a new script, CM 2, in a place where a perfectly efficient script, CM 1, had a long-standing tradition and was used island-wide. If we follow the general principle that 'different languages tend to use different scripts' (Baines 2008), then it may be linguistic differentiation.[19] And if it is true that CM 1 and CM 2 note two

---

[19] E. Masson advanced the idea that CM 2 registers Hurrian (E. Masson 1975). This is archaeologically untenable: there seems to be not a single shred of evidence to demonstrate Hurrian influence in any aspect of material culture on Cyprus (Knapp and Marchant 1982). From a philological perspective, the linguistic interpretation is conjectural, since the morphology of the Hurrian language has not been fully understood, nor can it be claimed that this is a cogent enough linguistic identification, as it is based on the application of phonetic values only on tablet fragment no. 1687. As we have already seen, the Hurrian language is actually recorded in more than one script at Ugarit (syllabic cuneiform as well as alphabetic cuneiform), but the idea that a Hurrian-speaking population, permanently installed in Cyprus, would adopt the Cypriot system of writing

different languages, then the agents responsible for the adaptation of CM I to create CM 2 did not possess an already functioning and active script of their own to use (the comparable case of Hurrian adopting cuneiform springs to mind) and were fully integrated into the society of Enkomi, because they did not leave traces of a differentiated material culture: this integration, if complete, would make the Enkomi society of that time fully bilingual. The same happened with the Hurrians at Ugarit, who used the same scripts as the indigenous Ugaritans: they would be invisible to us, were we not able to understand, albeit patchily, their language.

A methodological warning would prompt us not to expect a different linguistic group to leave a visible imprint on the archaeological record, and indeed one cannot be equipped with tools to identify such an imprint, in the presence of an undeciphered script. One ought also to see writing as a fluid instrument: even if it is generally conservative, and a feature usually retained by society rather than easily disposed of or replaced, it is by no means inert. A script can be modified and moulded into fitting the linguistic needs of any group that requires a visible counterpart to memory. But, and this is the real question, it is also never created in a vacuum. Observing it in the particular cultural environment that brings it into being is essential, not just to understand its fundamental usage and purpose but also to identify its significance in connection with the power structures of the society responsible for its creation. Its function is two-fold: that of being an efficient conveyor of language but also a powerful cultural artefact, profoundly embedded in the society that produces it. A natural consequence of such a definition is the necessity to frame the prospect of language differentiation in a close correlation with evidence that is also meta-linguistic.

The Cypriot literate elites and the archaeological context

The primary centres of Late Bronze Age Cyprus display a complex level of social organisation, and their urban elites used writing,

remains a mystery from an archaeological perspective. For a fuller account of all the possible linguistic interpretations or partial 'decipherments' of tablet fragment no. 1687, see Ferrara 2012a.

among other markers, as a specific means of asserting their identity and status through what could be defined, without overstating it, as an almost obsessive concern with marking ownership on precious, high-class material objects (Ferrara 2012a). This strategy of per-sonalising items seems to amount to a preoccupation with control-ling ownership as much as displaying status, and an epigraphic habit primarily observable at Enkomi. It appears that through this means, an influential group at the settlement was in control of the potential of writing and, while mastering this technology, managed to distance itself from, perhaps, the rest of the population, but more certainly from the rest of the other elites at other centres. Given the paucity of the Cypro-Minoan inscriptions, and the moot point relative to inscribed perishable materials (Sherratt, Chapter 4 in this volume), it is impossible to infer whether the extent of literacy was limited or not, or whether the individuals able to use and understand writing were few or otherwise. If, however, writing was a stunted or limited reality, at the hands of only a few people, its restricted usage may have been a symptomatic result of control imposed from the top.

With such caveats in mind, the scenario still remains puzzling. With a powerful elite at Enkomi, keen to continuously display status and mark property with their Cypro-Minoan script, was there room for another elite who developed CM 2 on the basis of CM 1, and who did so in an effort to distance itself linguistically in pretty much the same town quarters and definitely at the same time? An elite who chose a different epigraphic manifestation of such distance, using its modified writing system on tablets *uniquely*? Or are we dealing with the same elite, who manifested its bilingual skills by modifying phonologically a pre-existent script and using it on only one type of object, the tablets? If we look at the specific locations of these tablets, in one case (inv. no. 20.01) found in close proximity with CM 1, represented by a cluster of five balls (inv. nos. 20.02, 20.03, 20.04, 20.05, 20.253) on the road between Quartiers West 8 and East 8, close to the House of the Bronzes in southern Enkomi (Dikaios 1963, 1969–71; Ferrara 2008a), the situation is even more puzzling: could these elites have produced writing as part of two possibly separate administrations, and, in the absence of an established bilingual tradition or synergy, in a mutually incomprehensible environment? Either possibility seems unreasonable, if not an authentic oxymoron.

Conclusions: one script, too many?

In the light of the considerations and concerns manifested above, it seems that calling on linguistic differentiation to explain or justify the attested presence of more than one Cypro-Minoan script, appears either uneconomical or logically unwarranted. It would be tempting and fully solicited by the extant evidence to take this a step forward and conclude quite forcibly that CM 1 and CM 2 may well be one and the same script and that, one day, when surely more inscriptions are unearthed, the divergences seen today will be levelled out, if not perhaps altogether annulled. With so little material it is indeed counterproductive to assume otherwise, and we need to concede that calling on linguistic issues to solve a mere epigraphic problem complicates the picture more than it leaps its hurdles.

No conceptual impediment rules out the possibility that multilingualism was indeed a prominent trait of Cypriot society towards the end of the Late Bronze Age, and perhaps even before then, given the ever cosmopolitan nature of the island's make-up. But this cultural feature, whether ascribable to a multilingual or bilingual society, does not square with the written evidence we have for the late second millennium and is certainly not borne out by the Cypro-Minoan script, even if one presumes to win the argument for justifying its subgroups and varieties. Our view is that there is no reason to assume that Cypro-Minoan was used to record more than one language, just as there is, arguably, little reason to assume that Cypro-Minoan was represented by more than one script.

Indeed, the whole idea of thinking of it in the plural comes across as rather counter-intuitive, and one cannot help but consider this conclusion as the result of the often partial and sectarian slant that has tainted Cypro-Minoan studies for a long time. In concluding, in a spirit of utter epigraphic provocation, and in the wake of

75

the concerns already manifested by Palaima more than three decades ago, an appeal should be urgently launched again for a more integrated, holistic study of Cypro-Minoan and any other undeciphered script, with the hope that further, fully contextual analysis of writing will be ready to see the light.

4

LATE CYPRIOT WRITING IN CONTEXT

SUSAN SHERRATT

Context and the historical-intellectual context of context

By aiming to discuss Late Cypriot writing 'in context', I do not mean detailed archaeological context, such as the range and nature of Late Cypriot inscribed objects, where precisely they are found and what they are found with. Silvia Ferrara, following some very sensible advice offered by T. G. Palaima in an article published in 1989 (Palaima 1989a; see also Smith 2002), has already done this in meticulous detail, and as a result has been able to throw considerably more light on the Late Cypriot script, dispelling much of the obfuscation created by some of her predecessors (Ferrara 2005, 2012a, 2012b; Ferrara, Chapter 3 in this volume). She has given us an up-to-date, fully contextual corpus of Late Cypriot inscriptions, on clay tablets and other clay objects (including cylinders, balls and pots), and on metal and stone objects, such as gold rings, cylinder seals, bronze and silver bowls and bronze tools, and at a variety of sites spread widely – though not yet densely – throughout the island, starting chronologically (at least so far) at Enkomi in Late Cypriot I.[1]

Instead, what I would like to consider are wider forms of context: the context in which writing in general, and the first Cypriot Bronze Age script in particular, may have been taken up on Cyprus, and when this might have been and in what

I am grateful to Philippa Steele for inviting me to take part in one of the most congenial and stimulating conferences that I have experienced in a long time, and at which I learned much. My thanks, too, to Silvia Ferrara for her comments on a draft of this chapter and for her generosity in sending me copies of unpublished papers, including a draft of the one included in this volume; and to John Bennet for sparing time to read it, despite other more pressing calls on his attention. Any mistakes and all manifestations of wrong-headedness are, of course, entirely my own responsibility.

[1] For an even more recent complete corpus of Late Cypriot inscriptions, see *HoChyMin*.

circumstances; and the context in which our conventional views about this were originally formed. I would then like to go on to consider, not so much what we actually know, but what we know that we do not know, to see if factoring in such unknowns might make a difference to the way in which we approach these questions.

Taking the notion of writing in the Near East and the Mediterranean in the broadest of terms, we can see it spreading in the general direction of east to west over several millennia, from southern Mesopotamia in the late Uruk period to the central Mediterranean around the eighth century BC. One area which appears to buck this general trend is the Aegean, and it appears to do this twice: once in the matter of the relationship between the Aegean linear scripts and the Cypriot Bronze Age script in the mid second millennium, and again in the question of the relationship between Greek alphabetic writing and various first-millennium alphabetic scripts of western Anatolia, including Phrygian, Lydian, Carian and Lycian. In both cases, according to conventional wisdom, the spread is from west to east, from the Aegean area eastward.

I do not intend to pursue the matter of the Anatolian alphabetic scripts here, though I feel these suffer from similar problems of general intellectual background and approach as does the Cypriot script. What I would like to do is look more closely (or perhaps, rather, tangentially) at the question of the Cypriot Bronze Age script and its relationship to the Aegean. First, however, some account of my own background might help to explain where I am coming from.

When I was studying Classics (and later Classical archaeology) as an undergraduate and immediate post-graduate approximately forty years ago, Cyprus hardly ever received any mention, except perhaps in relation to the archaic dialect of Greek that its Greek-speaking inhabitants spoke in Classical times. It was regarded at best as a far-flung and rather uncivilised offshoot of the Greek world, its art and architecture too heavily tinged with eastern contamination to be regarded as either important or interesting, in this respect at least partly reflecting the attitudes of the historical Greeks (especially Athenians) themselves who, from Herodotus

on, were frequently very ambivalent towards the island.[2] My
particular interest was Aegean prehistory, specifically the later
part of the Late Bronze Age, and in this field too I encountered a
similar reticence concerning Cyprus, and usually dismissal of the
island as not being very important. In those days, its main point of
interest as far as the Late Bronze Age Aegean was concerned was
the apparent arrival of 'Achaeans' as refugee colonists, following
the collapse of the Mycenaean palaces around 1200 BC.[3] It was
commonly agreed, in this 'view from the west', that it was the
Aegean that was responsible for bringing some life (and art) to
the island, revolutionising its technological capabilities, and bringing it into the wider Mediterranean picture.[4] Those were still the
days of belief in Aegean thalassocracies, when everything of
Aegean origin in the eastern Mediterranean or everything eastern
in the Aegean was assumed to have been carried on Minoan
or Mycenaean ships (*PM* I: 15–25; *PM* II: 655–8; *PM* IV:
770–81; Kantor 1947; Furumark 1950; cf. Knapp and Cherry
1994: 128–30).

I not unnaturally, but rather unthinkingly, absorbed this point of
view; and, to cut a long story short, it was only after I started
looking properly at Cyprus that I realised that the answers to a
number of questions I had about the thirteenth and twelfth centuries
in the Aegean seemed to point to that island, where urban coastal
centres such as Enkomi were evidently booming at this time, and
on a scale and with a lay-out which made the palatial centres of
Mycenaean Greece and even the 'urban' centre of Neopalatial
Knossos look distinctly small or lacking in density by comparison.

What coloured the attitudes that I was absorbing, even up until
the late 1960s and early 1970s, was of course the fact that the
archaeology of Cyprus, at least from the point of view of

[2] E.g. Herodotus 1.199 for the practice in some parts of Cyprus of what he calls the 'most
shameful' (αἴσχιστος) Babylonian custom of temple-based prostitution on demand for all
young women.
[3] An idea which goes back at least as far as Tsountas (Tsountas and Manatt 1897: 364).
[4] See, for example, Casson 1949: 248: 'The Mycenaean contacts brought a widespread
change in the island which from 1400 onwards developed urban life and culture on
Mycenaean lines. All the main elements of Mycenaean life are found except architecture,
Mycenaean tomb types, and Mycenaean road-systems.' Cf. also Catling 1964: 300–2;
Stubbings 1975: 181–7.

archaeology further west, was still experiencing the patronising and somewhat antipathetical effects of what Edward Said has termed 'orientalism' (Said 1978), which had seeped through Europe when the vast Ottoman empire still had its grip on Cyprus and virtually the whole of the Near East. What these apparently rundown areas needed to revitalise them was liberation from the rule of the sultans in Istanbul and their stifling bureaucracies, and an injection of western European enterprise and advanced civilisation, based ultimately on that of Classical Greece. We are all familiar nowadays with the idea that we write history according to our own times (I should point out that I am no exception), and the attitudes of Said's 'orientalism' also pervaded interpretations of archaeology in the eastern Mediterranean from the nineteenth century onwards. In 1947, Helene Kantor, in discussing the role of the Greek mainland in the later second millennium, gave voice to what was then a widespread Aegeo-centric consensus of opinion in concluding that it was the source of 'cultural influence which was diffused along the eastern littoral of the Mediterranean' (Kantor 1947: 103). At the same time, archaeologists like Leonard Woolley and Claude Schaeffer were looking for, and in some cases claiming to have found, Late Bronze Age Aegean colonies and trading settlements in the Levant as well as on Cyprus (Woolley 1938, 1953: 156–7; Schaeffer 1930, 1939: 53–106). Even earlier, Arthur Evans very much shared (and indeed had a formative part in developing) this Aegeo-centric and rather dismissive view of Cyprus and the eastern Mediterranean, which coloured his attitude to his greatest interest, the Cretan scripts. In 1895, in *Cretan Pictographs and Prae-Phoenician Script*, he had already identified a relationship, in terms of forms, between the linear signs on inscribed objects from the prehistoric Aegean and the Cypriot syllabic script of the first millennium (Evans 1895: 83–5). After his discovery of tablets in linear scripts at Knossos in 1900 and the Italian discoveries at Ayia Triada, and following the recognition of the existence of a Bronze Age script on Cyprus similar to that of the later Cypriot Syllabary (Evans 1900: 216; Sayce 1905: 254; cf. Evans 1909: 70–3), the answer for Evans was natural: this Cypriot script, as 'a form of Minoan script', must have been introduced to the island by literate Aegean settlers. Along with other forms of art and culture found on Cyprus in the later second millennium he christened the script 'Cypro-Minoan' (Evans 1909: 70). It is perhaps worth remembering that, in the same publication (*Scripta Minoa*) in which the term 'Cypro-Minoan' first made an appearance, Evans also set out a complicated line of argument in which he proposed that the Phoenicians, and their alphabet, were also ultimately of Aegean origin (Evans 1909: 77–94). The wider intellectual and political context in which both these conclusions were reached can be gauged well from a footnote in which Evans, in self-consciously name-dropping mode, recalls a conversation he had with the Liberal statesman W. E. Gladstone at Hawarden (Evans 1909: 94). In response to Evans's expression of his opinion that 'the character of the Phoenician maritime enterprise, their eclectic religion, and the cosmopolitan colonial spirit generated by their great cities somewhat belies a purely Semitic origin', Gladstone is reported to have remarked: 'I have always believed that the Phoenicians were at bottom of non-Semitic stock.'

Current problems of context

A full century later I would not wish to deny the possibility – indeed the probability – of some relationship between Cretan Linear A (in particular) and the Cypriot script.[5] However, two aspects of the traditional view that the latter is derived from the former persistently worry me. One is that it is very difficult, as things stand at the moment, to imagine an appropriate context in which Crete could have introduced writing to Cyprus at any period, let alone around or somewhat before the middle of the second

---

[5] It is worth remembering that, at the time Evans was writing, he saw the main Aegean colonial impact on Cyprus (including the introduction of a form of Minoan script) as taking place in the fourteenth to thirteenth centuries BC (indeed he was largely responsible for pointing out that the Enkomi tombs excavated by the British Museum in the 1890s dated to this rather than a later period (Evans 1900)). At that time, the inscribed clay balls associated with the tombs at Enkomi and a gold ring from a tomb at Hala Sultan Tekke were, with the exception of an inscribed cylinder seal from the cemetery of Ayia Paraskevi which Sayce had dated to the Early Bronze Age (Sayce 1905) but which is almost certainly of Late Bronze Age date (Daniel 1941: 250; O. Masson 1957a: 15–17; Buchanan 1966: 192 no. 985), the earliest inscriptions known from Cyprus. Evans's comparisons between the Cretan linear scripts and the Bronze Age script of Cyprus were on the basis of signs drawn from all the Cretan scripts.

millennium BC (which is when it would have had to have been according to current evidence in the form of the earliest Cypriot inscriptions).[6] The other is that the very name 'Cypro-Minoan', which emerged against the particular intellectual and political background that I have just outlined, has, like many of Evans's confident terminological coinings or pronouncements, exerted a subliminal, but very powerful, influence over our views ever since. Even Palaima, who had some very perceptive and sensible remarks to make about approaches to the Cypriot Bronze Age script, took its Cretan origins for granted and never thought of these being questioned, except at a very detailed but arguably superficial level (Palaima 1989a: 136–40).[7] In the case of someone who above all laid admirable emphasis on micro-context, his failure (apart from a

---

[6] If one follows the conventional (Evansian) view of the derivation of the Cypriot Bronze Age script from Linear A, one would probably have to allow some time for the Cypriot offshoot to (apparently) lose the logograms which exist in the latter and persist into its Linear B successor. There is so far no certain attestation of logograms in the Cypriot script, and in particular none among its earlier manifestations, though it has been suggested that the two signs found immediately in front of each of the two rows of numerals on an inscribed sherd from a well at Enkomi (Dikaios 1969–71: 778 no. 4025 888 891 no. 131, pls. 149:21, 190:6, 319:131; E. Masson 1974: fig. 8), probably to be dated to Late Cypriot IIC or Late Cypriot IIIA, may be examples of these (Dikaios 1967: 84–5, 1969–71: 888; Ferrara 2005: Cat. no. ENK 109, where it is suggested that the 'logograms' might consist of the initial syllables of the relevant commodities). For a suggestion of logograms on two of the tablets from Ugarit (R.S. 19.01 and 19.02 (cf. E. Masson 1974: 20–3)), see Olivier, Chapter 1 in this volume; and for speculation concerning an independent development of logograms in the Cypriot script, which might well be thought of as having implications for the independence of the script as a whole, see Valério 2008.

[7] Even here, some of his counter-arguments seem a little strained. The 'archaic' tablet from Enkomi Level 1B may be flat-edged and flat-faced (Palaima 1989a: 136), but, as the photographs in Dikaios 1969–71: pl. 314A make clear, it is of an extraordinary thickness (at 3.3 cm. about half as thick as it is wide, and inscribed also on one of the lateral faces), quite unlike any inscribed tablet from the Aegean, as far as I am aware (see also Godart and Sacconi 1979: 129; Duhoux 2009: 31; Duhoux, Chapter 2 in this volume). Of the proposed sign matches, it seems to me (entirely subjectively) that there are five quite convincing parallels (AB 02 and AB 54 on the first line, AB 77 and AB 09 on the second line, and AB 01 (in the transcription used by Palaima) on the third line; cf. Hooker 1985: 178), three which might be seen as plausible (AB 57 and AB 01 on the first line (though if the third sign from the left on the third line is to be matched with AB 01, it seems unlikely that the third sign from the left on the first line can be intended as the same sign) and AB 70 (twice) on the second line), while the remainder seem distinctly less persuasive. It is perhaps also worth noting that most of the signs are relatively simple in their configurations and that, on the whole, those with the most persuasive matches are among the simplest. Of course, as Palaima (1989a: 138) points out, it is absolutely wrong procedure to compare the signs to those on standardised Linear A sign lists; and, of course, as he also points out, there are wide variations in the forms of individual Linear A signs themselves. However, his arguments on these grounds seem dangerously circular, since their efficacy depends on

conventional nod at a few pieces of travelling pottery, Palaima 1989a: 135) even to address the nature of the wider circumstances in which Crete might have bestowed a script upon Cyprus is perhaps rather a surprising omission.

Let us, therefore, address this question of context first of all. It is a question which has worried several generations of scholars since Evans, including Hector Catling (1964: 47–9), Machteld Mellink (quoted in Aström 1972b: 55), Emilia Masson (1979a: 137), Vassos Karageorghis (1982: 63) and Robert Merrillees (1993: 16; cf. also Grumach 1969: 284), but most have eventually bowed to the dominating personality (and celebrity) of Evans, and found themselves seeking refuge in sporadic evidence for some sort of direct contact between Crete and Cyprus in the relevant period. What this amounts to, even after all this time, is a single Early Minoan III pot and one or two putative Early Minoan III daggers from northern Cyprus (Karageorghis 1982: 46), a Middle Minoan Kamares pot also from northern Cyprus (Cadogan 1979: 63 n. 1; Catling in Jones 1986: 582–3), and an only slightly larger number of Late Minoan or Late Helladic I pots from Enkomi and the north coast sites of Ayia Irini and Toumba tou Skourou (Dikaios 1969–71: 836; Vermeule and Wolsky 1990: 381–3).[8] On the other side of the equation, we have evidence of a single Early Cypriot III Red Polished jar from Knossos (Catling and MacGillivray 1983) and small amounts of putatively Cypriot pottery at Kommos in southern Crete from Middle Minoan IB onwards (Shaw 1998; Rutter and Van de Moortel 2006: 287 Da/3, 293 H/1, 633–4, 641, 653–5, 711 N.211, pl. 3.20:Da/3, H/1). This is clearly not much to go on, but when one also begins to consider the distribution of the relatively small quantity of Middle Minoan (Kamares) pottery in the eastern

the assumption that we are in fact dealing with basically the same script, which is not an unreasonable assumption when it comes to Cretan inscriptions classed as Linear A, but is something that, in the case of the Enkomi tablet, needs to be demonstrated rather than assumed *ab initio*.

For recent discussions of this tablet, see Duhoux 2009, whose transcription, derived from HoChyMin, eliminates any similarity of the third sign from the left on the third line to AB 01, and who sees a maximum of ten sign matches with Linear A and B (Duhoux 2009: 20–1; see also Bombardieri and Jasink 2010: 145–9, who express doubts about most of these matches).

[8] The dozen or so Late Minoan IA pieces from Toumba tou Skourou are hardly enough to allow us to assume the presence of a Minoan emporium there (*pace* Betancourt 2008: 218; see Vermeule and Wolsky 1978: 307).

Mediterranean a certain pattern seems to emerge. Most of this turns up in small concentrations in Egyptian centres such as Abydos, Kahun and Haraga (Kemp and Merrillees 1980: 1–219), a lesser amount at such sites as Byblos, Ugarit and Sidon on the Levantine coast (Cadogan 1983: 514; Betancourt 1998: 6; MacGillivray 2003), and the smallest amount of all in northern Cyprus (S. Sherratt 1999: 206–7 table 1). This suggests that it is the result of an anti-clockwise sailing circuit,[9] along which possibly Aegean silver and Cretan textiles picked up in southern Crete were carried to Egypt (Barber 1991: 345–51), and perhaps things like ivory, gold, precious stones and other materials and objects travelled westward to the Aegean, with pottery for sale on the side being picked up along the way. One might conjecture that it was operated by ships based somewhere like Byblos or some other centre on the Levantine coast, and crewed by a motley mixture of experienced sailors, quite possibly including some Cypriots.

So far, so good. We are touching base in the right part of Crete and at roughly the right time for the newly adopted Linear A script to find its way eastward to Cyprus sometime in the period from Middle Minoan II (eighteenth century BC) to the early Late Bronze Age. But in what circumstances might this actually have happened? One of the general similarities between Linear A and the Cypriot Bronze Age syllabary is that both are found on a wide spread of materials and artefact types, which suggests that they were not confined to narrow administrative uses, or to a closed scribal class or even perhaps to a palatially based elite.[10] However, I am not sure how much further this gets us, unless we suppose that some Cypriot sailor docking at Kommos thought it would be a good idea to learn how to write using a system he had encountered briefly on Crete, and to take the knowledge back and introduce it at home. If he, or anyone from Cyprus, had decided that writing would be a useful accomplishment, he (or they) could have found

---

[9] See Kemp and Merrillees 1980: 268–84; Cline 1994: 91 map 4.
[10] Although, in the case of Linear A, the speed with which it seems to have disappeared from use after or at the time of the development of Linear B for writing Greek rather suggests that it was not deeply embedded in anything other than a relatively superficial stratum of Cretan society. In this it contrasts with the Cypriot script, which persisted in use for more than one language well down into the first millennium.

a variety of suitable multipurpose models much nearer home, in the Egyptian delta or further up the Nile, at Byblos, probably at Ugarit, or in fact at any largish maritime centre along the Levantine coast.

Knowns and unknowns – Cyprus

Let us return to Cyprus and see what information we have there. So far, the earliest proper inscriptions (and by that I mean two or more contiguous signs in apparently meaningful relationship to one another) both come from Enkomi: the inscribed clay loomweight (or whatever it may be)[11] from Schaeffer's Late Cypriot IA levels (Schaeffer, Courtois and Lagarce 1968: 266 fig. 3; Palaima 1989a: 152–3 fig. 12) and the surprisingly chunky tablet fragment from Dikaios's Level IB (Dikaios 1969–71: 882–3, 889 no. 10, pls. 126:55, 190:1, 314, 315:10). However, in addition to these we also have a range of isolated signs or marks on other objects from similar strata at Enkomi: a bronze ploughshare from the beginning of Dikaios's Level I (Dikaios 1969–71: 889 no. 1, pls. 126:19–19a, 153:13, 315:1), the handle of a Black Slip vessel from the destruction of Level IA (Dikaios 1969–71: 889 no. 2, pls. 153:19, 315:2), a White Slip I fragment from Level IB (Dikaios 1969–71: 889 no. 3, pls. 153:20, 315:3), a Painted Wheelmade I handle from the destruction of Level IB (Dikaios 1969–71: 889 no. 5, pls. 153:21, 315:5), a Bichrome handle from Level IB and four fragments of Plain Ware, also from Level IB (Dikaios 1969–71: 889 nos. 4, 6–9, pl. 315:4, 6–9). Of these, the ploughshare, according to Dikaios (1969–71: 624 no. 1820), appears to have been engraved, though other ploughshares from Enkomi are thought to have marks impressed during the manufacturing process, possibly while the metal was still in a semi-hard state (Catling 1964: 80; Buchholz and Karageorghis 1973: 171, 505 no. 1892). It is not clear in the case of

---

[11] For the alternative suggestion of a 'label', see e.g. Courtois, Lagarce and Lagarce 1986: 199; Olivier, Chapter 1 in this volume; Ferrara, Chapter 3 in this volume. However, although it seems flatter in shape than some uninscribed objects from Enkomi classified as loomweights (e.g. Courtois, Lagarce and Lagarce 1986: pl. XV:12; Dikaios 1969–71: 889 no. 16, pl. 160:5), it seems very similar to others (e.g. Dikaios 1969–71: 665 no. 3840/1, pls. 155:7, 161:3).

the pots and pot fragments whether the signs were added before or after firing. Both are known on Late Cypriot pottery, though on balance – with the exception of the problematic Red Lustrous Wheelmade ware, on which the marks were invariably impressed before firing (Eriksson 1993: 145–7) – those incised after firing seem to be more common (Hirschfeld 2002: 95), as on a Plain White Wheelmade jug from British Tomb 22 at Enkomi, dating somewhere in Late Cypriot I–II (BM 1897.0401.879: Hirschfeld 2002: 84 table 5 second entry).[12]

Quite properly, most of those studying the Cypriot script nowadays draw a firm line between 'proper' inscriptions and isolated signs such as these, which they prefer to call 'marks' and cannot assume to have anything to do with what they might recognise as 'writing'. However, just for the sake of thinking generally around the subject, I would like, at least temporarily, to blur the boundaries a little. This is because, as has long been noted, some (although by no means all) of the single marks found on pots or other articles, particularly in the Late Bronze Age, seem clearly to relate to signs, either literary or numerical, found in 'proper' inscriptions, or at least to have a generally similar 'linear' appearance. I further suggest a little blurring of boundaries may be in order because, although anyone can put a mark for whatever reason on a pot or any other object, in practice these marks cannot be assumed to be entirely arbitrary; and what people tend to do is to make use of marks, or types of marks, which are already available in their environment. Nicolle Hirschfeld, for instance, has made an extremely persuasive case for associating a substantial number of the post-firing marks found on Mycenaean pottery exported to the eastern Mediterranean with signs of the Cypriot Bronze Age script, and for further linking these with the distribution of this pottery in the east by Cypriot traders (Hirschfeld 1990: fig. 4, 1996, 2002: 96). It is also quite noticeable, for example, that, at sites such as Phylakopi on Melos or Ayia Irini on Kea in the Cyclades where 'potters' marks' made before firing start to appear on some pottery

---

[12] No. 22.16 in the excellent online catalogue of material from the British Museum Enkomi tombs (Ancient Cyprus in the British Museum, edited by T. Kiely: www.britishmuseum. org/system_pages/holding_area/ancient_cyprus_british_museum.aspx).

from around the end of the Early Bronze Age, from the later part of the Middle Bronze Age these begin to make use of signs taken from Linear A or of marks which look broadly like them (Bikaki 1984; Bennet 1994, 1995). Conversely, in the Aegean, 'potmarks' of any sort made before firing are very rarely encountered during the period of Linear B use on the Mycenaean mainland, at a time when we have good reason to believe that writing was very circumscribed, confined more or less to palatial elites who used it only in very limited circumstances.

I raise this because I think it may not always be helpful to separate the two phenomena too rigidly, and because making use of marks on objects – especially if these appear to relate to, or seem in general terms to resemble, signs from a known writing system in contemporary use – can be a sign of a form of para-literacy or at least of an awareness of literacy within one's general surroundings. Of course, this is all very well at times and in places when there is otherwise evidence (either direct or circumstantial) for the existence of literacy; and one cannot simply invert the logic of this to suggest that the use of marks on their own may themselves be evidence of the existence of a formal writing system in periods and regions where no evidence of such a system survives. Nevertheless, it may still be the case that marks inscribed or impressed on pots or other objects carry references to systems of recording or notation, even if the references are indirect and even if the referents have no transferred or systemic meaning where the marked objects themselves are concerned. For example, it is at least interesting that many, if not most, of the 'potmarks' which appear on pottery in the Aegean in the late Early Bronze Age and earlier Middle Bronze Age, like those on Early and Middle Cypriot pottery, take the form of round or oval impressions or simple linear configurations, which perhaps most resemble the systems of numerical notation known from Middle and Late Bronze Age scripts in the Aegean and Cyprus (Atkinson *et al.* 1904: 177–82; Daniel 1941: 251; E. Masson 1974: 22 fig. 8; Bikaki 1984; Bennet 1994, 1995; Smith 2002: 24–5 fig. 8; for examples of such marks on Cypriot pottery see Aström 1966: 149–73 figs. 135–58) and earlier (in the late Early Bronze Age) on what have plausibly been interpreted as weights (Rahmstorf 2003, 2006). Very similar types of marks also appear at Early Bronze Age Tarsus (e.g. Goldman 1956: 117 no. 206, 121 nos. 250–1, 124 no. 292, pls. 248:206, 253:250–1, 256:292) and in the Early Bronze Age Levant (Feldbacher and Fischer 2008: fig. 328a), as well as on weights in Old Kingdom Egypt and the east (Rahmstorf 2006: figs. 1–2). The possible implications of this – and of the coincidence of the timing of the appearance of marks on pots in both the Aegean and Cyprus – is something I have speculated a little about elsewhere (S. Sherratt n.d.), and will return to briefly below.

In Cyprus, isolated marks long pre-date the first 'proper' inscriptions in Late Cypriot I, and they continue to appear alongside the latter until at least the end of the Bronze Age. They are found surprisingly frequently on Middle Cypriot pottery (mainly on Red Polished and Black Slip wares), as Paul Aström's corpus of Middle Cypriot potmarks, compiled in 1966, shows (Aström 1966: 149–92). However, the earliest examples, so far, of such marks are found on a couple of perforated copper axes[13] and a chisel, a couple of Red Polished Philia jugs or juglets, and a Black Slip Combed ware bowl from Philia-Vasiliko, all of which can be dated to the Philia culture around the middle of the third millennium BC (Dikaios 1962: figs. 80.22, 82.25, 83.6; Buchholz and Karageorghis 1973: 170, 500 nos. 1867, 1869; Webb and Frankel 1999: 32; Webb et al. 2006: 261–6, 277–8, figs. 3–4).

This is particularly intriguing because, whatever one's views about immigration versus indigenous development at this time,[14] there is no doubt that the appearance of the Philia facies from shortly after the middle of the third millennium marks the culmination and intensification of a period of increasingly close and surprisingly intimate contacts between Cyprus and southern and western Anatolia from the second quarter of the millennium onwards, seen in ceramic types and forms as well as in a whole range of other objects (Swiny 1986; Frankel 2005; Peltenburg 2007; Webb and Frankel 2007). My own suggestion would be that it is at the time of the Philia horizon that seaborne (perhaps

---

[13] See Webb et al. 2006: 275 fig. 4 for the suggestion that these perforated axes also acted as ingots.
[14] Cf. e.g. Frankel 2000 and Knapp 2001.

by now sailborne) traffic from the Levantine coast begins to spread westward along the southern Anatolian coast, bouncing between this coast and northern Cyprus as it does so, and that, as a result, regular seaborne communications between Cyprus and southern Anatolia are intensified (S. Sherratt 2000: 18). As far as the marks on pots and metal objects are concerned, I find it especially interesting that: a) the perforated axe is a type which, though certainly made on Cyprus in the Philia phase, probably has its origins elsewhere;[15] and b) that marks on pots, some of them similar to the marks found on Cyprus, are also found, for example, in Early Bronze Age contexts at Tarsus (Goldman 1956: 98 no. 45, 121 nos. 250–1, 123–4 nos. 284, 286, 288, 290–2, pls. 235:45, 253:250–1, 256:284, 288, 290–2). A possible conclusion might therefore be that the Cypriot habit of marking objects spread to the island from somewhere along the southern Anatolian coast from roughly around the middle of the millennium in a period of what appear to be regular and fairly intimate contacts. Furthermore, the observation that this coincides roughly with the first appearance of very small numbers of marks on pots in the Aegean in the later part of Early Bronze 2 and Early Bronze 3 (Lindblom 2001: 15–16 table 1), some of the earliest of which also show similarities to marks found on pottery and other objects in Early Bronze Age Anatolia, might additionally suggest that a similar practice spread from Anatolia to the Aegean.[16]

This is not to say that, either in Cyprus or in the Aegean, such marks are directly script-related, though it is interesting that at least three of the (admittedly relatively simple) marks on the very few Philia marked objects can be compared to signs of the later Cypriot script.[17] In the Aegean at least, there is perhaps a case for linking their initial appearance with the *Metallschock* of the second half of

---

[15] Exampes are known from Cilicia, Syria and the Levant (Stewart 1962: 249, 276).

[16] For other similarities between Cyprus and the Aegean at this time, all linked through Anatolia, see Peltenburg 2007; Webb and Frankel 2007: 198.

[17] Perforated axe (Webb 2006: fig. 4): cf. Hirschfeld 2002: 71 table 1: Cypro-Minoan sign no. 82. Red Polished jug from Philia-Vasiliko (Dikaios 1962: fig. 80:22): cf. Hirschfeld 2002: 70 table 1: Cypro-Minoan no. 21. Red Polished jug from Philia-Vasiliko (Dikaios 1962: fig. 82:25): cf. Hirschfeld 2002: 70 table 1: Cypro-Minoan no. 23. In the case of the perforated axe and the mark on the base of the first of these jugs, allowance has to be made for the fact that it is not clear which way up the marks should be viewed.

the third millennium,[18] visible in the undeniably metallic-looking forms and surfaces of much of the new pottery of this period, which can often be closely related to the forms and appearances of surviving sheet-metal vessels at Anatolian sites. In a fit of unashamed speculation, fuelled almost entirely by limited circumstantial evidence, I have suggested elsewhere that the initial appearance of marks on Aegean pottery (which are particularly frequent on metal-derived shapes and wares with metallic echoes) has less to do with 'potters' marks' as such, but rather may be a matter of the skeuomorphic replication in clay of marks (as indications of weight, or as 'hallmarks' guaranteeing purity, authenticity, etc.) originally associated with metal vessels and other metal objects (S. Sherratt n.d.).[19] There is certainly no reason in either Cyprus or the Aegean to suppose that these are signs taken from a contemporary writing system of fully developed character (for which there is no evidence at all in either region before the beginning of the second millennium), though it remains an *a priori* possibility – if not a probability – that a pre-existing notational system for weights may eventually have merged with formal writing systems developed or adopted later (cf. Michailidou 2001), and it is perhaps not impossible that the forms, at least, of some standardised 'marks' of guarantee may subsequently have been incorporated as literate signs (ideographic or even phonetic) in such systems.[20] In the case of Anatolia, as I argue further below, we can perhaps be less certain about the existence or absence of

---

[18] For the effects of *Metallschock* on the pottery of the later Early Bronze 2 and Early Bronze 3 Aegean, see e.g. Nakou 2007; cf. also Webb and Frankel 2007: 198 for a similar effect on Cyprus at around the same time.

[19] In this connection, it may indeed be significant that almost half of the tiny number of Philia phase marks so far known are found on metal objects, and that this is the phase often credited with the introduction of new metal-working technologies to Cyprus (Webb and Frankel 1999: 31–3; Webb 2006). It may be even more significant if the perforated axe really can be regarded as an ingot, as has been suggested by Webb and others (see above, note 13). The presence of marks, some of them apparently comparable to signs of the Cypriot script, incised on copper and tin ingots from the much later Uluburun and Gelidonya wrecks, is well known (Bass 1967: 72–4; Sibella 1996; Hirschfeld 1999).

[20] One of the (admittedly very few) 'hallmarks' that may perhaps be detected on third-millennium Anatolian metalwork can possibly be seen on one of the silver 'standards' from Alacahöyük tomb A (Museum of Anatolian Civilisations, Ankara, no. 18794, the clearest photograph of which is probably that reproduced in Rijksmuseum van Oudheden Leiden 1986: 61 no. 43). It consists of what looks very like a bucranium, similar in appearance to one of the signs of the Cretan hieroglyphic script (Olivier and Godart 1995:

writing systems during the third millennium. The most we can say is that there is so far no evidence for this.

Knowns and unknowns – Anatolia

Let us leave it there meanwhile, and turn our attention to what else we know, and more particularly what we know that we do not know about Anatolia and the eastern Mediterranean generally. For a start, it has to be said that we still know pitifully little about southern and south-western Anatolia in the third and second millennia.[21] As far as southern Anatolian scripts are concerned, all our existing evidence belongs to the later second millennium at the earliest, and the majority of it to the first millennium. Luwian hieroglyphic inscriptions, which are written using a logosyllabary, are relatively sparse and mostly short in the second millennium; the earliest consists of three or four signs on a seal of Ispuhtahsu, a fifteenth-century king of Kizzuwatna, found in the form of an impression on a clay bulla at Tarsus (Goldman 1956: 246–7 no. 1, pls. 401:1, 405:1; Hawkins 1986: 371). Substantial hieroglyphic inscriptions, like those known from Hattusa, are relatively rare in the second millennium, and most belong to the Neo-Hittite period of the early first millennium. For what it is worth, in longer inscriptions, including those of the second millennium, Luwian hieroglyphic was written boustrophedon, like the early tablet from Enkomi may have been (Loprieno 1997: 25–6; Hawkins 2000: 4; Seeher 2002: 93; cf. Palaima 1989a: 140; but *contra* Duhoux 2009: 22–5).

As for other Anatolian scripts, apart from the cuneiform writing initially introduced via the karum (Old Assyrian trading post) at Kültepe-Kanesh, we know these only in the form of alphabetic scripts in the first millennium, when convention has it that they are borrowed from the Greek alphabet. For reasons primarily of context, which

---

390 no. 011) (especially those versions on a four-sided bar from the Mallia palace (168 no. 117) and a four-sided prism of unknown Cretan provenance (282–3 no. 304)); cf. Evans 1909: fig. 39:6).

[21] The TAY project database lists 37, 21 and 50 third-millennium sites in the provinces of Antalya, Mersin and Adana respectively (www.tayproject.org/veritabeng.html). The vast majority of these, however, are known only from surface finds and have not been excavated. For Middle and Late Bronze Age sites, see Kull and Röllig 1991; Forlanini 1992. See also Aksoy 2009 for Lycia.

would take too long to go into here, it seems equally likely that at least some of them have a more direct relationship with the Phoenician abjad, or perhaps a local variation of this. Moreover, if we take the case of the Lycian and Carian scripts, which we pick up only from the seventh and fifth centuries BC respectively, it has sometimes been speculated that certain additional letter forms may have been borrowed from, or influenced by, the Cypriot Syllabary (Evans 1909: 76–7; Roller 1987: 11; Jeffery 1990: 36–7; more generally, see also the recent discussion in Egetmeyer and Steele 2010: 129–30).

The point of all this is emphatically not to argue that either the Cretan or Cypriot Bronze Age scripts were derived from what we know as the Anatolian (Luwian) hieroglyphic script.[22] Rather, it is to point out that we really know very little about Anatolian scripts as a whole in the second millennium and quite conceivably earlier (Baurain 1980: 569–70). We know next to nothing about the range of variants of early scripts of which we do catch glimpses, and nothing at all about scripts which may have existed but did not survive, either as fossils in the archaeological record or in some form into the first millennium. As Machteld Mellink (1989: 329) once pointed out, Cilicia, in particular, from at least the middle of the Early Bronze Age was on the fringe of the literate Akkadian and Neo-Sumerian world (including the literate world of the Levant) and at the same time was increasingly in touch with both the south-western Anatolian and Cypriot spheres. Unlike in central Anatolia, where the natives probably did have to wait for the arrival of Assyrian merchants to introduce the notion of writing, more southerly and coastal areas arguably did not.

The question of unknowns brings me also to the question of media. It is a happy accident of history (at least from an archaeological point of view) that writing was first 'invented' in southern Mesopotamia, where virtually all they had was clay, so much so that they even made agricultural implements out of it. This – and the spread by one means or another of what can be called a Greater Mesopotamian culture – ensured that writing on clay became an elite convention of all sorts of

---

[22] Though cf. Hawkins 1986: 374 on the typological similarities between this and the Aegean scripts; and E. Masson 1979a: 136 for a comparison between signs of Anatolian hieroglyphic and those of Cypriot Bronze Age writing.

eastern rulers and those immediately around them well into the second and even first millennia. This is not to say, however, that clay was ever all that was used in areas like Anatolia and the eastern Mediterranean. The Egyptian practice of using papyrus is likely to have spread to the Levant and Syria already in the Old Kingdom (Bar-Ilan 1997), and other materials like wood, leather and even wax were available in most of the eastern Mediterranean. That wax was used at least in the later second millennium is strongly suggested by the hinged wooden tablet from the fourteenth-century Uluburun wreck (Bass *et al.* 1989: 10–11; Payton 1991) and later by a metal bowl with an inscription on a strip of wax beside the handle from early first-millennium Gordion (Lloyd 1967: 132 fig. 145). In addition, we know that in the Aegean Linear A was probably written on perishable materials (Krzyszkowska 2005: 155–8), although Linear B was probably not (Bennet 2001). On Cyprus, the use of paint to write inscriptions or make marks on Late Bronze Age pots after firing (Stubbings 1951: 41–52; Hirschfeld 1999, 2000), together with later traditions which associated writing with painting on leather or vellum (Hesychios, Lexicon s.v. διφθερολοιφός; Karageorghis and Karageorghis 1956: 355), make it extremely likely that perishable materials were used, possibly from a very early date. Although it is admittedly highly subjective, the general shapes of the signs (particularly perhaps of Luwian Hieroglyphic) might also suggest a background in media other than clay or stone – despite the fact that 'style' or appearance is likely to change according to the medium used – and there are indeed references in Hittite cuneiform texts to documents written on wooden boards or tablets (Hawkins 1986: 373; Symington 1991). Finally, in the case of the Cypriot syllabic script, we know that it survived through two to three centuries at the beginning of the first millennium when no visible sight of it remains. One conclusion that could very well be drawn from this is that it was written mainly on perishable materials.

Knowns and unknowns – the Levant

So much for Cyprus and Anatolia. Let us now think about Cyprus and the Levant, and what we know and do not know. We know that from at least the later part of the Middle Bronze Age Cyprus was

93

engaged in regular trading contacts with Syria and the Levant (Gerstenblith 1983: 70; Peltenburg 2008; Maguire 2009) and that, from at least the beginning of Late Cypriot II, Cyprus (particularly perhaps Enkomi) and Ugarit, in particular, were in what looks like fairly intimate contact with each other. We know this from Enkomi's adoption of typical Ugarit tomb types (Keswani 2004: 115; Crewe 2009: 27–9), from letters in Akkadian at Ugarit sent to and from people of Alashiya (Yon 1995; Beckman 1996a), and not least from the presence at Ugarit of texts written in the Cypriot Bronze Age script (O. Masson 1956a). What the letters from Ugarit, Tell el-Amarna (Moran 1996; Goren *et al.* 2003) and possibly Boğazköy (Beckman 1996b) tell us, among other things, is that some people living on Cyprus could also read and write Akkadian in syllabic cuneiform, and it is at least plausible that they could read other languages in other scripts as well.[23] At Ugarit we find inscriptions in a variety of languages and scripts, the latter including alphabetic cuneiform (Ugaritic), syllabic cuneiform, hieroglyphic Hittite and Egyptian hieroglyphic, as well as the Bronze Age Cypriot script. However, what we know about Ugarit, textually speaking, is concentrated mainly in the Late Bronze Age, particularly the period between *c.* 1400 and 1200 BC. We have far less idea of the range of scripts that may have been used there earlier than this (cf. Baurain 1980: 570).

Elsewhere in the Levant, however, we have traces of a variety of scripts other than cuneiform or the Egyptian scripts, ranging in date from the Middle to Late Bronze Age, some of them glimpsed in just one or two examples. There is the Byblos script, which seems to be a syllabic script with a pseudo-hieroglyphic appearance and which first occurs in the earlier second millennium. For what it is worth (probably not much more than other apparent similarities), it includes some linear signs which, superficially at least, would not look out of place in the Aegean and Cypriot scripts.[24] There is also

---

[23] For the intriguing possibility that the Alashiyan letters at Amarna were written by Ugarit-trained scribes, see Ferrara 2008b. I am most grateful to Silvia Ferrara for letting me see a copy of this unpublished paper.

[24] See e.g. Isserlin 1982: 794; Garbini 2001: 104–5 (who believes that the main influence behind the Byblos script was the Cretan, presumably Linear A, script); and cf. Baurain 1980: 569. One must beware, however, of falling into the trap that Evans (1909: 77–94

the proto-Sinaitic script, thought by some to be the earliest ancestor of the Phoenician abjad (Isserlin 1982: 800–2; Pardee 1997a: 76; Garbini 2001: 105–7;),[25] and alphabetic Canaanite, which almost certainly is. We catch other glimpses of apparently curious scripts, such as the clay tablet inscriptions from Deir' Alla with a *terminus ante quem* of *c*. 1200 BC (Isserlin 1982: 811),[26] the Kamid el-Loz ostraca of sixteenth- to fourteenth-century BC date (Isserlin 1982: 796; Hachmann 1993), signs engraved before firing on the sherd of a storage jar from Tel Haror in the western Negev, dating to the Middle Bronze Age (Oren *et al.* 1996), and the inscription engraved on a local stone vessel from Lachish which might at least in theory belong either to level IV (tenth to ninth century BC) or to level VI of the thirteenth to twelfth century (Finkelberg, Uchitel and Ussishkin 2004: 1629). Both of these last inscriptions have been hailed as examples of Aegean script; and, while the Haror sherd may well be,[27] the Lachish inscription – which has been identified as Linear A

figs. 41–3) fell into, in his belief that the Phoenician abjad was descended from the Aegean linear scripts, of seizing on mere visual similarities in the shapes of written signs (cf. Pope and Raison 1978: 17–18).

[25] Written boustrophedon, as well as dextroverse, sinistroverse and vertically (Isserlin 1982: 800).

[26] For these, which have persuasively been identified as written in a south Levantine variant of an early form of alphabetic script, see Shea 1989; Bron 2006: 190. They were thought by Albright (1975: 510) to be examples of 'Philistine' writing on the grounds of their suggested similarity to Minoan writing. In this respect, like the Lachish inscription discussed below, they seem a good illustration of the mesmerising effect that Evans's views of the influence of Aegeans and their scripts in the East Mediterranean has for long continued to exert over attitudes to the identification of uncanonical linear scripts and variants of scripts in that region.

[27] See Karnava 2005 for the suggestion that the signs on the Haror sherd comprise two early Cretan Hieroglyphic syllabograms (similar to those found together on one of the faces of a multifaced 'Archanes script' seal from Archanes, dated to Middle Minoan IA) and possibly a logogram (ideogram) or merely a drawing. While this poses problems in relation to the context in which the sherd was found (seventeenth–sixteenth century BC, in other words three or four centuries later than Middle Minoan IA), it could be said to make better sense than the three Linear A or Hieroglyphic logograms for 'figs', 'cloth' and 'bull' suggested by Olivier (Oren *et al.* 1996: 109), which are somewhat difficult to explain in terms of the inscribing, during the process of manufacture, of a pithos or storage jar. The composition of the sherd itself is compatible with manufacture in the area of Pyrgos in southern Crete (Day *et al.* 1999; Quinn and Day 2007), there is every reason to suppose that Crete and the Levant were already in trading contact in the first century or so of the second millennium and (since no other sherds of the same vessel were found) it may well be residual in its late Middle Bronze Age context at Haror. On the other hand, despite the ingenuity and appeal of Karnava's comparison, the fact that these signs appear to have been engraved before firing should perhaps alert us to the possibility that they do not represent writing as such but rather the kinds of marks (often characterised as 'potters'

or a script transitional between Linear A and B – is distinctly problematic (cf. Duhoux 2003: 149; Del Freo 2006: 164), and arguably has more to do with the centripetal urge to assimilate the unknown to the already known, however unlikely this may be contextually.[28] From a methodological and contextual point of view, it would seem rather more realistic (and cautious) to approach all such phenomena as possibly belonging to the unknown numbers and varieties of mysterious eastern Mediterranean logosyllabic, syllabic, proto-alphabetic or alphabetic scripts of which we catch mere glimpses in the second millennium, but which may not have survived beyond that.[29]

The point I am trying to make is how little we know about the variety of scripts (including some which would probably qualify as linear syllabic or logosyllabic scripts) and script variants in use in both the Levant and southern Anatolia from the end of the third millennium onwards. We are tantalised by puzzling glimpses here

marks') occasionally found on pottery and other objects in the late Early and Middle Bronze Age (for comparably complex 'potters' marks', not always found singly, on some of the Middle Bronze Age Aeginetan and Cycladic pottery, see Atkinson *et al.* 1904: 177–82; Bikaki 1984; Lindblom 2001: figs. 13–16, e.g. G53; and Feldbacher and Fischer 2008: figs. 328a–b for marks on Early Bronze Age Levantine pottery).

[28] The observation that the stone of which the vessel is made is found in the area of Lachish (Eshet 2004) suggests that the inscription itself was incised at the site or somewhere close to it rather than brought from anywhere in the Aegean. It is stated that it reads from right to left (very unusual in the Aegean linear scripts, if not entirely unknown in Linear A), though also that one of the asymmetrical signs has not been reversed as might be expected (Finkelberg, Uchitel and Ussishkin 2004: 1631). The conclusion that the script is Linear A (or rather a script transitional between Linear A and B) might be thought of as causing problems in terms of Aegean chronology, since the immediate (uncertain) context of the fragment is between two and five centuries later than the earliest Linear B inscriptions and the latest Linear A ones, though it could of course be residual in either context. The conclusion that it is transitional between Linear A and B raises methodological questions in any case, since it is based on a single sign identified as a specifically Linear B variant. No explanation is offered as to why someone at Lachish should be using Linear A or a transitional Linear A/B script in any period between the Middle Bronze Age and the ninth century BC, and the possible implications of its presence at Lachish (whether it was written by an Aegean visitor who arrived sometime shortly after the middle of the second millennium (Finkelberg 1998: 269–70), or whether we need to entertain the possibility that Linear B evolved out of Linear A in the Levant and perhaps remained in hitherto unsuspected use there for several centuries) are left curiously under-explored, submerged under the minute attention paid to the detailed consideration of classification, typology and terminology of Linear A and B sign forms. Nor is there much concern as to the possible implications of the language inscribed ('Minoan' is suggested, but not pressed; at least there is no suggestion that it is Greek).

[29] For other examples of second-millennium linear scripts glimpsed in the Levant, see Baurain 1980: 570; Isserlin 1982: 796.

and there, and I do not doubt that there are others that we still have not come across and perhaps never will encounter in the archaeological record. Given the likelihood of impermanent media, it seems extremely likely that we have only a tiny tip of the iceberg of varied forms and contexts of literacy that once existed in both regions, often side-by-side. Our difficulties are compounded by the probability that, outside elite official circles in the main administrative centres, scribal conventions (and therefore scripts) were not standardised, by the disconcerting ability of media used to affect the appearance of sign forms quite radically, and by the frequent cross-overs between scripts and languages which seem to have been characteristic of the east in the second millennium (Ferrara, Chapter 3 in this volume). In view of this, I believe we have to resist the positivist impulse to relate everything we come across to something we already know, and (for instance) to draw straight lines of connection going eastward from Aegean scripts to one or more Cypriot scripts or from Aegean scripts to the odd glimpses we may get from time to time of little-known linear scripts lurking around the East Mediterranean. Not only is it unduly positivistic, but it also betrays the heritage of a lingering Evansian Aegeo-centricism.

Broadening the context

Where does this leave Cypriot Bronze Age writing and the problem of its origins? For a start, I think we have to be willing to make the question a little more complex, as befits the contextual complexity which archaeology seems progressively to reveal. We also have to avoid simply combining the isolated micro-contexts of our regional specialisms and instead try to think in a joined-up macro-contextual manner, despite the areas of darkness and ignorance which bedevil this attempt. I am more than willing to believe that the Aegean and Cypriot Bronze Age scripts are in some way related,[30] but I find the idea that Crete simply bestowed its script

---

[30] They seem (as far as we can tell or guess) to be similar syllabic scripts with an emphasis on open consonant+vowel or simple vowel syllables, and they or their ancestors may well originally have been devised for languages with similar phonotactical structures.

on Cyprus at the beginning of the Late Bronze Age (or earlier) increasingly difficult to swallow (see Godart and Sacconi 1979: 133; and cf. Duhoux 2009: 30–2; Bombardieri and Jasink 2010: 149–50). Apart from the lack of a convincing context in which this might have happened, there are just too many unknowns. I certainly do not have any answers, and, until we can explain various other existing problems – such as the precise nature of the relationship between Cretan Hieroglyphic and Linear A (which is not simply one of chronological succession: e.g. Karnava 2002: 73–4) – we shall probably not get much further. Moreover, we cannot, it seems to me, simply and confidently appeal to the apparent antiquity of Cretan writing as long as we continue to know so pitifully little about the prehistory of large swathes of western and southern Anatolia.

Meanwhile, there are at least a couple of possibilities:

1) Linear A and the Cypriot Bronze Age script are both derived from a single logosyllabic parent script, perhaps at different times (since Linear A retains a logographic element and the Cypriot script – as far as we can see – does not appear to do so);[31] alternatively, the Cypriot script may have lost its logograms *in situ*, which would probably mean that it had existed on the island for some time before we currently see it.

2) They could each derive from different offshoots of what might once have been a single script (insofar as single scripts could be said to exist outside newly literate individuals or newly literate individual groups in the late third or early second millennia) or from otherwise related scripts.[32]

As for where Cyprus might have got hold of its script, almost anywhere on the northern coasts of the eastern Mediterranean seems a theoretical possibility, given the intimate interaction that

---

[31] See note 6 above. On current evidence, *if* the Cypriot script makes use of logographic elements, it seems as likely that Cypriot writers invented these for themselves.

[32] As with languages, we perhaps need to keep in mind the possibility of convergences as well as divergences, although the suggestion of Godart and Sacconi (1979: 133; cf. also Duhoux 2009; Bombardieri and Jasink 2010) that the earliest Cypriot writing in the form of the tablet from Late Cypriot I Enkomi was the result of a mingling of (mainly) oriental elements with a minority of Cretan elements deriving from Cretan mercantile activity on the Syro-Palestinian coast, while recognising the potential for complexity, seems not much easier to sustain on contextual grounds than a straightforward transmission from Crete to Cyprus.

Cyprus had with southern and south-western Anatolia from before the middle of the third millennium (Peltenburg 2007) and particularly during the Philia phase just after the middle of the millennium (Webb and Frankel 2007), at a time when the Aegean generally (including a couple of sites on the north coast of Crete: Lindblom 2001: 16 table 1) was beginning, like Cyprus, to experience the first appearance of the 'potmarks' which may have emanated, in one way or another, from Anatolia and the spread westwards of its contemporary metallurgical innovations and the possible pre-literate notation systems associated with them. Alternatively – and this need not preclude both – one might look to almost any major city in the coastal Levant at the end of the third or in the early second millennium (cf. Karageorghis 1958; Godart 1979: 37; Godart and Sacconi 1979: 133; Duhoux 2009: 31–2). In a context in which ships from places like Byblos or Ugarit were actively making contact with Crete, probably from the end of the third millennium (Gallagher 2008), and by the early second millennium were plying a circuit which certainly took in both Cyprus (and perhaps Cypriot crews) and almost certainly included parts of coastal southern Anatolia, the introduction of writing systems to both Cyprus and Crete from among the potentially many loosely interrelated ones which may have been washing around the coasts of the eastern Mediterranean seems not at all implausible. That Cyprus sat in illiterate ignorance, surrounded by a sea of literacy and waiting until distant Crete came to its rescue in the Late Bronze Age (as Evans imagined) seems, on the other hand, distinctly less plausible.

One more aspect that needs to be considered is that of language. So far, the languages which the Linear A and Hieroglyphic scripts of Crete and the Bronze Age script or scripts of Cyprus were used to write, or their affiliations, remain unidentified. There are, however, some circumstantial reasons for thinking that, on both islands, languages originally related to ones of southern or south-western Anatolia (whether classifiable as Indo-European or not) might well have been spoken.[33] Whether or not these might originally, in the

---

[33] The reasons are primarily archaeological and contextual, rather than linguistic: in the case of Crete, the probability that the earliest Neolithic colonists of around 7000 BC started off in the coastal regions of south-west Anatolia, and the links with this area which were

deep recesses of time, have been related or even mutually comprehensible languages there is no way of telling; but what one can probably postulate is that the process of script adoption would be afforded a head-start by a shared or similar language or (as is argued in the case of the Greek alphabet) at least some element of bilingualism. Whatever their earlier linguistic relationship, it seems unlikely that, by the beginning of the Late Bronze Age or even the Middle Bronze Age, any Anatolian-related languages on Crete and Cyprus were mutually intelligible, while the opportunities for bilingualism – on current archaeological evidence – would seem to have been limited to brief, and perhaps irregular, visits by a few individuals who travelled in their capacity as members of ships' crews. On the other hand, in the case of Cyprus – in view particularly of its geographical setting, but also of the archaeological data – it is not difficult to imagine rather more extensive bilingualism in relation to Levantine coastal centres from the Middle Bronze Age onwards, and in relation to southern Anatolia (with which shared language in the Philia horizon is a plausible possibility) perhaps continuously from the second half of the third millennium down to the beginning of the Late Bronze Age.[34] If one adds to that

maintained throughout the Neolithic and Early Bronze Age and possibly became more regular towards the end of the latter period. As far as Crete is concerned, there is also, however, the possible linguistic substrate, seen in certain pre-Greek place names, which appears to link the Aegean (including Crete) with the western fringes of Anatolia and is sometimes associated with the 'Pelasgians' of literary fame (Fick 1905; Evans 1909: 102; Blegen and Haley 1928; Hester 1957; Palmer 1958; but see Crossland 1962). In Cyprus, where fairly regular contacts with the probably still 'Mesolithic' inhabitants of coastal southern Anatolia can perhaps already be seen in the large quantities of Cappadocian obsidian which reached the island in the early aceramic Neolithic in the later ninth millennium (even if the earliest farming settlers themselves came from elsewhere), it is probably during the Philia horizon of the mid third millennium that the strongest case can be made for intimate and regular connections with southern and south-western Anatolia, if not actual immigration from there. Given the succession of multiple mixtures of different languages spoken on Cyprus over the last three millennia, place-name evidence for earlier languages on the island is at best unreliable and at worst non-existent.

[34] For evidence of relationships between Cyprus and Cilicia in the Middle Bronze Age (especially towards its end), see Seton-Williams 1954: 133; Goldman 1956: 164; Catling 1966: 44; Merrillees and Tubb 1979; Catling in Jones 1986: 585; Knapp 1990: table 3; Knapp and Cherry 1994: 43; Gates 2003: 18; Kozal 2005. Despite the shortage of imported Middle Cypriot I–II pottery in Cilicia, there is no compelling reason to suppose that some coming and going between the south coast of Anatolia and the north coast of Cyprus did not continue, particularly as long as the east–west sea route running between the two was regularly used, as it probably was from the late Early Bronze Age onwards. For the suggestion of Semitic personal names on some of the Cypriot tablets and speculation that her CM 2 texts from Enkomi may have been written in Hurrian, see

the possibility of a (re-)injection of Anatolian demographic and linguistic elements into Cyprus around the middle of the third millennium, then the chances that Cyprus derived its script directly from Anatolia at some point between the later third millennium and the mid second millennium, rather than from Crete, seem considerably more plausible.

Concluding thoughts

We could summarise some tentative conclusions and suggestions as follows:

- The Cypriot Bronze Age script (or, if one wants to be pernickety, scripts – though there seems little doubt that, if scripts in the plural, they are very closely related, however many languages they were used to write) and Linear A and its successor Linear B are very probably related in some way. The likelihood that all three are open-syllable syllabaries and the fact that some of the signs of Linear B and the later common Cypro-Archaic/Classical script share the same values seem to support this view.[35] However, a direct filial relationship

---

E. Masson 1974: 47–55; see also Knapp and Marchant 1982 for some further discussion of possible links between Cypriot Bronze Age script(s) and language(s) and those of Anatolia–Syria–Palestine.

[35] There are not, however, very many of these – perhaps not surprising in view of the span of time which separates them, and the spans of time which may separate both from their common ancestor, whatever this was. In addition, while some signs (e.g. Cypriot and Linear B 'pa'; 'se'; 'lo'='ro'; 'to'; 'ta'='da'; 'na' and perhaps 'po' and 'ti') remain fairly recognisable, there are other signs (such as 'ki' and 'ko') which one would probably be hard pressed to recognise as the 'same' signs without the prior knowledge that both are used to write Greek and have the same phonetic values. Of the eight Cypro-Archaic/Classical signs originally matched visually by Evans (1909: fig. 39) with Linear B signs, only four ('pa', 'lo'/'ro', 'ta'/'da' and 'na'), all among the structurally simplest signs, actually prove to match phonetically (cf. also Daniel 1941: figs. 1, 3), which says much about the dangers of relying on the subjective appearance of form alone to determine close relationships. While, as between Linear B and A, there is a strong likelihood that the same or similar forms in the Cypro-Archaic/Classical syllabary and the Cypriot Bronze Age script carry the same or similar values, one cannot discount the real possibility of shifts in the values of individual forms, of radical changes in the forms themselves which make their identification very difficult, or even of signs (in terms of their values) occasionally swapping places with other signs. All this is within series of comparatively standardised forms derived, in the case of each individual script, from similar media. How much more complicated we might expect it to become once we start to reckon on the effects on sign forms of quite different types of media within some of these scripts has been hinted at, in the case of the Cypriot Bronze Age script, by Ferrara (2005).

between Cypriot and Cretan Bronze Age writing is something that needs to be demonstrated rather than simply accepted because Evans said so.

- Such a demonstration not only requires evidence of the use of the same basic body of signs (or clearly derived signs) with the same values, which is difficult in the case of scripts which are undeciphered and when the languages they are used to write unknown or unidentified,[36] it also requires the existence of a suitable context in which direct transmission could have arisen – a context which includes consideration both of the opportunities for acquisition of literacy and also of the motives for it and the purpose to which the newly acquired technology of writing was intended to be put. Opportunity would typically consist of regular or extended contact between literate people and a group or critical mass of illiterate individuals engaged in similar activities, in a context in which the literacy of the former was deployed, rather than irregular or casual encounters between occasional individuals. There would also have to be a strong motive on the part of the illiterate to learn to write and some clearly perceived purpose for which writing was seen as an advantage.

- It seems likely that writing was first introduced to Cyprus some time before we currently first see it. This must certainly be the case if it was borrowed directly from Linear A in order for the apparent difference in ideogram use to develop. This, in turn, probably means sometime before the end of the Middle Bronze Age when, on archaeological grounds, the most we can envisage are casual and probably fairly irregular contacts between Cretans and Cypriot members of ships' crews at ports such as Kommos.[37] Even in the early Late Bronze Age, this is still likely to have been the case. In such circumstances, unless we can reasonably postulate that an important role for Linear A lay in providing documents to accompany the passage of goods traded overseas in the eastern Mediterranean (for which – though possible – there is as yet no evidence), it is hard to find an obvious motive at this comparatively early date, still less one that one might attribute

---

[36] Estimates vary as to how many signs Linear A and the Cypriot Bronze Age script may have in common, since comparing them tends to be a very subjective exercise. We can probably safely include the handful mentioned in the preceding note, which appear to change little as between Linear A and B on the one hand and the Cypriot Bronze Age and Archaic periods on the other, but when it comes to other signs we are on much shakier ground (see Olivier, Chapter I in this volume).

[37] The alternative – between Cypriots and Cretan members of ships' crews (or Cretan and Cypriot members of the same crews) – seems even less likely to produce a context conducive to the Cypriot adoption of a Cretan writing system, given that such Cypriot individuals would have been equally (if not more) exposed – and in similar circumstances – to literacy in a number of eastern Mediterranean ports.

particularly to a coherent group of Cypriots. Nor are there – as yet – any indications of an initial overriding purpose for the adoption of writing on Cyprus.

- The range both of media and types of inscriptions suggests that in Late Bronze Age Cyprus writing had a multitude of purposes both formal and informal, official and unofficial, and the possible use of perishable materials could theoretically expand these. In some of these respects at least, Late Bronze Age Cypriot literacy does seem to resemble that found in Neopalatial Crete. Where it differs is in the persistence of its literacy (and script) right through to the Archaic period and beyond, which suggests that writing was well embedded in various facets and probably strata of Cypriot society (Iacovou, Chapter 6 in this volume). Linear A, on the other hand, seems to have disappeared after the development of Linear B and to have lost its ability to be inscribed on a variety of different materials, suggesting that Linear A literacy may have been confined to limited social groups on Crete. Cyprus also differs from Protopalatial and Neopalatial Crete, however, in that, whereas in Crete writing and seal use are quite closely associated as aspects of the same administrative and transactional systems, Cyprus shows extremely limited evidence for the sphragistic use of seals, while the first seals found on the island (from the seventeenth to sixteenth centuries BC) are cylinder seals arriving from the east (Webb 2002: 113).[38] If Cyprus borrowed its writing system directly from Crete and for Cretan-related purposes, why did it not also borrow Cretan seal types and seal usage?[39]

- So far, this has largely been an exercise in deconstruction of a particularly long-lived assumption (that there is a direct line between Linear A and Cypriot Bronze Age writing), on the grounds mainly of context and of a daunting mixture of uncertainties inherent in that assumption and of unexplained obstacles to it. The exercise is hampered by

---

[38] With a single exception, which shows analogies to Near Eastern seal use and which Porada has suggested was not impressed on Cyprus (Porada in Dikaios 1969–71: 790–1, pls. 182A:1905/9, 322: fig. a–1, 324; contra Smith 2002: 14–16), clay sealings are conspicuous by their absence from the Late Bronze Age Cypriot archaeological record, as opposed to the apparently primarily decorative designs on pithoi which may have been made by wooden cylinders (Webb 2002: 126–8; e.g. Catling and Karageorghis 1960: 122, pl. 30:a–b). While a few seals have inscriptions in various scripts (including Egyptian hieroglyphic, cuneiform and Cypriot Bronze Age script), there is little to lead us to believe that seals were habitually used for sealing in the Cypriot Bronze Age, let alone in the manner in which they were on Crete.

[39] For one or two Late Cypriot cylinder seals which may have inscriptions intended to be read on sealings rather than on the seals themselves, see Smith 2002: 11–13. However, not only are these extremely few and often dependent on the apparent direction faced by a single asymmetrical sign, but, given that it is only an impression that most Cypriot Bronze Age inscriptions are written dextroverse, we cannot be sure that they were not intended to be read sinistroverse in the first place.

enormous gaps in our knowledge (the gaps created by our inability to read both Linear A and the Cypriot script, and by the fact that all those perishable documents have perished, for instance) – but, then, so was the original assumption. The same difficulties, and worse, beset any attempt to suggest an alternative construction, and I shall not dream of attempting one. However, it does seem possible – at least in theory – to consider other possibilities which seem to me to offer the potential of theoretically equally legitimate explanations, if not more so on the grounds of context.

- There seems no reason – other than that we know about the existence of Linear A on Crete much more definitely than we do about other early scripts in other areas – why both Linear A and Cypriot writing should not have a shared ancestry or even parentage, possibly originating somewhere in southern Anatolia or even in the Levant. While southern (especially perhaps south-western) Anatolia would provide plausible contexts in the form of the close material cultural connections between it and both Cyprus and the Aegean from the second half of the third millennium and might well provide a fundamental linguistic link between both regions (cf. also Hawkins 1986: 374), the Levant can also be seen as linking both regions from the later part of the same millennium onwards, particularly through the complex trade in metals[40] which has been suggested, for example, by Webb *et al.* 2006 and by the evidence for the initiation of an eastern Mediterranean–Cretan linkup (which would have had to traverse the westward passage between the intervisible coasts of southern Anatolia and northern Cyprus) at around the same time (Gallagher 2008; Wengrow 2010). Both the Anatolian and the Levantine coasts are very much closer to Cyprus than Cyprus is to Crete, and the regular coming and going which one can easily envisage between them would provide a much more intimate (if informal) form of contact conducive to the introduction of – and experimentation with – writing technology than is possible to imagine between Crete and Cyprus even as late as the early Late Bronze Age. Moreover, we know that literacy existed in the Levant (at Ebla) already in the third millennium, and this – together with the undoubtedly familiar model of Egyptian literacy – may well have encouraged other forms of writing to develop in the region for a variety of uses, unofficial and informal as well as official and formal; and, while we have no such definite knowledge for third-millennium southern coastal Anatolia, it seems highly likely that the inhabitants of more easterly regions like Cilicia, at least, were aware of the literacy of

---

[40] Again, I return to the association between metal objects and signs – some of them similar to those of later accredited scripts – mentioned above.

their neighbours. The fact that we have not found an obvious ancestral or parental script in either region means little or nothing. One need only reflect how recently alphabetic Canaanite was recognised at Ugarit (Courtois 1979: 1157–8; Pardee 1997b; Yon 2006: 18) or how even more recently 'proper' inscriptions have been discovered in Late Cypriot I Cyprus (Dikaios 1956).

- Finally – and at the very least – I would like to suggest that we consider dropping the term 'Cypro-Minoan' as applied to script on Cyprus in favour of 'Bronze Age Cypriot' or some such more neutral label. The term 'Cypro-Minoan' is so full of inherited intellectual baggage, which works subliminally to direct our thinking, that for the last hundred years, despite the enormous quantity of new understanding gained through archaeology on Cyprus, it has constricted our very approach to the problem of the origins of Cypriot literacy within unnecessarily narrow channels. Over that century, prehistoric Cyprus has emerged through its archaeology as a free-standing entity in its own right, with its own distinctive historical trajectories and cultural characteristics, no longer (as it once was) cast as a provincial outpost of the Aegean, on the one hand, or as a 'no man's land' on the other, passively accepting technological and cultural influences from west and east (Iacovou 2008a; Voskos and Knapp 2008). At the minimum, it seems desirable to credit Cyprus with some positive hand in the acquisition of its own first literacy and to confront the questions of where, when, why and in what circumstances it may have acquired it, rather than suppose that all problems are automatically solved by the simple remedy of attributing it to Evans's Minoan Crete.

5

FROM THE CYPRO-MINOAN TO THE CYPRO-GREEK SYLLABARIES: LINGUISTIC REMARKS ON THE SCRIPT REFORM

MARKUS EGETMEYER

Cypriot is considered a somewhat exotic ancient Greek dialect, mainly because of its script and also because of its geographical and thus cultural proximity to the Orient. Indeed, working on Cypriot leads one into a different world. But when the dialect is also labelled archaic, this could be denied and such a discussion would be idle.

Nevertheless, it is important to stress that the chronological distribution of the oldest inscriptions in the peculiar Cypriot script (Egetmeyer 2010a: § 10 and 'tableau III', 30–1) does not differ at all from what we observe for the other Greek dialects and also the Anatolian and Phrygian languages written in an alphabet: few inscriptions in the eighth century BC and an increasing amount only from the seventh century on. One has to add a discussion on scanty material from the end of the ninth/beginning of the eighth century, especially in the Phrygian, Euboian and perhaps also Carian area, and the subsequent hypothesis as to the invention of these alphabets not long before (Brixhe 2006, 2007: 23, 31; Theurillat 2007; Herda and Sauter 2010: 62–3). To express it in archaeological periods for Cyprus: very little material in Cypro-Geometric III, somewhat more only from Cypro-Archaic I on, and thus nothing during the preceding Cypro-Geometric I–II. The description of the evolution and relationship of all these alphabets, not only of the Greek ones, out of their Semitic model would be worth a monograph. In any case, the gap between the end of the Bronze Age and the first alphabetical inscriptions can be considered an illiterate period for Greece. It is here that the situation in Cyprus must differ. In both areas, Greece and Cyprus, Aegean syllabaries were used during the Bronze Age. The Linear B script used to write Mycenaean Greek was abandoned, and there is no link to the later alphabet. In Cyprus, however, the Cypro-Minoan script (CM) used to write non-Greek languages was abandoned, too, but one could rather say that it was replaced, because there is a direct link to the following script, which must be the result of a reform of Cypro-Minoan. This script is labelled here Cypro-Greek (CG), divided into a common (CG-C) and a Paphian (CG-P) branch (already Egetmeyer 2010a: 1), because the main bulk of its material is written in this language, and one can suppose that this language was the target of the adaptation. In Cyprus, the gap between the documentation of both scripts cannot be an illiterate one, it is just ours. But as the end of the Bronze Age signifies the end of a cultural period, it seemed natural to place the invention of the new script at the beginning of this new period. In other words, a high date, before 1000 BC, for the invention of the new Cypriot script was assumed, often implicitly, but more often still the subject is not discussed at all. The fact that the Cypro-Minoan script is attested until a later period (1050–950 BC) than Linear B, the example of the Luwian glyphs which demonstrates that a Bronze Age script can indeed survive under favourable conditions into the new period, and a comparison of the distributional data with the supposed script inventions for the alphabetic scripts described above, should have suggested that there is a need for real arguments. Behind this problem of the script reform lies the general one of the Hellenisation of Cyprus, which has been at the centre of an intense debate for a long time now (recent examples are Iacovou 2008a and Voskos and Knapp 2008).

But since 1983 all these considerations could be wiped away, because the Opheltas inscription (Figure 5.1), presenting a personal name in the proper Cypriot Greek dialect on an obelos in a tomb at Paphos, furnished the proof for the already supposed high date of the script reform (E. and O. Masson 1983). The missing link was found and a *terminus ante quem* fixed: 1050–950 BC. Arguing was abandoned before it even started. Alas, about twenty years later somebody disturbed this comfortable general opinion: Jean-Pierre Olivier directed his interest from the western branch of Aegean scripts to the eastern, Cypriot one, wishing to complete his research on the subject. From purely epigraphical considerations he came to the conviction

5.1 Opheltas inscription, ##170

that the Opheltas inscription was still written in a Cypro-Minoan syllabary (Olivier 2008: 608, 615). The *terminus ante quem* turned into a *terminus post quem*. The importance of this statement must be stressed, because one often has the impression that it is considered a witty observation without further implications, but in reality the whole question is open again. And as a linguist, one can immediately add that the importance of the indigenous non-Greek element is generally strongly underestimated (Egetmeyer 2010b).

The reasoning behind this new attribution is not obvious, because it is not simply founded on a different opinion on the outlook of the signs of the Opheltas inscription, and Olivier 2008 does not make his argument explicit. The scope of this chapter is a linguistic one, but once again a more detailed look at the history of the syllabograms is revealed to be necessary before one can move on to linguistic questions.

What gets forgotten in the excitement about the Greek, Opheltas, is that his obelos is part of an epigraphic ensemble in a wealthy tomb, which has to be taken into account, and this ensemble is all but Greek. All the epigraphical material from Paphos-*Skales* is well presented on a single page in E. and O. Masson (1983: 412) and is considered in the following:

Skales, tomb 49, obelos: (*HoChyMin*) ##170: CM 1: 064-011-024-004-012, neither CG-C: ⊻⌇8ⱶ Ⱬ nor CG-P: ⊥↯☷ⱶⱢ (Olivier 2008: 615)

The identification of the signs and the interpretation of the inscription by E. and O. Masson were perfect (also O. Masson 1994), but the inscription was not used to push our knowledge of the history of the scripts involved any further. From a standard view-point the five signs of the inscription present a <CØPØP> sequence (C = common, P = Paphian, Ø = non-characteristic sign form). The assumption of such a mix of signs does not, obviously, have much chance of corresponding with the facts. We have simply to admit that this is what a Paphian inscription of this time looked like, and that means that all the five signs belong to the CG-P signary. According to Olivier, we now have to go even further and consider the signs as belonging to a CM signary, more precisely the main CM 1 sub-branch (Table 5.1), and this despite its Greek reading.

Table 5.1 *Comparative Cypro-Minoan grid (after* HoChyMin: *413)*

CM 1, CM 2 ET « CM 3 » : TABLEAU DES SYLLABOGRAMMES

	CM 1	CM 2	« CM 3 »		CM 1	CM 2	« CM 3 »		CM 1	CM 2	« CM 3 »
001	[sign]	[sign]	[sign]	040	···	···	[sign]	079	···	[sign]	···
002	[sign]	···	[sign]	041	[sign]	···	···	080	···	[sign]	···
004	[sign]	[sign]	[sign]	044	[sign]	[sign]	[sign]	081	[sign]	[sign]	···
005	[sign]	[sign]	[sign]	046	[sign]	···	···	082	[sign]	[sign]	[sign]
006	[sign]	[sign]	[sign]	047	···	[sign]	···	083	[sign]	···	···
007	[sign]	···	[sign]	049	···	[sign]	···	084	[sign]	···	···
008	[sign]	[sign]	[sign]	050	[sign]	···	[sign]	085	[sign]	···	···
009	[sign]	[sign]	[sign]	051	···	[sign]	[sign]	086	[sign]	···	···
010	···	[sign]	···	052	···	[sign]	···	087	[sign]	[sign]	[sign]
011	[sign]	[sign]	[sign]	053	[sign]	···	[sign]	088	[sign]	···	···
012	[sign]	[sign]	···	054	···	[sign]	···	089	···	[sign]	···
012b	[sign]	···	···	055	[sign]	···	[sign]	090	···	[sign]	···
013	[sign]	[sign]	[sign]	056	[sign]	[sign]	[sign]	091	[sign]	[sign]	[sign]
015	[sign]	···	···	058	···	···	[sign]	092	[sign]	[sign]	[sign]
017	[sign]	[sign]	···	059	[sign]	[sign]	···	094	···	···	[sign]
019	[sign]	···	[sign]	060	···	[sign]	···	095	[sign]	[sign]	[sign]
021	[sign]	[sign]	[sign]	061	[sign]	[sign]	···	096	[sign]	[sign]	[sign]
023	[sign]	[sign]	[sign]	063	[sign]	···	···	097	[sign]	[sign]	[sign]
024	[sign]	[sign]	···	062	···	[sign]	···	098	···	···	[sign]
025	[sign]	[sign]	[sign]	064	[sign]	[sign]	···	099	[sign]	···	[sign]
026	[sign]	···	···	066	···	[sign]	···	100	···	···	[sign]
027	[sign]	[sign]	[sign]	067	[sign]	···	···	101	[sign]	···	···
028	[sign]	[sign]	[sign]	068	[sign]	[sign]	···	102	[sign]	[sign]	[sign]
029	···	[sign]	···	069	[sign]	[sign]	[sign]	103	[sign]	···	[sign]
030	[sign]	[sign]	···	070	[sign]	[sign]	[sign]	104	[sign]	[sign]	[sign]
033	[sign]	[sign]	···	071	···	···	[sign]	105	···	···	[sign]
034	[sign]	···	···	072	[sign]	[sign]	···	107	[sign]	[sign]	···
035	[sign]	[sign]	[sign]	073	[sign]	···	[sign]	108	[sign]	···	···
036	[sign]	[sign]	[sign]	074	···	[sign]	[sign]	109	[sign]	···	···
037	[sign]	[sign]	[sign]	075	[sign]	[sign]	[sign]	110	[sign]	[sign]	[sign]
038	[sign]	[sign]	[sign]	076	···	[sign]	···	112	[sign]	···	···
039	[sign]	···	···	078	···	[sign]	···	114	[sign]	···	···

Let us start to illustrate this with the main obstacle: sign 2, CM 011 ʃ corresponding to CG-C ʃ and CG-P ʕ <*pe*>. This CM 011 ~ CG <*pe*> equation was not known to E. and O. Masson, and this fact, combined with the obvious Greek reading, brought them automatically to identify the script as CG. The problem is that the sign form of ʃ CG <*pe*> is more elaborated, more angular, than the sign forms of CM 011 already mentioned, and that this sign was limited to the subbranch CM 2 (ɭ), used only in Enkomi, far away in the east of the island (E. Masson 1974: 13 and *HoChyMin*: 434). The sign figures in the two inscriptions ##207 and ##208. It is followed by the same sign CM 024 as in the Opheltas inscription in ##207 B.I.01, *HoChyMin*: 304–5:

]-104-011-024 | ~]-*i-pe-le* |

and B.I.10:

| 107-011-087 | ~ | *ma-pe-la*|

Four other examples in the same inscriptions can be indicated (*HoChyMin*: 434). But, what is decisive is that Olivier can now demonstrate that the sign CM 011 is part of all three CM syllabaries (*HoChyMin*: 413). In CM 3, used in Ugarit, one finds it in ##215, B.19, sign 8 (*HoChyMin*: 407), where it is to be distinguished from the divider, to be seen as the following and preceding signs 6 and 10. Most important are his identifications of the sign in the CM 1 inscription ##097, line 5–6 (sign 2):

| 104-011-024-006-012-023 & ~ | *i-pe-le-pa-u-ti* & (=stiktogram)

and lines 12 (sign 4)–13:

& 107-011-024-107-027-069-023 & ~ & *ma-pe-le-ma-si-•-ti* &

thus twice again with the sequence 011–024 ~ <*-pe-le-*>. Further examples figure in line 18, sign 6; line 24, sign 6 of the same inscription and in ##95 sign 3. For this last inscription Olivier thus integrates E. Masson's classification of the sign as n° I of a specifically archaic signary (E. Masson 1974: 11, with explication of the use of the Roman cipher, and 12 fig. 12) in the standard signaries. For Olivier, the CG sign <*pe*> has thus a CM antecedent and is not, with Palaima (1991: 453), a 'free invention' in these later CG signaries. This step opened the way for the CM classification of the Opheltas inscription.

Olivier proposed this identification of the second sign of the Opheltas inscription in letters to the author (especially that of November 2 2005), developing how a sign that he had formerly numbered CM 001bis should be considered identical to CM 011 ʃ and not to CM 001 Ɩ ~ CG <we>, which presents a similar sign form. However, one has to admit that the angular form of the sign in the Opheltas inscription remains remarkable and seems to be nearer to its CG form. But this is no reason to dismiss Olivier's proposal. The chronological distribution of the quoted inscriptions with sign CM 011 is the following table (F. Vandenabeele in *HoChyMin*: 33–8, where all dates for the CM inscriptions can be found):

LC I A–B	1650–1475	##95
	1400–1300	##097
LC II C	1325–1225 ?	##215
LC III A	1210–1200	##208
LC IIIB	1125–1100	##207
CG I	1050–950	##170 (Opheltas)

The example in question is thus the most recent one. Its form can be due to chronological reasons and demonstrate that the CG form had already been arrived at by CM times. In any case, the variation between these forms does not exceed by far the variations one has to accept for other signs: for example, the identification of CM 036 ⱳ in ##175, line 2, sign 2 (further examples are discussed below). We do not know enough about the Cypriot signaries to be able to decide, as for a phoneme, to what extent a graphical 'deviation' from the 'norm' is allowed for a grapheme unless a sign becomes unreadable or in danger of being confused with another one. In sum, this sign does not push for a CM attribution, but also does not impede it.

It seems that Nahm 1981: 59, 56 fig. 3 already proposed the equation CM 011 ~ CG <pe>, but without using sign numbers, and his whole presentation is difficult to use, because it is too tolerant in the comparison of sign forms and embedded in premature discussions on decipherment following E. Masson and C. Saporetti. The equation would have a graphic parallel in the evolution of the sign CG 𝔍 <po>, but it is not clear whether his CM sign corresponds only to CM 2 012 (or also to the stiktogram '&' of CM 1 (*HoChyMin*: 414–15).

The other signs had been well recognized as such, but it is useful to summarise them introducing linguistic terminology: CM 064 ⩊ ~ CG ⩊ <o> is the archaic Paphian form which corresponds to the later common form, and this grapheme represents there a conserved archaism, whereas the later Paphian form ⊥ probably represents an innovation. A few examples of this Paphian sign (but also of other ones) corresponding to common signs and found in contemporary inscriptions which generally use the innovated Paphian forms represent conserved Paphian archaisms or shared 'isographs', and confirm the view presented here. – CM 024 ⍥ ~ CG ⅚ <le> is also the later Paphian form, an inherited archaism which is replaced by an innovation in the common syllabary (𝟪). One might at least posit a link for this CG-C sign with CM 069 ⧓, supposing the frequent graphical 'H > X reduction' during CM > CG (cf. Smith 2003: 285 for Y-shaped/X-shaped CM marks). The most ancient example of this CG-C sign figures in the archaic, seventh-century inscription *ICS* 257, presenting an incised angular form (confirmed by O. Masson 1971: 51) (Figure 5.2). One can add that sign CM 033 ⩕ seems to correspond to CG-C (ⓝ) and CG-P (⋏ⁱ) <re>. The graphic distinction between /l/ and /r/, unknown to Linear B, would thus already be Cypro-Minoan. – CM 004 ⊢ ~ CG-C (⊢) and CG-P (⊢) is the sign corresponding to Linear A and B sign 01 (<da> in Linear B). The simplicity of this sign form can be supposed the reason for its consistency in these four Aegean syllabaries. – CM 012 (~ CG ⋏ <u>corresponds also to the later Paphian form, the common syllabary presenting an innovation (𝔐). This equation is

5.2 *ICS* 257.

far better than to suppose, with E. and O. Masson 1983: 413, that CG-P <*u*> has been simplified from CM 038 **ʍ**, conserving only its central element.

It is now important also to take into consideration the other epigraphic material from the same tomb, as well as material from the same place and region:

Skales, tomb 49, obelos: ##171:

023 | 023 ~ *ti* | *ti* (**Λ**~ CG-C ↑ and CG-P↑)
Skales, tomb 49, obelos: ##172:

a) 007 and c) 097 ~ a) • and c) *ro*

this last one (**Ꮋ**) also in an advanced 'H > X' form (*HoChyMin*: 414). All three obeloi are dated to CG I (1050–950) (*HoChyMin*: 36, 38).

Skales, tomb 49, stone: ##189. PPAP Pblo 001:

102 | • ~ *a* | *e*

The first sign (**Ж**) clearly presents a CM form, not showing the 'H > X reduction' of the later CG sign: CG-C ✳ and CG-P ✻. The second one lacks an obvious correspondence in CM. According to E. and O. Masson 1983: 413 this sign could be identified with CG-P **Ħ** <*e*>, and the inscription would thus be a CG one. This is not a bad idea, but seems finally unconvincing, because this Paphian sign, as also its CG-C variant (✳), is better considered the outcome of a great variety of more complex forms which go back to CM 037 **Ⴓ**. Its sign structure is still recurring in *Kouklia* 115 (Figure 5.3) (the remarks and the grid of O. Masson in *Kouklia* pp. 12–13 are insufficient for this sign, while the grid in Mitford 1961: pl. IV (after p. 6) is better). Another archaic variant figures in *Kouklia* 223, (a) line 3, sign 1 (Figure 5.4) presenting 'sept éléments graphiques' instead of four or only three in Masson's grid, resembling more a common <*e*>, though which Masson does not say, with his 'trait horizontal prolongé à droite'. These variants for <*e*> should be set against *Kouklia* 113, sign 4 (Figure 5.5), which is extremely simplified, with five strokes that are not super-imposed. But the presence of the CG sign <*e*> seems improbable here; the identification with CM 017 **ᑐ** by Olivier (*HoChyMin*:

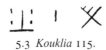

5.3 *Kouklia* 115.

5.4 *Kouklia* 223.

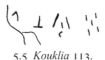

5.5 *Kouklia* 113.

262) seems better but the sign printed in the commentary of the holistic version seems to be an error, corresponding to the first sign of the inscription, CM 102; the right form is indicated in *HoChyMin*: 413. This sign may be related to the sign <*nu*> in CG-C (𐙀) and CG-P (𐠏) (Palaima 1991: 454–5 and Egetmeyer 2010a: § 36, p. 64–5).

Skales, three vase handles with a single sign (E. and O. Masson 1983: 413 fig. 7a–c, lacking in *HoChyMin* according to its editing principles). The first two come also from tomb 49: CM 006 𐙇 ~ CG-C 𐙇 and CG-P 𐙇 <*pa*>.
    Skales, tomb 49, vase handle: •. Thus an unknown sign, which is not astonishing, as the system of marks is not identical to the CM one.

Some other material from outside this tomb must be added:
    Skales, tomb 61, vase handle: CM 112 𐙩 ~ CG-C 𐙀 and CG-P 𐠐 <*ke*>, a sign limited to CM 1.
    Skales, tomb 67, stone, ##190:

109 | 023 ~ <u>wa</u> | ti

This could theoretically be the most recent CM document we have: from CG I–II ~ 1050–900 (*HoChyMin*: 37, 53), and, at least theoretically, we could have in every century an example of syllabic script in Cyprus (Egetmeyer 2010a: 30). The sign CM 109 𐙏 is known only in CM 1. It corresponds well to CG <*wa*>, but well only to CG-C 𐙁 and not to CG-P 𐠲. The reading /wa/ was already proposed by Palaima 1991: 455, who also proposes as an alternative CM 107 ⩊ ~ CG-C ⩊ and CG-P ⩓ <ma>. The alternative with this inversed form is not convenient, because one should retain the orientation of the inscription indicated by the second syllabogram CM 023 ⋀. The sign CM 109 is a rare sign: just seven attestations are known. Examples 2 and 3 figure in ##135 and ##139, where the same signs, CM 109 and 023, appear, but in reversed order, the sign CM 109 presenting a different, more advanced X-structure. Better-corresponding sign forms can be found in the other inscriptions, in example 4 in ##183, sign 2:

102-109-004-008-023 | 112 ~ *a-wa-ta-to-ti* | *ke*

The first sign, CM 102 ⩊, has a much more advanced form than indicated in the CM grid (*HoChyMin*: 413) and thus more resembles the CG form (CG-C ✳ and CG-P ✳). The inscription is not very early and belongs to LC II–LC III ~ 1230–1100. The fifth example figures in inscription ##179, with the same first sequence:

102-109-004-008-023 | 004-004-097 | 006-012 ~ *a-wa-ta-to-ti* | *ta-ta-ro* | *pa-u*

This inscription equally presents advanced sign forms in accordance with its recent date (LC III, 1225–1050). The sixth example figures in ##163, sign 3, and the seventh one in ##182 (LC III A, 1220–1190):

082-109-064-023 | CC XXX ~ *sa-wa-o-ti* | 230

E. and O. Masson 1983: 413 propose instead an identification of the first sign from ##190 under discussion not with this CM 109 sign (ᒳ), but with CM 051, a sign which is now absent from the CM 1 grid according to Olivier (*HoChyMin*: 413) and limited to CM 2 (ᐤ) and 3 (ᐤ). As we have the reverse situation for CM 109 – the sign is attested only in CM 1 – one could ask whether this reflects a complementary distribution which might allow us to combine both signs into a CM 1–3 051/109.

Skales, metal bowl, but without precise context (1050–1000?), ##186:

082-006-082-088-023 ~ *sa-pa-sa-la-ti*

This is the new reading instead of '48–6–48–88–23' by E. and O. Masson 1983: 411: signs CM 048 and 082 (E. Masson 1974: 14–15) are unified by Olivier in a single sign 082 Ⲩ. CM 088 Ⲩ can represent the predecessor of CG <la>, with a CM form not deprived of its two horizontal strokes, as later in CG-C 𝕏 and CG-P Ⴟ. Such a CM sign form reappears in ##161, line 2, sign 3. This Skales inscription is not discussed further by E. and O. Masson 1983 or anywhere else, but it can tentatively be read as well as the obelos presenting *o-pe-le-ta-u*, only that it does not give any Greek (Egetmeyer 2010a: § 454, p. 376). If it did, one could bet that it would have been considered a CG inscription, containing a <la> with an elaborated archaic sign form, as some other inscriptions do with other syllabograms (cf. <so> in *to-ro-to-so-si* below). This behaviour shows how our reasoning is distorted by our Greek perspective.

Paphos, but from an unknown find-spot, seal, LC III (1225–1050), ##206: 102–•
The second sign resembles in its structure the group of signs 102–110, but seems to lack an upper central element; if it were turned upside-down one could identify it with CM 104 ⵖ, but the first sign is not favourable to this.

Thus all but the last inscription come from Skales, and this is all we have for Paphos. Indeed, for the whole of western Cyprus, there is not much more: four very short inscriptions on vase handles from Maa-Palaeokastro can be added, which are also recent (*HoChyMin*: 35: LC IIIA, 1225–1150): ##153–156, and four other very short inscriptions from Kourion: ##149–152 *HoChyMin*: 35: no date).

From the corpus of the later CG inscriptions can be added one of the oldest from the eighth century, *ICS*[2] 18c from Paphos: *to-ro-to-so-si* (Egetmeyer 2010a: 736–7). All the signs are Paphian; notably the first and the third present the oldest examples of the innovated Paphian <to> (𝙓), whereas a later inscription from Paphos (*Rantidi* 1) still presents (twice) an archaic common *to* (ᚨ) (*Rantidi*, p. 31, grid, second variant, and p. 32, commentary). The fourth sign of the sequence *to-ro-to-so-si* seems instead to be part of the equation CM 067 Ⲯ ~ C̄G-C <so> (ᴪ), but ≠ CG-P <so> (ㅗ). This non-Greek inscription is thus a rare example demonstrating the emergence of the proper Paphian syllabary. One could be tempted to identify the Paphian <so> with CM 009 ⟁ (*HoChyMin*: 413) – thus it would not be an innovation in CG-P either, but heritage; this sign is, however, better linked to CG <li> (⟆/⟆) (with E. Masson 1979b: 406, but 402 and 405 with CM 009 twice leading to <li> in CG-C (⟆) and to <so> in CG-P (⟁), an improbable hypothesis. Her figure on page 402 does not correspond, and unfortunately the CM signs are not numbered). The sign CM 067 is known only in CM 1, and the equation with the <so> in *to-ro-to-so-si* had rightly been proposed by E. Masson 1979b: 399. It is thus another example of a preserved old form (there is more concerning <o> and <so> in Egetmeyer 2010b: 80–5).

Still later, in the sixth century, one finds a CG-C <tu> 𐠍 in *Kouklia* 128, sign 1, thus representing a preserved archaism in CG-P. This sign is the second variant in the grid (*Kouklia* p. 13); the first is the general Paphian form (𐠍), to which belongs another one in *Kouklia* 65 looking like an inverted CG-C <o> ⅍ (*Kouklia* p. 66, incomplete drawing, first sign right), a variant lacking in the grid but mentioned in the general commentary (*Kouklia* p. 14). The archaic Paphian text groups from Rantidi and Kouklia are the best known, and they are characterised as presenting the 'closest kinship', Rantidi being 'rustic' and Kouklia 'patronized by kings' (Mitford 1961: 7).

These Paphian examples already illustrate well the difficulties in determining the script system used in Cypriot syllabic inscriptions whose dates come near to the transitional phase between the Cypro-Minoan and Cypro-Greek scripts. The problem can also be illustrated outside the special Paphian case: the only other inscription dated to the Cypro-Geometric period is a very short one from Kition: ##147 from CG I (1050–1000):

023 | 107 ~ *ti* | *ma*

The form of the second syllabogram seems quite advanced but is comparable to the somewhat older example in ##137 (LC III A ~ 1190–1125/1100). The inscription is identical, but the sign CM 107 still presents the central horizontal stroke which is lacking in the younger example. It is from here that one would have to try to understand the history of this sign, which seems to be somewhat

Fig 5.6 *HoChyMin* ##092 = *ICS* 290.

particular also in one of the oldest CG inscriptions, that from Cilicia (Egetmeyer 2010a: 845). It is this type of graphical evolution one accepts for CM 102 ⩲ ~ CG <a> (✳/✷), but which can be demonstrated also for other signs, as for example CM 097 ⊦: an 'H > X reduction', visible in ##154, sign 2, and loss of the central horizontal stroke in the probably corresponding CG <ro>: CG-C ⩏ and CG-P ⩥.

An inscription from Golgoi, near to the opposing region of Enkomi, will be presented as the last example: ##092 = *ICS* 290 (Egetmeyer 2010a: 878) (see Figure 5.6):

064-027-004-006 ~ *o-si-ta-pa*

The inscription had been considered to have been written in CG but is now taken as written in CM script. In either case no Paphian sign forms are to be expected in this inscription. Its first sign is the same as in the Opheltas inscription, CM 064 ⩔ ~ CG-C <o> ⩔, the second one is CM 027⩘~ CG-C <si> ⩗, both presenting advanced sign forms from a CM view-point, the first an archaic form from a CG view-point. This first form is comparable to sign 7 on the weight ##095. The disc (##092) lacks an archaeological context and thus can only be placed in LC (1650–1050). The weight (##095) is dated to LC I A–B (1650–1475), but 'bien qu'il n'y ait pas de contexte ni de vrai parallèle' (*HoChyMin*: 34). But even with our limited knowledge of Cypriot sign forms, one can again say that both inscriptions look old from a CG view-point but young from a CM view-point.

The attribution of the disc to the CM corpus cannot thus be considered absolutely sure. On the weight signs 097 (ꟼ), 108 (𐙄) and 064 (ꟾ) show again a 'H > X reduction'. CM 108 is the first variant in *HoChyMin*: 414, and the second one figures in ##197, sign 1. On both inscriptions, the disc and the weight, CM 064 presents an intermediate form between the 'regular' CM and CG forms (and not an archaic one on the weight, as for E. Masson 1974: 12, sign V, comparable to what has been said above, p. 111, on CM 011). It might be linked (with *HoChyMin*: 118, holistic commentary on the weight) to a split in two sign forms in CG-C and CG-P, thus hinting at different simplifications, not simply a CM > CG-C/P(archaic) (ꙮ) > CG-P (ꓕ) evolution. This last Paphian form with its vertical stroke would then be linked to older, unattested CG forms, still nearer to CM. According to these epigraphical considerations one would thus like to attribute a late LC date to both inscriptions, which is satisfactory for the disc, but not at all so for the weight. Thus, either its archaeological date is wrong or the reasoning demonstrates how unable we are to date according to sign forms.

It becomes clear from this discussion of late CM and early CG material that some graphical evolution, which we have to assume has taken place to arrive at the CG signary, is already present in CM inscriptions; it is also clear that a certain amount of common CG signs figure in archaic Paphian inscriptions. These common forms are probably nothing other than the original forms before the emergence of a proper Paphian signary, which then remains a productive one. The best example is the sign for <o> discussed above. The fact is not surprising in itself: the coexistence of old and young letters is a well-known fact for inscriptions in the Greek alphabet (Wachter 1989: 22–3). This means that the desire of the Paphians to distinguish themselves from the rest of Cyprus by their script is already an archaic phenomenon, comparable to what happens in the realm of the local Greek alphabets (Luraghi 2010), but it is not as old as the Opheltas inscription, because, as in linguistics, what are important are innovations and not shared archaisms. The Opheltas inscription does not contain Paphian innovations. There is no proof that the CG-C/CG-P split has taken place: it is simply a Cypriot syllabic inscription. But in CM or in CG?

The uncertainties present in the above discussion prevent us from assigning absolute certainty to Olivier's CM attribution. Only the Greek reading urges us to consider the Opheltas inscription as written in a new CG signary. This, however, cannot be considered a sufficient argument, unless someone sustains that different language necessarily means different script, and there is no further reasoning behind this attribution. If we widen our view, all the further context, archaeological and epigraphical, of tomb 49 is indigenous Cypriot, i.e. Cypro-Minoan. Nothing urges us to consider the Opheltas inscription as written in a script different from the others, that there are two scripts present in the tomb. The high date and the context render it much more probable that we are dealing with only one script: CM.

The other inscriptions of the tomb are of no help for determining the language used. They contain only single signs of inscription types still in use in later periods of the first millennium. Once we have another longer inscription, the metal bowl (##186), we are certainly back to Cypro-Minoan language. Nevertheless, the Opheltas inscription does not simply present a proper name, which happens to be Greek, as in the later Eteocypriot inscriptions, where these integrated Greek names do not have Greek endings other than that of the nominative or else Eteocypriot endings. It is really an inscription in Greek language, because the name is in the genitive. Let us also stress that the name element itself is archaic, even unique in our rich knowledge of Cypriot onomastics, but a smiling god has delivered to us a name which is lexically linked to, of all things, *Onāsi-*, the name element which becomes the most frequent in first millennium Cyprus (Egetmeyer 2010a: §§ 311, 676).

The above examples demonstrate that attributing an inscription to one or other script by its simple palaeographic appearance is not always an easy task. Sometimes inscriptions defy an immediate classification, and the attribution might remain in suspense, were it not for one sign or the other that allows a decision. The Opheltas inscription is not such a case, because by mere chance all its signs have correspondences in both signaries, CM and CG. But is it thus at all necessary to assume a script reform? With Greeks writing in CM and non-Greeks writing in CG, could one not simply assume a script continuum with evolving sign forms, nothing more? Thus,

Paphos trying to be something particular? One could also ask in the opposite sense, whether one should not go a step further back and hold that we do not know what 064–011–024–004–012 means.

One should not forget the historical situation in the Cypro-Geometric period: two competitors trying to expand their influence on the island, Greeks and Phoenicians, the latter with a script, the former without. It is only logical that the Greeks would not adopt a script from their competitor, but rather take it from the indigenous Cypriot population, the advantage of this being that they could gain the latter's sympathy and themselves appear finally as indigenous. Such a cultural argument is generally rightly used to describe the relationship between the Cypro-Greek syllabary and the Greek alphabet (for example Brixhe 2007: 21 n. 5), but it can already be invoked for this earlier period and perhaps earlier still to understand the borrowing of a Cretan script by Bronze Age Cypriots. Anatolians, though they already had a script, cuneiform, also invented one of their own, the glyphs (Yakubovich 2008). Already for these reasons it seems oversceptical to doubt even the interpretation of 064–011–024–004–012 as /$Op^h eltau$/, but we ought to try to interpret the situation we have and suppose that we know approximately the phonetic value of five CM signs.

It would be an interesting task to describe what exactly distinguishes CM from CG, and we also lack a Cypriot 'Jeffery' (*The Local Scripts of Archaic Greece*), but let us now leave these considerations on epigraphy and palaeography and turn our attention to the linguistic problems. These will also underline that we have indeed to assume a script reform.

In the above paragraphs other CM sequences are sometimes also transliterated, because what is allowed for Opheltas must be allowed for other inscriptions, too. However, the readings serve only to illustrate some possibilities and are nothing more than a curious game. Whether the supposed graphical sign relations between CM and CG are all justified, and, if they are, then to what extent the phonetic values of the CM signs correspond to the CG ones, remains an open question. One needs to find out whether anything can be said about the phonological system of the CM-language(s), which is generally not a matter considered by those attracted to this material.

Let us look at the vowel system: for the language of CM I the existence of the middle vowels /e/ and /o/ was denied, this leading to the assumption of a three-vowel system with only the vowels /a/, /u/ and /i/ on the edges of the vocalic triangle (E. Masson 1974: 39, 1979b: 400, 409, with an improbable hypothesis for the creation of CG <e> ✳ as a variant of CM 102 Ӈ /CG <a> ✳). The Opheltas inscription obliged us to accept the existence of the vowel /o/ (E. and O. Masson 1983: 413). Finally, the hypothesis that CM 037 Ѡ is the source of CG <e> is no worse than others. The acceptance of the Opheltas inscription containing the sign <pe> as CM strongly favours the existence also of this vowel. It is thus easily possible that five vowels are present in the CM script:

CM 102/*a*, 037/*e*, 104/*i*, 064/*o* and 012/*u*

Almost all these signs are present in CM 1–3; only 064 and 012 are lacking in CM 3. These considerations are of great importance for the structure of the syllabary, because for every vowel sign one can also suppose the existence of accompanying CV signs, so typical of the Aegean scripts. A given grid for a language with only a three-vowel system and CV_{1-3} sign series needs a higher amount of consonant series than one for a five-vowel system and CV_{1-5} sign series. In the first case one would need more consonant phonemes or even complex signs. These considerations concerning the vowel system of the donor language should have made us sceptical right at the beginning.

What is the numerical relationship between the donor grid and the receiver grid? A first glance at *HoChyMin*: 413 gives us a total of 114 syllabograms. But this number is almost worthless: it is the total of all syllabograms known in CM 1–3, i.e. in different, even if related, scripts, and only reflects the history of the research. There are numbers missing, and not all numbers exist in every script. One thus has to count for oneself (or be among the lucky few who already have access to Olivier: in press): seventy-two syllabograms in CM 1, seventy-one in CM 2 and fifty in CM 3. These last two, limited to two cities, are left aside in the following, and it is supposed that the script loan takes place from CM 1 to CG (already E. Masson 1979b: 408). Accepting the existence of five vowels and permitting errors in our sign list, the existence of further signs and incomplete syllabogram series, this leaves us with $72 - 5 = 67$ signs for the syllabogram series; divided by 5 one arrives at about $13/14$ CV_{1-5} series. This does not mean thirteen/fourteen consonantal phonemes, because we have no idea how many phonemes, partaking in one basic phoneme trait, are bundled in one and the same series, as happened in Linear B and CG. For this CG we can be much more certain of making a count which corresponds to reality: 5 vowels and 12 consonant series (more precisely: 11 simple consonant and 1 complex series), which would give a theoretical grid of $5 + (5 \times 12 =) 60 = 65$ signs. This leaves us with a difference of seven syllabograms or one or two CV_{1-5} series. Even if this very hypothetical count corresponds to reality, this does not mean that the CG series corresponds to the CM series, reducing it by one or two series, because, as in the LA > LB process, the change can be more profound than the absolute numbers suggest: Linear A possesses about 100 signs, Linear B almost 90, but during the loan process about 30 signs were suppressed, about 20 created, and the mere difference of 10 in the total number does not indicate the amount of the change, and we thus cannot know how much the two phonological systems differ (for a possible non-Greek phoneme, cf. the different rendering of $/t^h/$ in the city name *Lapethos*: Egetmeyer 2010a: § 214, p. 197). For our purpose it suffices to say that we have to deal with a reduction process concerning the whole grid. To what extent we also have a substitution and a creation process we do not know, because we cannot read CM. But the general reduction process is what happens during all the other Aegean script loans, every adaptation probably presenting an adaptation to another language (leaving aside the Cretan glyphs): LA > LB, LA > CM (reduction of about thirty signs), CM 1 > CM 2, CM 1 > CM 3 (?) and CM > CG.

The CG grid must, however, be described in a more precise way: one can distinguish five vowel signs and nine complete CV series which both constitute the core grid present everywhere. Then there are three incomplete additional series whose chronological and geographical distribution is not exactly known. The core grid consists of:

$a, o, e, u, i - wV_{1-4}$ (without wu), $rV_{1-5}, lV_{1-5}, nV_{1-5}, mV_{1-5}, sV_{1-5}, kV_{1-5}, tV_{1-5}, pV_{1-5}$

The incomplete additional series consists of two simple series and one complex series, i.e. alternating with the use of two signs:

jV_{1-3} ($ja, je, jo; ji$ and ju missing), zo (ze and zu might exist, but are not attested, za is doubtful and always represents an expected /ga/), xa, xe (xo probably did not exist, so one can thus doubt the existence also of xi and xu).

The total of the core signs is forty-nine (instead of fifty, because of the lacking wu). With the exception of zo, the signs of the incomplete series are not attested at any time everywhere, and some might be secondary additions, most probably je. The total of these additional signs is seven, and the total of the whole syllabary thus fifty-six. If one adds ze and zu (no word where these signs were expected is known), one would arrive at fifty-eight. The maximum possible total of sixty-five signs certainly did not exist. For the CG proto-syllabary one can suppose the existence of at least fifty signs (the forty-nine core signs + zo), perhaps fifty-one, if ja ($\lozenge$) is to be included and perhaps linked to CM 015 $\lozenge$ (only CM 1). No other additional CG sign has an attractive correspondent in CM, but, among the core signs, the vowels and at least one CV sign of every core series have possible correspondents in CM. The existence of one correspondence in a series would render the existence of the whole series probable, if one could be sure that a phonetic correspondence was maintained, but that is not the case. The example of the name *Opheltas* with the syllabograms *pe, le* and *ta* demonstrates, however, that the situation is not hopeless.

The creation of the Cypriot proto-syllabary is primarily a linguistic challenge and not an epigraphic one: to adopt a graphic system that was used for the notation of a phonetic system of the non-Indo-European 'Cypro-Minoan' language for the phonetic system of the Greek language. The loan takes place from a script for one language (CM 1, excluding CM 2 and 3) to another language for which a new script is to be created. This other language is thought to be the Greek language, because otherwise the reason for a script reform cannot be understood.

This does not mean to neglect the presence of at least one non-Greek language, certainly a survivor of the Cypro-Minoan language(s), also written with the new script, but this was not the target of the reform. It is probable that for some time both scripts, CM and CG, coexisted, but at some point the indigenous population ceased to use their old system. The situation is not that astonishing, because on Crete, too, Eteocretan was written in a Greek alphabet. On Cyprus, there is no Eteocypriot signary (Egetmeyer 2010b: 74–85). This means that the new syllabary might be less well adapted to the indigenous language(s) than the CM script(s). It also means that it is not certain, or that it is even improbable, that the CG syllabograms indicate identical phonetic values when used in a Greek inscription or in a non-Greek one. It is also supposed that the division into a CG-C and a CG-P syllabary is secondary. But the further history of this distinction lies beyond the scope of this chapter: the basic phonetic structure is the same for both, the distinction being only a graphic one.

One could speak of a pre-Cypriot (dialect) period (meaning the period between a certain mainland Greek at the end of the Bronze Age, the migration to Cyprus and including the period on Cyprus before the invention of the script), a proto-Cypriot period (meaning the period between the invention of the script and a somewhat better attestation of the dialect, i.e. not before the sixth/fifth century) and a Cypriot period. The linguistic missing link of the Opheltas inscription gives us the information that the evolution /-o #/ > /-u #/ is accomplished. Can the CG grid itself tell us something more?

These kinds of questions were already asked by others concerning the creation of the two other Greek scripts, Linear B from Linear A and the Greek alphabet from Phoenician abjad LA > LB and PA > GA (Lejeune 1976 and Palaima and Sikkenga 1999; Brixhe 1991, 1994 and Wachter 1989, 1996). Two phonemes reveal themselves as important also for the discussion of the CG syllabary: the semi-vowels and the labiovelars, the first the main concern of Lejeune, the second treated by Brixhe.

Linear B has a triple structure: a simple CV series and two (incomplete) complex ones, CjV and CwV. This structure renders some of the main clusters of Greek at that period, and the phoneme pairs *i/i̯ and u/u̯* are extremely important for the ablaut phenomena of Indo-European grammar. But all this is gone in Greek during the first millennium, Greek losing the consonantal player in this system. It is thus not astonishing that the structure of CG is different. It is further admitted here that the Greeks who instal themselves in Cyprus are illiterate and that the syllabic structure of the grid, the rules of use of the syllabograms and the sign forms are to be explained starting with Cypro-Minoan alone.

We do not know much about the way the Aegean syllabaries were taught (Duhoux 1986), we have no such thing as a *Musteralphabet* and we ignore the order of the signs in teaching. But something of the sort certainly existed (##001 was hypothesised as being something similar, because no sign is repeated in it). One may wonder whether there existed additional syllabograms which were added at the end, like in the alphabet tradition, an important factor (Wachter 1989: 29–34). The CG grid might have evolved a little, but there is no reason to doubt that it essentially reflects the phonetic system at the moment of its invention.

Concerning the pair *j*/*w*, both phonemes were still present in the phonemic system of Greek at the moment of the invention of Linear B. But already Lejeune 1976: 202 considers the loss of /*j*/ a proto-Mycenaean phenomenon, whereas /*w*/ is still a stable phoneme in the Mycenaean texts. At the moment of the invention of the CG grid, there surely existed no phoneme /*j*/ in the dialect. It is thus astonishing that the CG grid presents in its most complete form three signs for such a sound: <*ja*>, <*jo*>, <*je*>. One could say that these signs are good for nothing: they only render the syllabary more complicated, without any gain. In fact, as there is no such phoneme, the signs are exclusively used for the subphonemic glide [*j*], and its use is not constant (Egetmeyer 2000, 2010a: §§ 119–28). Such a glide is also written in the neighbouring Pamphylian dialect, but the situation there is different, because the glide is written with the already existing letter *iota*: no additional sign had to be learned. In Cypriot, <*i*> is never used to express a glide. If we knew the phonemic system of the CM I language better, it could perhaps help us to understand what happens. It must be stressed that in the earliest phase of the Greek alphabet <*j*> and <*i*> coexisted, and the distinction was exploited in the Phrygian and Sidetic alphabets to express different phonemes (Brixhe 2007: 16–17, 23 n. 7). However, the phenomenon does not seem to give us any information

127

useful for our question as to the date of the script reform, because the phoneme was absent for the whole period here in question. It is, however, important once one takes into account the loss of the labiovelars.

In fact, the situation is completely different concerning the labiovelars: they are stable phonemes in Mycenaean Greek, written with their own sign series, but they are absent from Cypriot Greek (Egetmeyer 2010a: §§ 196, 223–35). Their loss is later than the loss of /j/. Thus, was the syllabary invented before or after the loss of the labiovelars? And when were these lost? They were lost in three phases, the first one already attained in Mycenaean Greek, but it did not put the existence of the phoneme in danger; only the second and the third phases did, but they are post-Mycenaean (Brixhe 1996: 84–90). The loss of these phonemes is a pan-Greek phenomenon, but there are differences in the evolution and the consequence of their disappearance, and the time of their disappearance may vary too.

One must admit that the time span between the fall of the Mycenaean palaces and the date of the Opheltas inscription would be sufficient for such a loss to happen. The non-identical development of the labiovelars in Arcadian and Cypriot does not favour an immediate loss of these phonemes in the post-Mycenaean period. There are even good arguments for traces of their existence still being visible in the primitive history of the Greek alphabet, related to the distinction of the letters *kappa* and *qoppa* (Brixhe 1991: 338–40, 2007: 24). In the Cypriot syllabary there are no such traces. This does not, of course, mean that the Cypro-Greek syllabary is a later invention than the Greek alphabet, but it renders the assumption of a very high date, i.e. quickly after the collapse of the Mycenaean palaces, doubtful. One might suppose that six instead of three values were expressed by the series for velar stops (not only /k/, /g/, /k^h/, but also /k^w/, /g^w/, /k^{wh}/), but this seems to be way too heavy for a single series. It would be easier to assume that a separate sign series existed, which was then abolished before our first possible examples, and so it remains unknown to us. This cannot be proved wrong and would have to be taken into account for the CM > CG process, but it also seems doubtful. At least one might ask whether the problem of the *ga*/*za* sign can be linked to this problem, revealing one such trace (Egetmeyer 2010a: § 202). The easiest hypothesis is to assume that the labiovelars simply did not exist any more at the moment of the script reform. Further, one has to consider that, concerning the second phase, not only the writing of the labiovelars itself was a problem, but also of its intermediate stages, especially for /k^w/ > /s/ in the position before /i/ and the hypothetical existence of a complete <zV> series (Egetmeyer 2010a: §§ 195–6, 228). The third and latest phase results in labial phonemes. It is this result which has to be accepted more frequently as a regular result in the Cypriot dialect, as often admitted (Egetmeyer 2010a: § 233). It means that at the end of this evolution a higher quantitative amount of words with preserved labiovelars existed in Cypriot than in many other dialects. This increases the doubts as to their disappearance without any trace.

Other regions equally preserve some traits of the existence of earlier labiovelars: Arcadian presents in the fifth century a sign (~ /ts/) related to the evolution of *k^w before /e/ and /i/, but it is used for a new sound, probably presents a limited orthographic reform (Duhoux 2006: 22, 55, 57) and cannot be used as an argument for their late disappearance in this dialect. Better examples for a late existence of labiolevars seem to exist for another peripheral region, the north of Greece (Hatzopoulos 2007: 230–1).

In Ionic-Attic the loss of labiovelars precedes the change of /$\bar{a}$/ to /$\bar{e}$/, because the result corresponds to what is to be expected before /$\bar{a}$/ (Lejeune 1972: §§ 39,249 and Gusmani 1976). Near to Cyprus, the forms of the personal name *Mopsos* in the (glyphic) Luwian-Phoenician bilingual of Çineköy in Cilicia from about 725–700 BC may add a further element. The forms present the result of a former *Mok^w sos* (Mycenaean *mo-qo-so(-)*). The velar in the Luwian form *Muksas (mu-ka-sa-)* is the already earlier result of the integration of the name of a Greco-Anatolian hero (Liebhart and Brixhe 2009: 147–9) according to the rules of Anatolian phonetics, whereas the Phoenician form *mpš* seems to reflect the contemporaneous Greek form *Mopsos*, after the loss of the labiovelar, thus indicating the presence of Greeks in this region. In sum, labiovelars may have been present in Greek until the tenth century BC.

Another fact must be stressed for Cypriot: the phoneme /w/ is present in the dialect at the moment of the invention of the script, but during the following centuries it becomes obsolete, even if it is written until the end of the use of the syllabic script in Cyprus, when it can even appear as a hyperdialectal sound. The phoneme /w/ and its corresponding signs can thus be reactivated at any time. Nothing of this kind can be observed for the labiovelars. In sum, the absence of labiovelars in the CG syllabary argues against a high date for the script reform.

As already indicated, we do not know which signs of the theoretically possible series (*)<za>, *<ze>, *<zi>, <zo>, *<zu> really existed. The distribution with only one certain sign of the series, <zo>, two possible and even probable further ones, *<ze> and *<zu>, and one of doubtful reading, (*)<za>, fits well with the distributional frequency of the phoneme before vowels in the Greek language in general. Even if we lack syllabic examples, the testimony of the glosses with words containing a ζ demonstrates that such examples are to be expected in Cypriot, too (Egetmeyer 2010a: §§ 22, 126). As already mentioned, further examples might be expected at a high date linked to the disappearance of the labiovelars. The inscriptions in non-Greek language do not change the picture.

The existence of at least two signs for a complex series /ksV/, <xa> and <xe> may confirm this impression. Both signs would have been very practical in the conjugation of the *alpha*-thematic aorist (Egetmeyer 2010a: § 245). Cypriot Greek seems to have a certain preference for verbs in -ίζω (Egetmeyer 2010a: § 589–92), which would increase the need for the use of signs *<ze> and <zo> expressing the thematic vowels *e/o* in the present tense (but the inscriptions do not attest any example of a second/third person singular or a second plural – only the glosses do), and one might even be tempted to search here for an argument for the distribution of the dental and velar conjugation of the aorist in the dialect (Egetmeyer 2010a: § 606).

In sum, linguistic considerations make the assumption of a lower date of the script reform preferable. Olivier's classification of the Opheltas inscription as a Cypro-Minoan and not as a Cypro-Greek inscription fits well into this picture and warns us of linguistic trouble. We no longer need to assume a script reform before 1050–950, i.e. approximately 1100–1000 at the latest. A lower date corresponds well to the general situation in Cypro-Geometric Cyprus. Greeks integrated themselves in Cyprus in a literate society. They did not take it over, and thus CM was certainly not 'killed', as Linear A was by Linear B (Bennet 2008: 22). To find first attempts at simply writing their Greek language in the script their new society had lived with for a long time is only normal. Cypro-Minoan had already undergone script loans, for CM 2 and CM 3. Greeks just did it again. Nevertheless such a script reform is more likely to have taken place when the Hellenisation of the island had advanced, and this is probably a slower process than was generally thought. More precise conclusions are difficult to assert, and I do not pretend to have given the right answers, but I hope to have asked useful questions.

6

THE CYPRIOT SYLLABARY AS A ROYAL SIGNATURE: THE POLITICAL CONTEXT OF THE SYLLABIC SCRIPT IN THE IRON AGE

MARIA IACOVOU

Introduction

It is a widely acknowledged fact that the syllabic script attested in Cyprus during the better part of the first millennium BC was not a novel scribal tool; it was, rather, the Iron Age version of the Late Cypriot script that we know as Cypro-Minoan.[1] We are unable to identify the languages written in the four subcategories of Cypro-Minoan,[2] but we are fairly certain that it was the only writing system used on the island in the course of the Late Bronze Age and almost to the end of the second millennium BC.

This privileged, one-to-one relation between a locally developed writing system and the human environment of Cyprus was evidently altered in the Iron Age when, first, the Phoenician and, later, the Greek alphabet were introduced to the island. In Cyprus the Phoenician alphabet remained the exclusive tool of only one Semitic language, whose written evidence is confined to a period ranging from the ninth to the third centuries BC.[3] During this time, the Cypriot Syllabary was used by two different languages. The one has been identified as Greek – specifically, as the Arcado-Cypriot dialect, the only Greek dialect that retained a very close kinship to the Greek of Linear B.[4] The other language has been christened Eteocypriot because its indecipherable inscriptions are

---

[1] According to Olivier (Chapter 1 in this volume), it probably evolved from the CM 1 syllabary, which is attested between the fifteenth and the eleventh centuries (*HoChyMin*).

[2] Olivier, Duhoux and Ferrara (Chapters 1,2 and 3 respectively in this volume).

[3] Cf. Masson and Sznycer 1972; Collombier 1991: 429, 438–9; Lipinski 2004.

[4] Cf. Morpurgo Davies 1992: 422. 'Du point de vue linguistique, l'arcado-chypriote se présente comme le groupe dialectal le plus proche de la langue notée dans les tablettes mycéniennes en linéaire B' (Baurain 1997: 129);

133

suspected of preserving one or more of the island's indigenous languages that had survived into the first millennium.[5]

The inscriptional evidence, therefore, underscores a major transformation of the island's human environment in the Iron Age. It discloses that Cyprus had become home to three distinct linguistic groups. The two identifiable languages, Greek and Phoenician, which do not appear in the textual evidence of Cyprus until the first millennium BC, are believed to be languages introduced to the island by immigrant groups at the end, or shortly after the end, of the Late Bronze Age. The origin of the third, the unreadable Eteocypriot, remains mysterious, but, from the point of view of archaeology, there is hardly any possibility that it could have been introduced in the Late Bronze or Early Iron Age. It seems more likely that the origin of its carriers is lost in the prehistoric era of Cyprus.[6]

Signatures of power and authority

My contribution will *not* focus on how literate laymen may have used the syllabic and/or alphabetic scripts of Iron Age Cyprus. I am instead concerned with *how, where* and for *how long* these scripts, and the languages that employed them, were used as signatures of power and authority on an island where trilingualism (or even multilingualism) did not have a material culture equivalent. I wish to emphasise this crucial point because, to this day, young scholars fall into the trap of assuming *a priori* that these three linguistic terms – Greek, Phoenician and Eteocypriot – represent ethnic identities: they do not.[7] The three languages did not match three different cultures. Iron Age Cyprus, much like Bronze Age Cyprus, which was probably also multilingual,[8] had its own distinct and easily recognisable material culture; a culture that cannot be neatly broken up into Greek, Phoenician and Eteocypriot components. Concerted

---

[5] Friedrich 1932: 49–52. The term Eteocypriot is, according to O. Masson (*ICS*[1] p. 85), 'une heureuse suggestion de J. Friedrich'. Egetmeyer has suggested there are two different languages in the non-Greek syllabic (Eteocypriot) inscriptions.

[6] '[A] pre-Hellenic and pre-Semitic language, probably related to the native Cypriot tongue' (Lipinski 2004: 42).

[7] Iacovou 2005: 125.   [8] Ferrara (Chapter 3 in this volume).

efforts that would have led to the development of three sharply defined ethno-cultural groups are not identified in the mortuary or sacred landscapes of Iron Age Cyprus.[9] Nor were the territories of the Iron Age polities ethnically cleansed enclaves, where only one of the three language groups lived. Nevertheless, as we shall see below, on the level of political authority, a patterned cultural attitude can be traced between ruling dynasties and the script, or scripts, they used.[10] It would appear that this attitude was in each case conditioned by the linguistic identity of the ruler.

The evidence currently at our disposal reveals that from the seventh century BC to the end of the fourth the syllabic script had been extensively used almost throughout Cyprus, for (mostly short) documents (dedications, epitaphs, agreements, ownership claims and coin legends) issued by, or in the name of, Cypriot kings.[11] To the extent that this evidence preserves its spatial and temporal context, it can assist in the reconstruction of the island's political geography in the Cypro-Archaic and Cypro-Classical periods. We should be warned, however, that the degree of success of this difficult task is conditioned by our readiness to interpret the intra-island circumstances that helped the scribal system of Bronze Age Cyprus to survive as the writing tool of two unrelated languages in the Iron Age and, more importantly, to be upgraded into a vehicle of royal authority.

The long life of the Cypriot writing system

How and why, then, did the Late Cypriot syllabic system survive? The long-term persistence of something as potentially sensitive as an ancient scribal system, especially in a period of political instability, social change and population movements caused by the 'total disappearance of the Late Bronze Age palaces and all the special features of life associated with these palaces, most notably the art of writing',[12] implies that Cypro-Minoan was part-and-parcel of a

---

[9] Iacovou 2006a: 44.   [10] *Ibid.*, 53.
[11] E.g. *ICS*[1] 15, p. 110, 90–91, p. 145 (dedications); 16–17, p. 112 (epitaphs); 217, p. 235 (agreement); 176, p. 192, *ICS*[2] 180a, p. 412 (ownership); *ICS*[1] 319–326, pp. 318–23 (coins).
[12] Muhly 2003a: 24.

far more important continuity: that of the island's politico-economic system. In effect, what this means is that the Iron Age polities of Cyprus, which we tend to refer to as city kingdoms, continued to operate on much the same decentralised management system as their Late Cypriot predecessors in the thirteenth and twelfth centuries.[13]

Irrespective of the abandonment of a number of urban centres at the end of the thirteenth century and the economic recession that affected the regions they represented – Alassa-*Paliotaverna* in the Kouris river valley and Kalavassos-*Ayios Demetrios* in the Vasilikos valley are prime examples of the effects of the crisis in Cyprus[14] – the absence of a central, island-wide administration meant that some other centres, like Enkomi and Hala Sultan Tekke, were able to survive, while others still, like Kition and Paphos, may have even benefited from the crisis.[15] If all the regional economies of Cyprus had failed, if the crisis had 'killed' the industry and export trade of metals throughout Cyprus, the chances are that the island's scribal tool would also have died, and then we would have had a genuine Cypriot 'Dark Age'.[16]

We may, therefore, ascribe the survival of the Late Cypriot script to the following factors. It had not been the recording tool of a palatial economy, nor a system of writing closely guarded by scribes employed by royal authorities (like, say, Linear B).[17] Establishing with precision the range of functions for which the Cypro-Minoan was used since it first appeared around the middle of the second millennium BC is severely handicapped by its limited inscriptional corpus.[18] Nevertheless, there can hardly be any doubt that it existed in, and served, a decentralised economic environment.[19] This environment was curtailed by the crisis but survived nonetheless. A small number of twelfth-century BC harbour towns continued to trade in copper.[20] They were also involved – Enkomi

---

[13] Iacovou 2008a: 625, 640.   [14] Cf. Hadjisavvas 1996, 2002; South 1996, 2002.
[15] Iacovou 2007: 17.
[16] On the continuity of the copper trade with Crete, see Muhly 1998: 323.
[17] 'We may not be able to read the written documents from Bronze Age Cyprus, but we know what they are not: they are not the inventories and transaction-records of a centralised bureaucracy' (Snodgrass 1994: 172); also, E. S. Sherratt 1998: 297.
[18] Cf. Smith 2002; *HoChyMin*.
[19] Cf. Pickles and Peltenburg 1998: 90; Peltenburg 2012: 345–51.
[20] Cf. E. S. Sherratt 1998: 300, 304; Webb 1999: 287; Bell 2006: 102–3.

and Paphos in particular – in the production and circulation of probably the earliest tools and weapons made of iron, whose number and distribution (in the Aegean, the Levant, Anatolia and Egypt) increased in the eleventh century.[21] The profile, however, of their trading partners must have changed 100 per cent: no longer were they heads of palatial administrations; they were instead independent merchants involved in entrepreneurial activities in a highly fragmented but, from a different point of view, liberated Mediterranean economy that transformed 'the trading landscape in the earliest decades of the Iron Age'.[22] What one has to bear in mind is that, in much the same way that all the disasters of the crisis years have been collectively attributed to a single agent, the 'Sea People',[23] the mercantile societies that began to emerge in the Mediterranean after the collapse of the palace economies have been almost exclusively credited to Phoenician activities.[24] As a matter of fact, in the Late Bronze to Early Iron Age transition the Cypriots, like the Canaanite people living on the Levantine coast (but now renamed Phoenician), 'capitalised on the opportunities that arose from the power vacuum (which followed the withdrawal of the influence of the Great Powers of Egypt and Hatti)'.[25]

The fact that formal syllabic writing is still attested in a twelfth – eleventh-century urban context sets the stage for its adoption by a new linguistic group,[26] which is held responsible for the introduction of an early Greek dialect to the island. The reasons behind the establishment of Greek-speaking people in Cyprus were almost certainly economic. The pattern of their establishment – they seem to have targeted the surviving urban polities – suggests that they infiltrated the island not as colonists but as economic migrants.[27] They did not set themselves up in new settlements, as colonists would probably have done. Nowhere on the island do we find

---

[21] Consult Appendix I in E. S. Sherratt 1994: 85–92; also E. S. Sherratt 1998: 300. On Cypriot metalworkers having played a 'major role in unlocking the secrets of working with iron', see Muhly 2003b: 145–6.

[22] Cf. Bell 2006: 105.

[23] Cf. on the crisis in the different regions of the Mediterranean, papers in Ward and Joukowsky 1992.

[24] For a wider view-point, Muhly 1998: 314.   [25] Bell 2006: 61, 112.

[26] Cf. Hirschfeld 2002: 99; Smith 2003: 281.   [27] Iacovou 2008a: 640.

evidence for the foundation of a Greek colony.[28] As a matter of fact, had it been left to material culture indicators, we would never have suspected the arrival of Greek-speaking people on Cyprus. Their presence is not revealed by the introduction of an ethnically distinct cultural package. The permanence of their establishment is heralded by a relation of phenomenal endurance that the Arcado-Cypriot Greek dialect developed with the local syllabic script, spanning the whole of the first millennium. Its early stages are epigraphically manifested in Old Paphos in the tenth century BC, while the last joint appearance of the syllabary and the Greek language occurs on first-century BC sealings from the Roman archive of Nea Paphos, close to a thousand years later.[29]

Syllabic writing, Greek language and Cypriot metals

According to Jean-Pierre Olivier, the five syllabic signs used to inscribe the earliest known Greek inscription of Cyprus with the proper name *Opheltas* are still in the Cypro-Minoan script.[30] The specifically Arcado-Cypriot genitive case of 'o-pe-le-ta-u' supports the presence of people in the population of Paphos who belonged to the Arcado-Cypriot dialectal group.[31] The discovery of the Opheltas inscription on a bronze obelos (skewer or spit), which had been deposited in a tenth-century Cypro-Geometric chamber tomb at Palaepaphos-Skales,[32] is an insightful addition to the transformations that the environment of Cyprus in general and Paphos in particular had been undergoing since the end of the Late Bronze Age (twelfth to eleventh centuries); but it is not the only one. Like Greek itself, the 87 cm.-long bronze spit, which Opheltas took the trouble to have inscribed with his name, is an object not recorded in the material culture of Cyprus before the first millennium BC.[33] In fact Skales, Tomb 49 contained two more bronze spits – and they also are inscribed with signs.[34] Of all his peers buried during the

---

[28] Iacovou 2008b: 229–32.   [29] Michaelidou-Nicolaou 1993: 346–7.
[30] Olivier, Chapter 1 in this volume; *contra* Duhoux, Chapter 2 in this volume.
[31] Cf. E. and O. Masson 1983: 414; Deger-Jalkotzy 1994: 11–12.
[32] Karageorghis 1983: 60, 75.   [33] Consult Catling 1964.
[34] Karageorghis 1983: 60–1, pl. 88 (Skales, Tomb 49: nos. 16–18); E. and O. Masson 1983: 412–13.

Cypro-Geometric period in the burial grounds of Palaepaphos (at least among those that have been published), Opheltas alone owned three of these rare and prestigious objects.

Spits found in eleventh- and tenth-century Cypro-Geometric tombs are usually in bronze (e.g. the Early Iron Age tomb from Kition), although spits made of iron are reported from CGI-III tombs at Lapethos.[35] In the Cypro-Archaic I–II period they were mostly of iron and were deposited, often together with a pair of fire-dogs, in warrior burials (e.g. Paphos-Kato Alonia); some of these elite burials come from monumental built tombs (e.g. Patriki, Tomb 1, Tamassos, Tomb 12).[36] A pair of iron fire-dogs in Salamis, Tomb 79 (which is also a built tomb) was accompanied by a bundle of twelve iron skewers bound together with two rings. The burial dates to the seventh century BC.[37] Interestingly, an eighth-century BC warrior tomb from Argos also contained a pair of fire-dogs and twelve iron spits.[38]

Although, as shown by Karageorghis, their original function as spits for roasting meat is not in doubt,[39] these thin rods (the hand could grasp six at once) were clearly an acknowledged symbol of status. Could they have also had a value as exchange units? The number in which they are found is either divisible by or a multiple of six: there were three in Skales, Tomb 49 and in the Early Iron Age tomb from Kition; twelve in Salamis, Tomb 79; and eighteen in Paphos-Kato Alonia and Patriki, Tomb I.[40] '[I]n the Argolid, there was effected, probably in the eighth century BC, an innovation which is attributed by accurate research to king Pheidon of Argos. This innovation resulted in the official authorization of metal for coinage in the form of spits, in every way similar to cooking spits (skewers).'[41] A bundle of iron spits found in the Argive Heraion is, in fact, thought to have been deposited as an offering by Pheidon himself.[42] In Cyprus a bronze obelos was also found in an eighth-

---

[35] Myres 1910: 107 for the Early Iron Age tomb from Kition; Gjerstad *et al.* 1934, Lapethos, Tomb 409:7, Tomb 11: 32a–c, Tomb 417:12a, Tomb 422:10.

[36] Karageorghis, 1963, 1970: 41 (Paphos-Kato Alonia), 1972: 169 (Patriki, Tomb I); Buchholz, Matthäus and Walcher 2002: 228–9 (Tamassos, Tomb 12); Matthäus 2009: 140, Abb.15 (iron oboloi from Tamassos, Tomb 12 photographed by Max Ohnefalsch-Richter);

[37] Karageorghis 1973: 118.   [38] Courbin 1957: 368–70 figs. 52–4.

[39] Karageorghis 1970.   [40] Karageorghis 1972: 172.

[41] Karamessini-Oeconomides 1969: 443.   [42] *Ibid.*, 444.

century sacred context: on the 'Phoenician-period' floor of the temple at Kition.[43]

In Early Iron Age Greece metal was exchanged in the form of cauldrons, tripods or axes, but, admittedly, we have no evidence regarding the shape or weight of the units in which Cyprus traded its metal in the first millennium BC. The oxhide ingot, the exchange unit of Cypriot copper *par excellence*, is not recorded after the twelfth century. Each weighed about 28 kg.; 'the shape was standardised but the weight varied considerably'.[44] Judging from the shipwrecks that carried oxhide ingots and the Alashiya textual sources, they were shipped in considerable numbers, and the recipients were invariably heads of Late Bronze Age states.[45] Inevitably, the oxhide copper ingot had to be abandoned after the collapse of the second-millennium BC state economies. It is, therefore, not altogether unlikely that spits were used as exchange units in the pre-monetary economy of Cyprus.

From Opheltas to the first Cypro-Archaic *basileis*

An old (Late Bronze Age) syllabic script, a new language (i.e. Greek) and (possibly units of) metal, the island's primary export commodity, make their first joint appearance in Paphos in the tenth century BC. It was the beginning of a long and intimate relation. Opheltas is apparently the first Greek immigrant known to us to attempt to become literate in an environment where syllabic literacy was, evidently, alive. He succeeded in establishing his ownership of the spit but, other than that, we cannot claim that Opheltas also had a political career. Three hundred years later, however, in the seventh century BC, two of his Greek-speaking kin, who bore the names Akestor and Eteandros, used the syllabic script to claim possession of high-value metal objects: a silver plate and a pair of solid gold bracelets, which almost certainly had reached the island as finished products.[46] In addition, Akestor and Eteandros took a

[43] Karageorghis 1970: 38.   [44] Knapp 2008: 310.
[45] Cf. Bass 1997; Bell 2006: 83 table 17; Knapp 2008: 308–12.
[46] Silver plate: Mitford 1971: 373–6; *ICS²* 180a, p. 412; Marcoe 1985: 177–9; Matthäus 1985: 164 no. 429; Karageorghis 2000: 182 no. 299 (dated 725–675). Pair of solid gold bracelets: Mitford 1971: 7–11; *ICS¹* 176, p. 192; O. Masson 1984: 75–6 n. 23; recently, Egetmeyer 2008: 1005 fig. 6.

further step in using the script: they identified themselves as *pa-si-le-wo-se*. They were kings of Paphos.[47]

These two objects bear the earliest known inscriptions in which the Greek term *basileus* is written in the Cypriot Syllabary. The Mycenaean *basileus* – *qa-si-re-u* on the Linear B tablets from the palace archives of Knossos and Pylos – was not in the chain of administrative command during the palatial period,[48] but in the post-palatial horizon of Mycenaean Greece the authority of this local community chieftain was upgraded.[49] The fact that from the beginning the supreme secular rulers in the kingdoms of Cyprus were identified with just this one Mycenaean Greek term, which was inscribed in syllabic Greek until the end of Cypriot kingship around 300 BC,[50] allows us to conjecture that some of these regional leaders may have actually reached Cyprus in the twelfth century BC at the head of immigrant groups.[51] Although the Greek alphabet began to be used cautiously in Cyprus towards the end of the fifth century,[52] the title *basileus* does not appear in alphabetic Greek until the fourth century BC, and not to the exclusion of the syllabic term.[53] In Amathous, where the syllabary expressed the Eteocypriot language,[54] it was the only script used on the coinage of the Amathousian rulers, whose names were mostly Greek.[55] The earliest known coins of Amathous are assigned to the middle of the fifth century.[56]

Despite the fact that the Phoenician alphabet is reported on inscriptions from a number of different locations around Cyprus from the ninth century on, we have to wait until the fifth century before we can see it used as a royal signature.[57] What this amounts

---

[47] Iacovou 2006b: 319.   [48] Palaima 2006: 68–9.   [49] Cf. Carlier 1984.

[50] Cf. Michaelidou-Nikolaou 1976: 17–21, syllabic inscriptions of the last king of Paphos, Nikokles.

[51] Iacovou 2006b: 327–8.   [52] Cf. Collombier 1991: 433–7.

[53] The shorthand inscription B or BA (for *basileus*) is first inscribed on coins of Salamis: cf. Collombier 1991: 435–6 nn. 27–8. The earliest known official document issued digraph-ically, with Greek syllabic and alphabetic letters, also comes from Salamis and preserves the name of Evagoras I (411–374): cf. Yon 1993: 145 fig. 7.

[54] The earliest securely documented use of the syllabary in Amathous is found on a monumental pictorial vase of the seventh century, which was dedicated to the sanctuary on the summit of the acropolis of Amathous: Hermary and Masson 1990.

[55] On Greek-named Amathousian kings, cf. *ICS* 199 (Zotimos), 201 (Lysandros), 202 (Epipalos), 203 (Rhoikos), 207, 211.

[56] On the coinage of Amathous: cf. Amandry 1984: 57–76, 1997: 31–44.

[57] Consult Collombier 1991: 438–9.

to is that in the Cypro-Archaic period the syllabary was the only script employed by state authorities in Cyprus, mostly on coin issues, and these authorities were Greek. For those who advocate that state formation in Iron Age Cyprus was a late event, triggered by an exogenous, most probably Phoenician intervention, this is a frustrating observation. As we shall see below, this may not be the only evidence that works against this claim.

The Neo-Assyrians recognise the Cypriot kings

The earliest external acknowledgement of Cypriot kingdoms is inscribed on a royal stele and dates to 709/707 BC. It was issued by the Assyrian ruler Sargon II (*c.* 721–705) and is in cuneiform.[58] In recognising the Cypriot rulers as kings, Sargon II used the Akkadian term *sharru*. How do we explain, then, that after Sargon II had ordered a stele to be erected in the harbour of Kition, on which he recorded his supremacy over the (seven) statesmen of Cyprus, the local chiefs did not adopt cuneiform as their state script, or the term *sharru* by which they had just been internationally recognised? Nor did they adopt the Phoenician alphabet as their state script, or the widely recognised Semitic term *mlk* to define their constitutional role as kings. Instead, starting with Akestor and Eteandros of Paphos, the Cypriot statesmen employed that same old syllabic writing system, which nobody could possibly read outside Cyprus. Are we to assume that they, all of a sudden, remembered to resuscitate the syllabary that had remained dormant for over 300 years and elevate it to the status of a royal script? Or is it more likely that throughout this time the syllabary had retained a degree of visibility, and that, in the eyes of the Cypriot people, syllabic writing continued to represent an instrument of economic management and authority? The evidence seems to point to a straightforward answer: in seeking to establish their authority the Cypriot monarchs did not consider other options. Decisively and consistently, they employed the syllabary, and not another script. But where were the seats of these Archaic *basileis* located?

---

[58] On the discovery of the stele of Sargon II in Larnaca (ancient Kition), and for a critical commentary of the text (with earlier bibliography), see Yon and Malbran-Labat 1995: 161–8, 169–79; also Yon 2004: 345.

One would be justified in thinking that the answer can be found on an invaluable royal Assyrian prism, inscribed by Esarhaddon (*c.* 680–669) on the occasion of the rebuilding of his palace at Nineveh. Securely dated to 673/672 BC, the prism inscription contains the only known list of Cypriot kingdoms and their heads of state.[59] The transliteration of the geographical names identifies eight out of the ten sites with Cypriot toponyms: Idalion, Chytroi, Soloi, Paphos, Salamis, Kourion, Tamassos and Ledra. On the identification of the remaining two, Qartihadasti and Noure, there is no consensus. Based on the assumption that Tyre had established a colony in Kition, some like to believe that Qartihadasti, meaning 'new city', should be identified with Kition. Others claim, with good reason, that the term applies far better to Amathous, which was a new establishment. Noure, for which Amathous was until recently the only candidate, has now been identified with Marion by Lipinski.[60]

Shifting polities

Although some of the most prominent kingdoms of the island are readily identifiable on the list, we have to bear in mind that the number as well as the geographical locus of these ten polities represent only one early phase in the development of the political geography of the first millennium BC.[61] Suffice it to say that at the end of the fourth century BC, when Ptolemy I decided to abolish the segmented political system of the island, the kingdoms were no more than seven.[62] The reduction of their number – and, consequently, the increase of the territorial size of (some of) the rest – is only half the story. The other half is the transfer of all kingdom capitals to the coast, so that each region's administrative centre was at the same time the main port of trade. This amounts to a lot of major politico-economic changes that took place in the time frame of the seventh to the fourth centuries BC. How and when these events may have taken place eludes us at the moment: too many

[59] Luckenbill 1927: 690; Borger 1956: 60. For the Assyrian texts that refer to Cyprus, see Saporetti 1976: 83–8.
[60] Baurain 1981; Lipinski 2004: 75. see Hermary 1987: 379–81 on Amathous as 'la Carthage de Chypre'; *contra* Yon 2004: 21.
[61] Iacovou 2002.   [62] Based on Diodorus Siculus: Iacovou 2004: 272.

pieces of the puzzle are still missing. Nevertheless, a macro-historic approach will reveal a number of key patterns.

For instance, what can the prism list tell us – in combination with epigraphical and archaeological evidence – about the Early Iron Age phase in the history of the kingdoms? The settlements that can be identified on the prism of Esarhaddon and on local inscriptions as state capitals in the early phase of the Cypro-Archaic period were founded (according to archaeological evidence) no later than the beginning of the Cypro-Geometric period. They had either been urban establishments since the Late Bronze Age (e.g. Paphos) or were new foundations (e.g. Amathous) that had been established in the eleventh to tenth centuries.[63] This would suggest that it did not take long for the power vacuum, created in regions where the primary centre had succumbed after the thirteenth-century BC crisis, to heal.[64]

Thus we begin to see that, like the continuity of the open-air cult and ritual architecture, the continuity of the syllabic script into the Iron Age is a component of the island's Late Cypriot settlement hierarchy system, which survived into the first millennium: Cyprus remained divided into self-sufficient economic territories.[65] Waiting for the Assyrians or the Phoenicians to provide a new state formation model for Archaic Cyprus was superfluous, because the economic basis of the island's own system did not die out at the end of the Bronze Age.

State-level polities did not *reappear* in Cyprus belatedly during the eighth century, as some scholars suggest: they had never altogether *disappeared*.[66] Sargon II did not introduce kingship to Cyprus at the end of the eighth century: he simply acknowledged the existence of Cypriot kings.

Coastal versus inland polities

In spite of these fundamental continuities, half the names of the secular rulers on the prism inscription may be read as Greek, which

---

[63] Cf. Iacovou 1994.   [64] Cf. South 2002: 68; Iacovou 2008a: 112.
[65] Consult 'The continuum: A region-bound economic system' in Iacovou 2008a: 640.
[66] Knapp 1994: 290; Rupp 1987: 147.

was not the linguistic identity of the people that first used the Cypro-Minoan script. The king of Idalion was named Ekishtura/Akestor, of Chytroi Pilâgura/Pylagoras, of Paphos Ituandar/Eteandros, of Kourion Damasu/Damasos, of Ledra Unasagusu/Onasagoras and of Tamassos Admêsu/Admatos (the latter with reservations).[67] In the 400 years that had elapsed since the Greek migration, which we consider a twelfth-century episode, at least 50 per cent of the island's economic territories had passed into the hands of rulers that *were* Greek, or *had become* Greek.

There seems to be more, however, to the geographical distribution of the Greeks' regions of authority: all four inland sites, Idalion, Chytroi, Tamassos and Ledra, appear to have kings with Greek names. We may infer that after their establishment in some of the promising coastal polities that existed in the twelfth century (e.g. Paphos and Enkomi-Salamis) the Greek immigrants targeted next the copper-rich heart of the island. Their success notwithstanding, had it not been for the prism of Esarhaddon, we would not have suspected that Chytroi, Ledra or Tamassos had achieved political autonomy for any length of time in the Cypro-Archaic period. Despite the fact that they must have had between them a major percentage of the island's copper mining areas, these three polities do not seem to have survived as independent economic regions in the Cypro-Classical period. There is to this day not one inscription with the name of a king of Chytroi, Tamassos or Ledra. The literary sources are equally silent as regards their status, although a cryptic, or at least peculiar, reference (in Athenaios's *Deipnosophists*) to a king Pasikypros, who sold his kingdom for 50 talents to Pumayyaton (362–312), the last king of Kition, and retired to Amathous, is rightly believed to refer to Tamassos.[68] Inscriptions confirm that for a period in his reign, but not to the end, Pumayyaton was addressed as king of Kition, Idalion and Tamassos.[69]

What is even more infuriating is that despite the recent discovery of the Lefkosia coin hoard, which dates to about 500–498, and is thus the oldest that has ever been found in Cyprus, numismatic experts are unable to associate with any degree of certainty the

---

[67] Lipinski 1991; O. Masson 1992: 27–9.   [68] Cf. Yon 2004: 83.
[69] Yon 2004: 174 no. 1002.

thirty-six silver *sigloi* to any one of the inland polities: 'For the time being, it may only be suggested that kings of Ledra, Tamassos, Idalion or Soloi, whose names are hardly known, might have been responsible for the issuing of this remarkable coin series.'[70] It is not at all unlikely that either Ledra or Tamassos, or even both, may have lasted long enough into the sixth century to issue coins that have not yet been identified. But there is little at the moment to support their being able to function independently after 500 BC.[71] Idalion, therefore, is to this day the only inland polity known to have maintained its independence as late as the first half of the fifth century, by which time the coastal polities – Salamis, Lapethos, Soloi, Marion, Paphos, Kourion, Amathous and Kition – had won the day.

Political geography and numismatic economy

Numismatic experts underline that the introduction of coinage in Cyprus was a surprisingly early phenomenon in the third quarter of the sixth century.[72] Despite the fact that around this time the Cypriot kings had offered their allegiance to the Persian empire, the style and weight of the silver *sigloi* of Cyprus do not imitate the Persian *sigloi*. In the Phoenician city states numismatic economy was introduced almost a century later than in Cyprus – around the middle of the fifth century. As Elayi remarks, even the earliest coins of Byblos and Tyre are later than the fifth-century issues of Kition and Lapethos, which have Phoenician inscriptions.[73]

As the matter stands, the earliest recorded association of script and language with a numismatic economy in Cyprus is expressed in the Greek syllabary in Salamis, Paphos, Kourion and Idalion before the end of the sixth century.[74] Idalion, the inland kingdom, which comes first on the list of Esarhaddon – a list from which Kition is conspicuously absent – was attacked, defeated and annexed by Kition. A glimpse of the dramatic events of what must have been a long drawnout confrontation between Kition and Idalion is preserved on the

---

[70] Pilides and Destrooper-Georgiades 2008: 327.   [71] Iacovou 2002: 79.
[72] Kraay 1976: 301.   [73] Cf. Elayi 1992: 21–2, 26.
[74] Cf. *ICS*¹ p. 115 (Paphos), p. 250 (Idalion), p. 318 (Salamis); Kagan 1999: 33–43 (Kourion); see Destrooper-Georgiades 1993: 88–9 n. 7. On the Larnaca hoard which contained some 700 coins of the Cypro-Archaic period, see Destrooper-Georgiades 1984.

famous bronze tablet of Idalion. The tablet, which holds the longest surviving syllabic Greek text, was issued by king Stasikypros and the *polis* of Idalion during a moment of great distress (after the Ionian Revolt but early in the fifth century BC).[75]

Since when, then, did Kition become the capital of an independent kingdom? The debate over the geographical identification of the Cypriot *Qardihadasti* is in fact directly related to the political status of Kition before the fifth century, and Antoine Hermary was the first to confront this key issue.[76] *Qardihadasti*, which appears on the prism of Esarhaddon as an alternative name for a Cypriot kingdom, is essentially a *hapax*. Its only other occurrence is on a notorious Phoenician inscription which mentions not a king but a governor of *Qardihadasti* who was a servant of the Sidonian king Hiram. Inscribed on the fragments of two bronze bowls found in an antique shop in Limassol, this *Qardihadasti* has little in terms of provenance to safely associate it either with Kition or any other site in Cyprus.[77]

Kition, despite its being an affluent urban centre during and after the Late Bronze Age crisis, is a polity in which the syllabary is rarely encountered in the first millennium, and *never* in association with royal functions. But to say that the syllabary was never used there for state functions is not all the truth. The point is that to this day there is no evidence in *any* script or language to support the view that Kition had become the seat of a king before the fifth century – in spite of the long-term excavation programmes that have revealed a lot of data on the history of Kition in the first millennium, and in spite of the presence of an alphabetic inscription in the temple courtyard issued by a Phoenician pilgrim around 800 BC.[78] The first coins that can be safely attributed to Kition date

---

[75] Cf. *ICS*¹ 233–244, on the text of the bronze tablet of Idalion; see Stylianou 1989: 403–4, Destrooper-Georgiades 2002: 353 n. 16 on the problem of the chronology of the attack(s) of the Phoenicians of Kition against Idalion.

[76] Hermary 1997.

[77] O. Masson and Sznycer 1972: 77–8; O. Masson 1985: 33–46; Lipinski 2004: 46–7; Yon 2004: 51 no. 34a–b.

[78] Inscription incised after firing on a fragmentary Red Slip bowl imported from the Phoenician coast and found in the sanctuary. The inscription records a pilgrim's sacrifice to a female deity. The pilgrim is a Phoenician individual named Moula and the divinity is identified for the first time by the name of Lady Astarte: cf. Lipinski 2004: 45; Yon 2004: 169 (no. 1100).

from the fifth century, and they were struck by Baalmilk, whose name is inscribed on the coins in the Phoenician alphabet. He is considered the founder of the Phoenician dynasty of Kition.[79] Lapethos is the only other kingdom that has not produced evidence of the Greek syllabary. The fifth and fourth century coins of Lapethos carry Phoenician inscriptions in spite of the fact that some of the kings have Greek names.[80] Had the Phoenicians been responsible for Iron Age state formation in Cyprus, Phoenician and its script should have become the tool for state functions before the fifth century, certainly ahead of the Greek syllabary, and in more than just two Cypriot polities.

Kition and Idalion: an 'either or' situation

I should like to propose an unconventional interpretation as to why Kition fails to provide evidence of having been an independent authority before the fifth century. A Cypriot kingdom is a territorial formula; the potential to carry out an independent economy is based on a geographically consolidated territory that provides access to mineral resources and to a port of export.[81] Idalion and Kition, however, belong to the same geo-economic region: one (Idalion) was nearer, and in control of, the mines, the other (Kition) was its port of export. It seems like an 'either or' situation, which would also explain why there is minimum overlap between the last coin issues of Idalion and the first of Kition (e.g. a stater of Idalion is struck over a stater of Baalmilk I).[82] For Kition to take over as the region's administrative capital and port of trade, it had to undermine the supremacy of the last remaining inland capital that blocked the route to the mining region. And it did just that, in the years after the Ionian Revolt but probably not until the second quarter of the fifth century. Following the abolition of the Greek dynasty of Idalion, Ozibaal, son of Baalmilk I, began to identify himself as king of Kition and Idalion. The takeover is now

---

[79] 'Ce n'est qu'à partir de 479 av. J.-C. au plus tôt que des monnaies sont attribuées avec certitude à Kition' (Destrooper-Georgiades 2002: 352).
[80] Cf. *ICS*[1] 267; Collombier 1991: 438; Destrooper-Georgiades 1993: 89 n. 7.
[81] On the territorial formula, see Iacovou 2007: 348.
[82] Destrooper-Georgiades 2002: 353–5 nn. 16, 22.

confirmed by the fascinating discovery of an economic archive – the first ever to be found in Cyprus – in a building identified as the administrative centre of Idalion in the fourth century BC. The archive rooms were full of accounts inscribed on ostraca or written on gypsum plaques, all in the Phoenician alphabet.[83]

Use of the Greek syllabary and the Greek alphabet by non-Greek authorities

The epigraphic data of the fifth and fourth centuries, the final phase in the history of Cypriot kingship, allow us to make a number of observations regarding what has been described above as the development of a patterned cultural attitude of the ruling dynasties towards the scripts they used.

In Kition, the kingdom's capital centre, the Phoenician dynasty made exclusive use of the Phoenician alphabet until the day its last member, Pumayyaton, was executed (312 BC) by Ptolemy I.[84] In Idalion, where the Greek monarchy had developed a strong bond with syllabic Greek literacy in the Cypro-Archaic period, we observe the following paradox after its annexation by Kition: on the one hand, Phoenician scribes – most probably under the authority of a governor appointed by the Kitian king – kept accounts in the Phoenician alphabet;[85] on the other, a Phoenician *adon* (prince) named Baalrom considered it necessary, despite his being a member of the royal family, to have his sumptuous dedication of a statue to Reshef Mikal (Apollo Amyklos in Greek) inscribed not only in the Phoenician alphabet but also in the Greek syllabary. This precious digraphic and bilingual inscription, which was issued in the reign of the most celebrated Kitian king, Milkyaton (392–362), provided the key for the decipherment of the Greek syllabary. It also confirms that the Phoenicians of Kition acknowledged that the Semitic term *mlk* (king) held the same political value as the term

---

[83] Hadjicosti 1997: 58–9 fig. 24.

[84] Cf. Yon 1992: 249; 'Pour la période qui va du IXe à la fin du IVe s. av. J.-C., on ne s'étonnera pas de trouver presque uniquement des inscriptions en phénicien (environ 150 numéros)' (Yon 2004: 159).

[85] Note that a 'chef des scribes' is mentioned on a Phoenician inscription of the fourth century BC from Kition: Yon 1989: 369.

basileus in syllabic Greek and that the term *adon* (prince) was the equivalent of the Greek *wanax*.[86] In Amathous, digraphic and bilingual inscriptions were also issued by royal authorities in the fourth century. The last king, Androkles, who, like most Amathousian kings, had a Greek name, issued two dedicatory inscriptions in the Eteocypriot syllabary and in the Greek alphabet. Both are inscribed on the bases of statues of his sons, which Androkles dedicated to the sanctuary of the Amathousian goddess on the summit of the acropolis of Amathous. On the one, Androkles invokes the goddess as *Kypria*, and on the other, as *Aphrodite*; he also renders in Greek his otherwise unidentified Eteocypriot title as *basileus*.[87] Furthermore, the study of inscribed vessels collected from the destruction stratum of the last palace of Amathous shows that 'l'utilisation conjointe des syllabaire chypriote et de l'alphabet grec n'était donc pas restreinte aux seuls textes lapidaires publics'. Of all the language groups of Cyprus, the Amathousians, kings and craftsmen, appear to have taken the lead in using the Greek alphabet alongside the syllabary. Before the end of the fourth century they were a 'population alphabétisée'.[88]

There is no evidence that a bilingual text was ever issued by a king whose linguistic identity was Greek. Apparently, Greek-speaking *basileis* did not feel obliged to render their syllabic signature, or their title, in another language. They had no need to advertise their authority in either Phoenician or Eteocypriot, probably because they were already using the island's majority language and the best-known script. This may be the main reason behind their reluctance to let go of the Greek syllabary in the name of the Greek alphabet. In the fourth century, they began to accept that the Greek alphabet could coexist with the Greek syllabary in digraphic inscriptions, but the occasions on which the alphabet

---

[86] Cf. *ICS*[1] 220, p.246; Collombier 1991: 440. On the use of the terms *basileus* and *wanax* and their Semitic equivalents in Cyprus, see Yon 1989: 365–6, 1992: 250; Iacovou 2006: 329.

[87] This is the first time that the goddess is named Aphrodite in Cyprus. Hellmann and Hermary 1980: 259–72; Hermary and Masson 1982: 235–42.

[88] Petit 1991: 489–90.

appears on its own as a royal signature remain rare to the end (e.g. on the coins of Salamis).

Scripts and languages after the abolition of kingship

With these observations in mind we should now turn to the day after the abolition of the kingdoms. For as long as territorial boundaries had existed between Cypriot polities, linguistic groups like the Eteocypriot of Amathous and the Phoenician of Kition were able to promote their language into a state language. What happened, however, to the phenomenon of Cypriot *trilingualism* in the third century BC, after the last kings were ruthlessly extermi-nated in the political agenda of Ptolemy's newly founded empire? None of the three languages, not even Arcado-Cypriot Greek, was accepted as the administrative language of the politically unified island. The Ptolemaic colonial administration made use of the Greek *koine* in the alphabet. Once regional authorities and the boundaries between them were eliminated, syllabic Eteocypriot and alphabetic Phoenician disappeared from the written record of Cyprus in no time. It is as if they had a precise expiry date, which coincided with the termination of their respective dynas-ties.[89] The speed with which alphabetic Greek replaced alphabetic Phoenician in Kition in the third century was, as Yon has shown, phenomenal.[90]

But the Greek dialect of Cyprus and its scribal tool, the syllabary, refused to die.[91] In the last quarter of the third century BC, 'the Cypro-Arcadian dialect and the syllabary, which was exclusively its vehicle, still flourished in the chora of Idalion' – despite the fact that it had remained under Phoenician rule since the fifth century.[92] Syllabic Greek was no longer inscribed by kings or members of their family but by Cypriot craftsmen; not on marble bases or on objects of precious metal but on humble earthen pots deposited in a sacred grotto at Kafizin. In over thirty cases the inscriptions are digraphic (syllabic and alphabetic).[93]

---

[89] 'Les premiers textes phéniciens trouvés à Kition commencent vers 800 et les derniers sont de la fin du IVe s. ou du début du IIIe s. av. J.-C.' (Yon 2004: 154).
[90] Yon 1992: 251, 2004: 160–1.   [91] Palaima 1991.   [92] Mitford 1980: 264.   [93] *Ibid.*

The inscriptions of Kafizin and, more recently, the discovery of syllabic Greek in the Roman archive of Paphos as late as the first century BC, make the Cypriot Syllabary one of the hardiest ancient writing systems that has ever been developed in the Mediterranean. This longevity is associated with the unknown prehistoric language(s) for which it was originally developed and, even more, with the antique Greek dialect that was introduced to Cyprus at the end of the second millennium BC and which became the official language in the majority of the Iron Age kingdoms.

Paphos and the Syllabary

It is no coincidence that the earliest and the latest known uses of the syllabic script by the Greek language are associated with Paphos, whether Old or Nea Paphos. It was there that Greeks learned to use the Cypro-Minoan script (in the tenth century BC); it was there that Greeks were first identified as *basileis* (in the seventh century BC) and later on (in the fourth century) as king-priests: *basileus* of Paphos and *hiereus* of the *wanassa*.[94] In this manner they explicitly stated their dual authority over the sacred and secular landscape of their kingdom; and for all this time their royal signature was inscribed in the Cypriot Syllabary.

[94] Cf. Maier 1989.

7

RETHINKING SOME ALPHABETIC AND SYLLABIC CYPRIOT INSCRIPTIONS

MASSIMO PERNA

In 2006 the private collection of Alessandro Palma di Cesnola preserved by the Palma di Cesnola family in Florence was donated by the last descendant of the family to the Museo di Antichità of Turin. Thanks to the kindness of the museum's Director, M. C. Preacco, I was able to study the inscriptions in Cypriot syllabic writing of the first millennium BC belonging to this collection.[1] A period of study at the Museo di Antichità provided a certain number of developments, some of which were surprising. This period of study is part of the work for the preparation of the first tome of the Corpus of first-millennium Cypriot syllabic inscriptions, volume XV of the *Inscriptiones Graecae*, at the present time in preparation with the collaboration of Markus Egetmeyer and Artemis Karnava, about which I shall give some details at the end of this chapter.

In this chapter I shall take into consideration only two documents from this collection, in a very preliminary way, in order to demonstrate that there is still much work to do, not only on new documents but also on old documents published a long time ago, but sometimes incorrectly. Cypriot inscriptions of the A. Palma di Cesnola collection will be published shortly in collaboration with Maria Giulia Amadasi Guzzo, Markus Egetmeyer and Maria Letizia Lazzarini.[2]

---

[1] I wish to thank M. C. Preacco, who provided me with the photos for the study and publication of these inscriptions, and the Institute for Aegean Prehistory of Philadelphia for its constant support, which has allowed me to spend periods of study in various museums.
[2] Perna 2010: 147–54; Egetmeyer et al. (in press).

Inscribed limestone tablet

The first document of the Cesnola Collection provides the first sensational surprise. It is a rose-coloured limestone tablet, published in 1887 by A. Palma di Cesnola as an inscription in Cypriot syllabic writing.[3] Later, in 1957, the inscription was published by O. Masson in the article 'Les inscriptions étéochypriotes'[4], and then in *Les inscriptions chypriotes syllabiques* (*ICS*),[5] among the inscriptions *'Dubia et Spuria'*, in vertical position, as you can see in Figure 7.1. Masson did not observe the document personally but based his analysis on the observations of S. Sauneron, who had had the opportunity to study the collection in Florence. However, by rotating the tablet you can see that the inscription is not in syllabic Cypriot at all but in alphabetic Greek (see figure 7.2).

The inscription is composed of eight signs placed on two lines and in four columns. It has been incised with the help of a burin, which was used to trace the vertical lines from the top to the

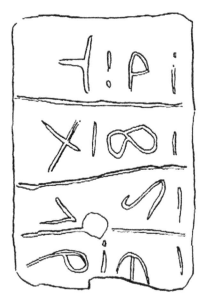

7.1 Drawing of the limestone tablet (after O. Masson in *ICS*[1] p. 390).

---

[3] Palma di Cesnola 1887: 197. [4] O. Masson 1957b: 69. [5] *ICS*[1] 460, p. 390.

7.2 Limestone tablet inscribed in alphabetic Greek. © Museo di Antichità, Turin. Collezione 'Alessandro Palma di Cesnola' (inv. 89361).

bottom. On each sign is incised a horizontal line preceded and then followed by a point incised not very deeply. The tablet is broken on its right side, and the fracture affects, just partially, the fourth sign of the first line; nevertheless, the sign can be identified as ε. There is a large hole in the middle of the third column, but it does not touch any sign, and it does not pass completely through the thickness of the tablet.

The inscription is unusual. It does not give the impression of a true inscription, but rather of a series of isolated and pigeonholed signs, as if it were a writing exercise. It is not impossible that here four of the first five letters of the Greek alphabet follow one another in the right order, but with the absence of the letter γ. The four signs on the second line do not seem to form a word (at least, not a complete word), because it is composed of four consonants, i.e. τ, χ, λ and ρ. The writing has quite a cursive form. Moreover, these letters could be also numbers, as in examples from the second and third centuries AD: in this period, cursive letters were in fact used as numerals.

Inscribed seal

Among the inscriptions of the A. Palma di Cesnola Collection there is also a seal with a Cypriot syllabic inscription of the first millennium (see Figures 7.3–7.4). The only mention of the seal appears in the volume *Salaminia* by Palma di Cesnola.[6] The inscription is

---

[6] Palma di Cesnola 1887: 166.

7.3 Seal with Cypriot syllabic inscription. © Museo di Antichità, Turin. Collezione 'Alessandro Palma di Cesnola' (inv. 89388).

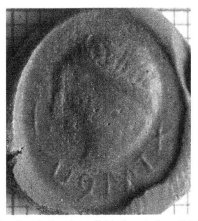

7.4 Impression of seal with Cypriot syllabic inscription. © Museo di Antichità, Turin. Collezione 'Alessandro Palma di Cesnola' (inv. 89388).

completely unpublished, because although it is briefly mentioned by Palma di Cesnola, it is considered by him as a Greek alphabetic inscription. In fact he reports it as 'a head, on the left side, and an inscription, read by Sayce: IAⲰ MIX[AHL'.

The seal is probably made of chalcedony, has an irregular circular shape and is yellow to amber-coloured. The inscription is composed of six signs. Looking at the impression, on which conventionally the inscription is read, and starting from left to right, the first two signs (*lo* and *we*) and also the fourth (*ko*) belong to the category of signs that does not supply useful detail in order to understand the direction of the reading (and the direction of writing), since they are symmetrical, while the last sign, with an uncertain reading, cannot help us. The third sign, however, the *no*, is oriented to the right. This is the only clue for a reading of the inscription from right to left, but, as underlined by Olivier,[7] 'Toutefois, comme il semblerait qu'environ la moitié de la trentaine de sceaux inscrits l'aient été de façon à pouvoir être lus directement sur le sceau alors que l'autre moitié semble avoir été gravée pour être lue sur l'impreinte, toute recherche de « logique » en ce domain semble vaine.'

On the seal the first five signs have a deep incision, while the sixth is quite shallowly incised:

1 The first sign, *lo*, does not have the classic cross shape but an X shape that is more frequent in the inscriptions in the ancient Paphian syllabary of Kourion.
2 The second sign, *we*, has its usual form both in the ancient Paphian syllabary and in the common syllabary.
3 The third sign, *no*, is composed of two identical lines, well known in the ancient Paphian syllabary.
4 The fourth sign has a shape that in the ancient Paphian syllabary corresponds to *ko*; in the common syllabary, the same sign is read *ro*.
5 The fifth sign has to be read with much doubt as *la*. It appears as a square without its upper part. A small horizontal line, less evident, seems to originate from the left side of the square, forming a right angle. The sign appears a little bit different from its basic shape as attested more frequently and has instead a triangle (or an angle) with a lateral appendix. It has to be stressed that the sign is similar to the Cypro-Minoan sign 087 of CM 1 and CM 2, which is the ancestor of the *la* both in the Paphian and in the common syllabary.
6 For the sixth sign the reading is uncertain. The only convincing comparison is with the sign *mi* of the Paphian syllabary.

If the inscription, as we hypothesised, is in the ancient Paphian syllabary, the anthroponym *lo-we-no-ko-la-mi* that results is without doubt a non-Greek name.

---

[7] Garcia Ramón, Olivier and Perna 2006: 26.

***

As stated above, the period of study that I spent in the Museo di Antichità of Turin is part of the work for the preparation of the first tome of the corpus of first-millennium Cypriot syllabic inscriptions. I would like to give an update on the work we have been doing and to outline what has been achieved during these first years. The initial agreement to embark on such an adventure was reached by a core group consisting of Markus Egetmeyer, Artemis Karnava and myself during the Mycenological conference held in Rome in February 2006. Since then, more collaborators have been added, namely Hedvig Enegren-Landenius and Evangelini Markou, who will work from time to time on specific groups of documents.

It is our belief that a corpus of Cypriot syllabic inscriptions, since the documents are dispersed in so many different countries and museums around the world, cannot be the task of one or even two people. The two-member team has worked out successfully in the past with regard to the documents with Cretan Hieroglyphic and Linear A inscriptions from the island of Crete, since these are, in their overwhelming majority, kept in museum stores in just one country, Greece. In the case of material dispersed all over the world, only a joint venture following the same guidelines will be able to succeed where more than one team has already failed in the past.

So far, we have completed the study of inscriptions kept in the museums of Turin, Naples and Policoro in Italy, Thessaloniki, Athens (Museum of the Agora, Numismatic Museum, National Archaeological Museum and Cycladic Art Museum) and Delphi in Greece, as well as the documents kept in the British Museum in London and the Fitzwilliam Museum of Cambridge, in the Louvre in Paris, in the Museum of Mediterranean Antiquities Medelshavmuseet in Stockholm, in the castle of Goluchow in central Poland, and in the Metropolitan Museum of New York and the Philadelphia Museum of Art. Another visit to Cyprus was planned for October 2011. Over three periods of study more than 200 inscriptions have also been photographed in the Cyprus Museum in Nicosia, where we have received great help and collaboration from our Cypriot colleagues and the museum personnel.

Table 7.1 Inscriptiones Graecae XV, *vol. 1. In total, 343 inscriptions from Marion (259), Kourion (43) and Amathous (41).*

Region of MARION-ARSINOE	
London, British Museum	10
Cambridge, Fitzwilliam Museum	3
Oxford, Ashmolean Museum	3
Stockholm, Medelshavmuseet	6
Lund, Univ. Dept. of Classics	2
Bruxelles, Musées Royaux d'Art et d'Histoire	1
Berlin, Staatliche Museen	11
Paris, Louvre	3
Goluchow castle (Poland)	7
Bank of Cyprus – Foundation (Nicosia)	4
Polis District Museum/Marion/Arsinoe	15
Paphos District Museum	9
Nicosia, Cyprus Museum	162
Coins	5
TOTAL	241 (+18 lost) = 259
Region of KOURION	
New York, Metropolitan Museum	15
London, British Museum	3
Nicosia, Cyprus Museum	4
Kourion/Episkopi Museum	8
Limassol, District Museum	3
In situ	7
TOTAL	40 (+ 3 lost) = 43
Region of AMATHOUS	
Paris, Louvre	4
Paris, Cabinet de Medailles	1
Oxford, Ashmolean Museum	2
Amathous/EFA	3
Limassol District Museum	15
Coins	8
Nicosia, Cyprus Museum	4
TOTAL	37 (+ 4 lost) = 41

The corpus now has a home. It will be published, as mentioned above, as part of volume XV of the *Inscriptiones Graecae*, subdivided into three fascicles. The first will contain the inscriptions discovered in the regions of Marion, Kourion and Amathous in Cyprus. These total 343 of the 1,360 documents included in the remarkable database compiled by Jean-Pierre Olivier with the assistance of Frieda

Vandenabeele (see Table 7.1). The precious database was generously handed to us, and naturally it represents an excellent point of departure for our work. If we ever bring our project to completion, this will also be thanks to Olivier and Vandenabeele's foundational work over the past ten years. Of those 1,360 documents some 350 were photographed in 2007 and 2010; thus most of the inscriptions that will appear in the first volume have already been photographed.

In this endeavour we need the help of all colleagues who work in the field of Cypriot archaeology. It would be of extreme importance to let us know of any newly discovered documents or, for that matter, of any documents found when visiting museum stores, where documents, old and new, sometimes re-emerge. For example, during my last study visit to the British Museum, four previously unknown inscriptions were pointed out to me by Thomas Kiely, the curator of the Cyprus Collection.[8] Also in the Museo di Antichità of Turin, five were rediscovered, and in the Museum in Nicosia an Italian colleague, who was working 2 metres away from us, showed us an unpublished inscription consisting of two signs incised on the bottom of a vase from Marion. In short, only with the help of all colleagues working in the field can we overcome this challenge and bring our work to completion.

[8] Kiely and Perna 2011.

BIBLIOGRAPHY

General

Agresti, A. (1990) *Categorical Data Analysis*, New York.

Aksoy, B. (2009) 'Some remarks on the later prehistory of the southwestern Anatolia' in Ç. O. Aygün (ed.) *SOMA 2007. Proceedings of the XI Symposium on Mediterranean Archaeology, Istanbul Technical University, 24–9 April 2007*, British Archaeological Reports International Series 1900, Oxford, 1–7.

Albright, W. F. (1975) 'Syria, the Philistines, and Phoenicia' in I. E. S. Edwards (ed.) *Cambridge Ancient History*, 3rd edn, vol. II, part II: *History of the Middle East and the Aegean region, c.1380–1000 BC*, Cambridge, 507–36.

Amandry, M. (1984) 'Le monnayage d'Amathonte' in P. Aupert and M.-C. Hellmann (eds.) *Amathonte I, Testimonia 1, Etudes chypriotes IV*, Paris, 57–76.

— (1997) 'Le monnayage d'Amathonte revisité', *Cahiers du centre d'études chypriotes* 27, 35–44.

Aström, P. (1966) *Excavations at Kalopsidha and Ayios Iakovos in Cyprus*. Studies in Mediterranean Archaeology 2. Lund.

— (1972a) 'Absolute chronology' in P. Aström (ed.) *The Swedish Cyprus Expedition*, vol. IV, part ID, Lund, 755–62.

— (1972b) 'Some aspects of the Late Cypriote I period', *Report of the Department of Antiquities, Cyprus*, 46–57.

— (1989) *Katydhata: A Bronze Age Site in Cyprus*, Gothenburg.

Atkinson, T. D., Bosanquet, R. C., Edgar, C. C., Evans, A. J., Hogarth, D. G., Mackenzie, D., Smith, C. H. and Welch, F. B. (1904) *Excavations at Phylakopi in Melos*, London.

Baines, J. (2008) 'Writing and its multiple disappearances' in J. Baines, J. Bennet and S. Houston (eds.) *The Disappearance of Writing Systems: Perspectives on Literacy and Communication*, Oxford, 347–62.

Barber, E. J. W. (1991) *Prehistoric Textiles: The Development of Cloth in the Neolithic and Bronze Ages with Special Reference to the Aegean*, Princeton.

Bar-Ilan, M. (1997) 'Papyrus' in E. M. Meyers (ed.) *The Oxford Encyclopedia of Archaeology in the Near East*, vol. IV, Oxford, 246–7.

Bass, G. F. (1967) *Cape Gelidonya: A Bronze Age shipwreck*, Philadelphia.

— (1997) 'Prolegomena to a study of maritime traffic in raw materials to the Aegean during the fourteenth and thirteenth centuries BC' in R. Laffineur and

P. P. Betancourt (eds.) *TEXNH: Craftsmen, Craftswomen and Craftsmanship in the Aegean Bronze Age, Aegaeum 16*, Liège, 153–70.

Bass, G. F., Pulak, C., Collon, D. and Weinstein, J. (1989) 'The Bronze Age shipwreck at Ulu Burun: 1986 campaign', *AJA* 93, 1–29.

Bataille, A. (1954) *Pour une terminologie en paléographie grecque*, Paris.

Baurain, C. (1980) 'Chypre et le monde égéen', *BCH* 104, 565–80.

(1981) 'Un autre nom pour Amathonte de Chypre', *BCH* 105, 361–72.

(1997) *Les Grecs et la Méditerranée orientale: des siècles obscurs à la fin de l'époque archaïque*, Paris.

Beckman, G. (1996a) 'Akkadian documents from Ugarit' in A. B. Knapp (ed.) *Sources for the History of Cyprus*, vol. II: *Near Eastern and Aegean Texts from the Third to the First Millennia BC*, Altamont, NY, 26–8.

(1996b) 'Akkadian documents from Hattusa' in A. B. Knapp (ed.) *Sources for the History of Cyprus*, vol. II: *Near Eastern and Aegean Texts from the Third to the First Millennia BC*, Altamont, NY, 29.

Bell, C. (2006) *The Evolution of Long-Distance Trading Relationships across the LBA/Iron Age Transition on the Northern Levantine Coast*. BAR International Series 1574. Oxford.

Bennet, J. (1994) 'Two new marks on Bronze Age pottery from Kommos', *Kadmos* 33, 153–9.

(1995) 'Marks on Bronze Age pottery from Kommos' in J. W. Shaw and M. C. Shaw (eds.) *Kommos I:2. The Kommos Region and Houses of the Minoan Town. The Minoan Hilltop and Hillside Houses*, Princeton, 313–21.

(2001) 'Agency and bureaucracy: Thoughts on the nature and extent of administration in Bronze Age Pylos' in S. Voutsaki and J. Killen (eds.) *Economy and Politics in the Mycenaean Palace States. Proceedings of a Conference Held on 1–3 July 1999 in the Faculty of Classics, Cambridge*, Cambridge Philological Society Supplement 27, Cambridge, 25–37.

(2008) 'Now you see it; now you don't! The disappearance of the Linear A script on Crete' in J. Baines, J. Bennet, and S. Houston (eds.) *The Disappearance of Writing Systems: Perspectives on Literacy and Communication*, London, 1–29.

Betancourt, P. P. (1998) 'Middle Minoan objects in the Near East' in E. H. Cline and D. Harris-Cline (eds.) *The Aegean and the Orient in the Second Millennium. Proceedings of the 50th Anniversary Symposium, Cincinnati, 18–20 April 1997*, Aegaeum 18, Liège/Austin, 5–12.

(2008) 'Minoan trade' in C. W. Shelmerdine (ed.) *The Cambridge Companion to the Aegean Bronze Age*, Cambridge, 209–29.

Bikaki, A. H. (1984) *Keos IV: Ayia Irini: The Potters' Marks*, Mainz am Rhein.

Blegen, C. W. and Haley J. B. (1928) 'The coming of the Greeks', *AJA* 32, 141–54.

Bombardieri, L. and Jasink, A. M. (2010) 'Decorative repertoire and script signs: A complex "origin" for the writing system in Cyprus?', *Kadmos* 49, 133–59.

Borger, R. (1956) *Die Inschriften Asarhaddons, Königs von Assyrien*, Graz.

Brixhe, C. (1991) 'De la phonologie à l'écriture: quelques aspects de l'adaptation de l'alphabet cananéen au grec' in C. Baurain, C. Bonnet and V. Krings (eds.) *Phoinikeia Grammata. Lire et écrire en Méditerranée. Actes du colloque de Liège, 15–18 novembre 1989*, Liège/Namur, 313–56.

(1994) 'La saga de l'alphabet et la collaboration des cultures' in D. Conso, N. Fick and B. Poulle (eds.) *Mélanges François Kerlouégan*, Besançon/ Paris, 78–94.

(1996) *Phonétique et phonologie du grec ancien I. Quelques grandes questions*, Louvain-la-Neuve.

(2006) 'Nouvelle chronologie anatolienne et date d'élaboration des alphabets grec et phrygien', *CRAI* (2004) 2006, 271–89.

(2007) 'Les alphabets du Fayoum', *Kadmos* 46, 15–38.

Bron, F. (2006) 'Les écritures sud-sémitiques: origine et diffusion' in A. Lemaire (ed.) *Langues et écritures de la Méditerranée. Actes du forum des 9, 10 et 11 mars 2001*, Paris, 183–97.

Buchanan, B. (1966) *Catalogue of Ancient Near Eastern Seals in the Ashmolean Museum 1. Cylinder Seals*, Oxford.

Buchholz, H.-G., and Karageorghis, V. (1973) *Prehistoric Greece and Cyprus: An Archaeological Handbook*, London.

Buchholz, H.-G., Matthäus, H. and Walcher, K. (2002) 'The royal tombs of Tamassos', *Cahiers du centre d'études chypriotes* 32, 219–42.

Cadogan, G. (1979) 'Cyprus and Crete c. 2000–1400 BC' in V. Karageorghis (ed.) *Acts of the International Archaeological Symposium 'The Relations Between Cyprus and Crete, c. 2000–500 BC', Nicosia, 16–22 April 1978*, Nicosia, 63–8.

(1983) 'Early Minoan and Middle Minoan chronology', *AJA* 87, 507–18.

Carlier, P. (1984) *La royauté en Grèce avant Alexandre*, Strasburg.

Casson, S. (1949) 'Cyprus' in M. Cary (ed.) *The Oxford Classical Dictionary*, Oxford, 248–9.

Catling, H. W. (1964) *Cypriot Bronzework in the Mycenaean World*, Oxford.

(1966) *Cyprus in the Neolithic and Bronze Age Periods*. Cambridge Ancient History, vols. I–II, rev. edn, fascicle, Cambridge.

Catling, H. W. and Karageorghis, V. (1960) 'Minoika in Cyprus', *Annual of the British School at Athens* 55, 109–27.

Catling, H. W. and MacGillivray, J. A. (1983) 'An Early Cypriot III vase from the Palace at Knossos', *Annual of the British School at Athens* 78, 1–8.

Cline, E. H. (1994) *Sailing the Wine-Dark Sea: International Trade and the Late Bronze Age Aegean*. BAR International Series 591. Oxford.

Collombier, A.-M. (1991) 'Ecritures et sociétés à Chypre à l'âge du fer' in C. Baurain, C. Bonnet and V. Krings (eds.) *Phoinikeia Grammata. Lire et écrire en Méditerranée, Studia Phoenicia*, Collection d'études classiques 6, Namur/Liège, 425–47.

Courbin, P. (1957) 'Une tombe géométrique d'Argos', *BCH* 81, 322–86.

Courtois, J.-C. (1979) 'Ras Shamra (Ugarit ou Ougarit)' in H. Cazelles and A. Feuillet (eds.) *Dictionnaire de la Bible, Supplément*, vol. IX, Paris, 1124–295.

(1990) 'Yabninu et le Palais Sud d'Ougarit', *Syria* 67, 103–41.

Courtois, J.-C., Lagarce, J. and Lagarce, E. (1986) *Enkomi et le Bronze Récent à Chypre*, Nicosia.

Crewe, L. (2009) 'Feasting with the dead? Tomb 66 at Enkomi' in T. Kiely (ed.) *Ancient Cyprus in the British Museum. Essays in Honour of Veronica Tatton-Brown*, London, 26–48.

Crossland, R. A. (1962) 'The supposed Anatolian origin of the place-name formants in -ss- and -tt-' in C. Battisti and C. A. Mastrelli (eds.) *Atti del VIIº Congresso Internazionale di Scienze Onomastiche I*, Florence, 375–6.

Daniel, J. F. (1941) 'Prolegomena to the Cypro-Minoan script', *AJA* 45, 249–82.

Day, P. M., Oren, E. D., Joyner, L. and Quinn, P. S. (1999) 'Petrographic analysis of the Tel Haror inscribed sherd: Seeking provenance within Crete' in P. P. Betancourt, V. Karageorghis, R. Laffineur and W.-D. Niemeier (eds.) *MELETEMATA: Studies in Aegean Archaeology Presented to Malcolm H. Wiener as He Enters his 65th Year*, Aegaeum 20, Liège/Austin, 191–6.

Deger-Jalkotzy, S. (1994) 'The post-palatial period of Greece: An Aegean prelude to the 11th century BC in Cyprus' in V. Karageorghis (ed.) *Cyprus in the 11th century BC*, Nicosia, 11–30.

Del Freo, M. (2006) 'Les premières écritures du monde égéen' in A. Lemaire (ed.) *Langues et écritures de la Méditerranée. Actes du forum des 9, 10 et 11 mars 2001*, Paris, 159–80.

Destrooper-Georgiades, A. (1984) 'Le trésor de Larnaca (IGCH) 1272 réexaminé', *Report of the Department of Antiquities, Cyprus*, 140–61.

(1993) 'Continuités et ruptures dans le monnayage chypriote à l'époque achéménide', *Transeuphratène* 6, 87–101.

(2002) 'Les royaumes de Kition et Idalion aux Vᵉ et IVᵉ siècles', *Cahiers du centre d'études chypriotes* 32, 351–68.

Dikaios, P. (1956) 'A new inscribed clay tablet from Enkomi', *Antiquity* 30, 40–1.

(1962) 'The Stone Age' in P. Dikaios and J. R. Stewart *The Swedish Cyprus Expedition*, vol. IV, part IA: *The Stone Age and the Early Bronze Age in Cyprus*, Lund, 1–203.

(1963) 'The context of the Enkomi tablets', *Kadmos* 2, 39–52.

(1967) 'More Cypro-Minoan inscriptions from Enkomi' in W. C. Brice (ed.) *Europa: Studien zur Geschichte und Epigraphik der frühen Aegaeis. Festschrift für Ernst Grumach*, Berlin, 80–7.

(1969–71) *Enkomi: Excavations 1948–1958*, vol. I, Mainz am Rhein.

Dikaios, P. (1971) *Enkomi: Excavations 1948–1958*, vol. II, Mainz am Rhein.

Driessen, J. (2000) *The Scribes of the Room of the Chariot Tablets*, Salamanca.

Duhoux Y. (1978) 'Une analyse linguistique du linéaire A' in Y. Duhoux (ed.) *Etudes minoennes I. Le linéaire A*, Louvain, 65–129.

(1986) 'The teaching of orthography in Mycenaean Pylos', *Kadmos* 25, 147–54.

(1998) 'Pre-Hellenic language(s) of Crete', *The Journal of Indo-European Studies* 26, 1–39.

(2003) *Des Minoens en Egypte? 'Keftiou' et 'les îles au milieu du Grand Vert'*, Louvain-la-Neuve.

(2006) 'La lettre Ϻ et quelques problèmes connexes en arcadien archaïque (*IG* V 2.262)', *Kadmos* 45, 20–68.

(2009) 'The Cypro-Minoan Tablet 1885 (Enkomi): an analysis', *Kadmos* 48, 5–38.

(in press) 'The most ancient Cypriot text written in Greek: The Opheltas spit', *Kadmos* 50.

Egetmeyer, M. (1992) *Wörterbuch zu den Inschriften im kyprischen Syllabar*, Berlin/New York.

(2000) 'Les syllabogrammes en *y*- dans le syllabaire chypriote' in L. Dubois and E. Masson (eds.) *Philokypros: Mélanges de philologie et d'antiquités grecques et proche-orientales en mémoire d'Olivier Masson (= Minos*, suppl. 16), Salamanca, 137–52.

(2001) 'Sceau chypriote' in H. Poncy, O. Casabonne, J. de Vos, M. Egetmeyer, R. Lebrun and A. Lemaire 'Sceaux du musée d'Adana. Groupe du "Joueur de lyre" (VIIIe siècle av. J.-C.) – Sceaux en verre et cachets anépigraphes d'époque achéménide – Scaraboïdes inscrits – Scarabées et sceaux égyptisants', *Anatolia Antiqua* 9, 18–20.

(2002) 'Notes ciliciennes', *Anatolia Antiqua* 10, 177–81.

(2008) 'Langues et écritures chypriotes: nouvelles perspectives', *Académie des Inscriptions et Belles-Lettres, Comptes Rendus*, 997–1020.

(2010a) *Le dialecte grec ancien de Chypre*. vol. I, *Grammaire*. vol. II, *Répertoire des inscriptions en syllabaire chypro-grec*, Berlin/New York.

(2010b) 'The recent debate on Eteocypriote people and language' (*Mycenological Colloquium 11, Austin/Texas 2000), Pasiphae* 3 (2009) 2010, 69–90.

(2012) '"Sprechen Sie Golgisch?" Anmerkungen zu einer übersehenen Sprache' in P. Carlier, C. de Lamberterie, M. Egetmeyer, N. Guilleux, F. Rougemont and J. Zurbach (eds.) *Études mycéniennes 2010. Actes du XIIIᵉ colloque international sur les textes égéens, Sèvres, Paris, Nanterre, 20–3 Septembre 2010*, Pisa/Rome, 427–34.

(in press) 'Syllabaires chypriotes' in R. Mugnaioni, M. Savelli and Chr. Touratier (eds.) *Ecritures du monde*, Paris (manuscript from June 2007).

Egetmeyer, M. and Steele, P. M. (2010) 'A new archaic and possibly Cypriot inscription from Cilicia', *Kadmos* 49, 127–32.

Egetmeyer M., Amadasi Guzzo M. G., Lazzarini M. L. and Perna M. (in press) 'Le iscrizioni cipriote sillabiche ed alfabetiche conservate presso la Collezione Alessandro Palma di Cesnola del Museo di Antichità di Torino'.

Elayi, J. (1992) 'Le phénomène monétaire dans les cités phéniciennes à l'époque perse' in T. Hackens and G. Moucharte (eds.) *Numismatique et histoire économique phéniciennes et puniques*, *Studia Phoenicia* 9, Louvain, 21–31.

BIBLIOGRAPHY

Eriksson, K. (1993) *Red Lustrous Wheel-Made Ware*, Studies in Mediterranean Archaeology 103, Jonsered.

Eshet, Y. (2004) 'Micropaleontological examination of the bowl bearing the Linear A inscription' in D. Ussishkin (ed.) *The Renewed Archaeological Excavations at Lachish (1973–1994)*, vol. III, Tel Aviv, 1639.

Evans, A. J. (1895) *Cretan Pictographs and Prae-Phoenician Script: With an Account of a Sepulchral Deposit at Hagios Onuphrios near Phaestos in its Relation to Primitive Cretan and Aegean Culture*, London.

(1900) 'Mycenaean Cyprus as illustrated in the British Museum Excavations', *Journal of the Anthropological Institute of Great Britain and Ireland* 30, 199–220.

(1909) *Scripta Minoa: The Written Documents of Minoan Crete, with Special Reference to the Archives of Knossos*, Oxford.

Feldbacher, R. and Fischer, P. M. (2008) 'Potmarks on ceramic containers from Early Bronze Age Tell Abu al-Kharaz, Jordan valley' in P. M. Fischer *Tell Abu al-Kharaz in the Jordan Valley*, vol. I: *The Early Bronze Age*, Vienna, 391–8.

Ferrara, S. (2005) 'An interdisciplinary approach to the Cypro-Minoan script.' Unpublished PhD thesis, University of London.

(2008a) 'The archaeology of the Cypro-Minoan script: views from Enkomi and Ugarit' in A. Demetriou (ed.) *Proceedings of the IV International Cyprological Congress*, Nicosia.

(2008b) 'Writing without reading: The Cypro-Minoan script between the linear and cuneiform traditions', Mycenaean Seminar, Institute of Classical Studies, London, 10 December 2008. Summary in *Bulletin of the Institute of Classical Studies* 52 (2009).

(2012a) *Cypro-Minoan Inscriptions*, vol. I: *Analysis*, Oxford.

(2012b) *Cypro-Minoan Inscriptions*, vol. II: *Corpus*, Oxford.

Fick, A. (1905) *Vorgriechische Ortsnamen als Quelle für die Vorgeschichte Griechenlands, Göttingen.*

Finkelberg, M. (1998) 'Bronze Age writing: Contacts between east and west' in E. H. Cline and D. Harris-Cline (eds.) *The Aegean and the Orient in the Second Millennium. Proceedings of the 50th Anniversary Symposinm, Cincinnati, 18–20 April 1997, Aegeum 18*, Liège, 265–72.

Finkelberg, M., Uchitel, A. and Ussishkin, D. (2004) 'The Linear A inscription (LACH Za 1)' in D. Ussishkin *The Renewed Archaeological Excavations at Lachish (1973–1994)*, vol. III, Tel Aviv, 1629–38.

Forlanini, M. (1992) 'Das hethitische Reich im 14. bis 13. Jahrhundert v. Chr.', *Tübinger Atlas des vorderen Orients*, vol. III, Tübingen, 6.

Frankel, D. (2000) 'Migration and ethnicity in prehistoric Cyprus: technology as *habitus*', *European Journal of Archaeology* 3, 167–87.

(2005) 'Becoming Bronze Age: Acculturation and enculturation in third-millennium BC Cyprus' in J. Clarke (ed.) *Archaeological Perspectives on the Transmission and Transformation of Culture in the Eastern Mediterranean*, Oxford, 18–24.

BIBLIOGRAPHY

Friedrich, J. (1932) *Kleinasiatische Sprachdenkmäler*, Berlin.
Furumark, A. (1950) 'The settlement at Ialysos and Aegean history, *c.* 1550–1400 BC', *Opuscula Archaeologica* 6, 150–271.
Gallagher, J. V. (2008) 'The arrival of sailing technology in the Aegean', unpublished DPhil thesis, University College, Oxford.
Garbini, G. (2001) 'The question of the alphabet' in S. Moscati (ed.) *The Phoenicians*, London, 101–19.
García Ramón, J. L., Olivier, J.-P. and Perna, M. (2006) 'Un scarabée avec inscription syllabique chypriote du premier millénaire au Musée archéologique de Naples', *Cahiers du centre d'études chypriotes* 36, 23–30.
Gates, M.-H. (2003) 'Kinet Höyük 2002', *ANMED* 1, 17–18.
Gerstenblith, P. (1983) *The Levant at the Beginning of the Middle Bronze Age*, Philadelphia.
Gilboa, A. and Sharon, I. (2003) 'An archaeological contribution to the early Iron Age chronological debate: Alternative chronologies for Phoenicia and their effects on the Levant, Cyprus and Greece', *BASOR* 332 (November), 7–80.
Gjerstad, E., Lindros, J., Sjöqvist, E. and Westholm, A. (1934) *The Swedish Cyprus Expedition, vol. I*, Stockholm.
Godart, L. (1979) 'Le linéaire A et son environnement', *Studi micenei ed egeoanatolici* 20, 27–42.
Godart, L. and Olivier, J.-P. (1978) 'Ecriture hiéroglyphique crétoise' in J.-C. Poursat, L. Godart and J.-P. Olivier (eds.) *Fouilles exécutées à Mallia. Le Quartier Mu I, Etudes crétoises* XXIII, Paris, 31–217.
(1985) *Recueil des inscriptions en linéaire A*, vol. V, Paris.
Godart L. and Sacconi, A. (1979) 'La plus ancienne tablette d'Enkomi et le linéaire A' in V. Karageorghis (ed.) *Acts of the International Archaeological Symposium 'The Relations between Cyprus and Crete, c. 2000–500 BC.'*, Nicosia, 128–33.
Goldman, H. (1956) *Excavations at Gözlü Kule, Tarsus, vol. II, From the Neolithic through the Bronze Age*, Princeton.
Goren, Y., Bunimovitz, S., Finkelstein, I. and Na'aman N. (2003) 'The location of Alashiya: New evidence from petrographic investigation of Alashiyan tablets from El-Amarna and Ugarit', *AJA* 107, 233–55.
Grumach, E. (1969) 'Die kretischen und kyprischen Schriftsysteme' in U. Hausmann (ed.) *Allgemeine Grundlagen der Archäologie*, Munich, 234–88.
Gusmani, R. (1976) 'Zum Alter des jonischen Wandels ā > η' in A. Morpurgo Davies and W. Meid (eds.) *Studies in Greek, Italic and Indo-European Linguistics Offered to Leonard R. Palmer*, Innsbruck, 77–82.
Hachmann, R. (1993) 'Ostraka mit eingeritzten und eingestempelten Zeichen aus Kāmid el-Lōz (Libanon): Probleme der phönikischen Buchstabenschrift und der ugaritischen Keilschrift' in M. J. Mellink, E. Porada and T. Ozgüç (eds.) *Aspects of Art and Iconography: Anatolia and its Neighbors. Studies in Honor of Nimet Ozgüç*, Ankara, 227–72.
Hadjicosti, M. (1997) 'The kingdom of Idalion in the light of new evidence', *BASOR* 308, 49–63.

Hadjisavvas, S. (1996) 'Alassa: a regional centre of Alasia?' in P. Aström and E. Herscher (eds.) *Late Bronze Age Settlement in Cyprus: Function and Relationship*, SIMA-PB 126, Jonsered, 6–8.

(2002) 'The contribution of the LC economy to the emergence of kingship in Cyprus', *Cahiers du centre d'études chypriotes* 32, 53–8.

Hamilton, G. J. (2002) 'W. F. Albright and early alphabetic epigraphy', *Near Eastern Archaeology* 65, 35–42.

Hatzopoulos, M. B. (2007) 'Μακεδονικὰ Παραλειπόμενα: le cheval, le loup et la source' in M. B Hatzopoulos (ed.) *Actes du Ve congrès international de dialectologie grecque (Athens 2006)*, Paris, 227–35.

Hawkins, D. (1986) 'Writing in Anatolia: Imported and indigenous systems', *World Archaeology* 17:3, 383–76.

(2000) *Corpus of Hieroglyphic Luwian Inscriptions*, vol. 1: *Inscriptions of the Iron Age*, Berlin.

Hellmann M.-C. and Hermary, A. (1980) 'Inscriptions d'Amathonte III', *BCH* 104, 259–72.

Herda, A. and Sauter, E. (2010) 'Karerinnen und Karer in Milet: Zu einem spätklassischen Schüsselchen mit karischem Graffito aus Milet', *AA* (2009) 2010, 51–112.

Hermary, A. (1987) 'Amathonte de Chypre et les Phéniciens' in E. Lipiński (ed.) *Phoenicia and the East Mediterranean in the First Millennium BC*, Studia Phoenicia 5, Louvain, 375–88.

(1997) 'Le statut de Kition avant le Ve s. av. J.-C.' in E. Acquaro (ed.) *Studi in onore de Sabbatino Moscati*, Rome, 222–30.

Hermary, A. and Masson, O. (1982) 'Inscriptions d'Amathonte IV', *BCH* 106, 235–42.

(1990) 'Deux vases inscrits du sanctuaire d'Aphrodite à Amathonte', *BCH* 14, 187–206.

Hester, D. H. (1957) 'Pre-Greek place names in Greece and Asia Minor', *Revue Hittite et Asianique* 61, 107–19.

Hiller, S. (1985) 'Die kyprominoischen Schriftsysteme', *AO*, Beiheft 20, 61–102.

Hirschfeld, N. (1990) 'Incised marks on Late Helladic and Late Minoan III pottery.' Unpublished MA dissertation, Texas A&M University.

(1996) 'Cypriots in the Mycenaean Aegean' in E. De Miro, L. Godart and A. Sacconi (eds.) *Atti e Memorie del Secondo Congresso Internazionale di Micenologia*, Rome, 289–97.

(1999) 'Potmarks of the Late Bronze Age eastern Mediterranean.' Unpublished PhD thesis, University of Texas at Austin.

(2000) 'Marked Late Bronze Age pottery from the Kingdom of Ugarit' in M. Yon, V. Karageorghis and N. Hirschfeld (eds.) *Céramiques mycéniennes*, Ras Shamra-Ougarit XIII, Paris, 163–200.

(2002) 'Marks on pots: patterns of use in the archaeological record at Enkomi' in J. S. Smith (ed.) *Script and Seal Use on Cyprus in the Bronze and Iron Ages*, Boston, MA, 49–109.

Hooker, J. T. (1985) 'Minoan and Mycenaean settlement in Cyprus: A note' in T. Papadopoulos (ed.) *Acts of the Second International Congress of Cypriot Studies. I. Ancient Section*, Nicosia, 175–9.

Iacovou, M. (1994) 'The Topography of 11th century BC Cyprus' in V. Karageorghis (ed.) *Cyprus in the 11th century BC*, Nicosia, 149–65.

(2002) 'From ten to naught: Formation, consolidation and abolition of Cyprus' Iron Age polities', *Cahiers du centre d'études chypriotes* 32, 73–87.

(2004) 'Mapping the ancient kingdoms of Cyprus: Cartography and Classical scholarship during the Enlightenment' in G. Tolias and D. Loupis (eds.) *Eastern Mediterranean Cartographies*, Athens, 263–85.

(2005) 'Cyprus at the dawn of the first millennium BC: Cultural homogenization versus the tyranny of ethnic identifications' in J. Clarke (ed.) *Archaeological Perspectives on the Transmission and Transformation of Culture in the Eastern Mediterranean*, Levant Supplementary Series 2, Oxford, 125–34.

(2006a) '"Greeks," "Phoenicians" and "Eteocypriots": Ethnic identities in the Cypriote kingdoms' in J. Chrysostomides and C. Dendrinos (eds.) *Sweet Land . . . : Cyprus through the Ages*, Camberley, 27–59.

(2006b) 'From the Mycenaean QA-SI-RE-U to the Cypriote PA-SI-LE-WO-SE: The *basileus* in the kingdoms of Cyprus' in S. Deger-Jalkotzy and I. Lemos (eds.) *Ancient Greece from the Mycenaean Palaces to the Age of Homer*, Edinburgh, 315–35.

(2007) 'Site size estimates and the diversity factor in Late Cypriote settlement histories', *BASOR* 348, 1–23.

(2008a) 'Cultural and political configurations in Iron Age Cyprus: The sequel to a protohistoric episode', *AJA* 112, 625–58.

(2008b) 'Cyprus from Migration to Hellenisation' in G. R. Tsetskhladje (ed.) *Greek Colonisation: An Account of Greek Colonies and Other Settlements Overseas*, vol. II, Leiden, 219–88.

Isserlin, B. S. J. (1982) 'The earliest alphabetic writing' in J. Boardman (ed.) *Cambridge Ancient History*, 2nd edn, vol. III, part I: *The Prehistory of the Balkans; and the Middle East and the Aegean World, Tenth to Eighth Centuries BC*, Cambridge, 794–818.

Janko, R. (1987) 'Linear A and the direction of the earliest Cypro-Minoan writing', *Minos* 20–2, 311–17.

Jeffery, L. H. (1990) *The Local Scripts of Archaic Greece: A Study of the Origin of the Greek Alphabet and its Development from the Eighth to the Fifth Centuries BC*, rev. edn with corrections and supplement by A.W. Johnston, Oxford.

Jones, R. E. (1986) *Greek and Cypriot Pottery: A Review of Scientific Studies*, Athens.

Kagan, J. (1999) 'The archaic and early Classical coinage of Kourion', *Cahiers du centre d'études chypriotes* 29, 33–43.

Kantor, H. J. (1947) *The Aegean and the Orient in the Second Millennium BC*, Bloomington, IN.

Karageorghis, J. (1958) 'Quelques observations sur l'origine du syllabaire chypro-minoen', *RA*, 1–19.

Karageorghis, J. and Masson, O. (eds.) (1988) *The History of the Greek Language in Cyprus. Proceedings of an International Symposium Sponsored by the Pierides Foundation, Larnaca, Cyprus, 8–13 September, 1986*, Nicosia.

Karageorghis, V. (1963) 'Une tombe de guerrier à Palaepaphos', *BCH* 87, 265–300.

(1970) 'Note on Sigynnae and Obeloi', *BCH* 94, 35–44.

(1972) 'Two built tombs at Patriki, Cyprus', *Report of the Department of Antiquities, Cyprus*, 161–82.

(1973) *Excavations in the Necropolis of Salamis*, vol. III, Nicosia.

(1982) *Cyprus from the Stone Age to the Romans*, London.

(1983) *Palaepaphos-Skales: An Iron Age Cemetery in Cyprus*, Constance.

(1987) 'A Cypro-Archaic I tomb at Palaepaphos-Skales', *Report of the Department of Antiquities, Cyprus*, 85–96.

(2000) *Ancient Art from Cyprus: The Cesnola Collection*, New York.

(2002) Κύπρος, το σταυροδρόμι της Ανατολικής Μεσογείου, Athens.

Karageorghis, V. and Demas, M. (1985) *Excavations at Kition V*, part II, Nicosia.

Karageorghis, V. and Karageorghis, J. (1956) 'Some inscribed Iron-Age vases from Cyprus', *AJA* 60, 351–9.

Karamessini-Oeconomides, M. (1969) 'Iron spits', *Archaiologika Analekta Athinon* 2, 442–5.

Karnava, A. (2002) 'Επτά διευκρινήσεις σχετικά με τις προϊστορικές γραφές του Αιγαίου', Αρχαιολογία και Τέχνες 84, 69–77.

(2005) 'The Tel Haror inscription and Crete: A further link' in R. Laffineur and E. Greco (eds.) *EMPORIA: Aegeans in the Central and Eastern Mediterranean. Proceedings of the 10th International Aegean Conference*, Aegaeum 25, Liège, 837–43.

(2007) 'Tradition and innovation: The scripts in the Old Palatial period', *BICS* 50, 199–200.

Kemp, B. J. and Merrillees, R. S. (1980) *Minoan Pottery in Second Millennium Egypt*, Mainz.

Keswani, P. (2004) *Mortuary Ritual and Society in Bronze Age Cyprus*, London.

Kiely, T. and Perna, M. (2011) 'Four unpublished inscriptions in Cypriot syllabic script in the British Museum', *Kadmos* 49, 93–116.

Knapp, A. B. (1990) 'Production, location and integration in Bronze Age Cyprus', *Current Anthropology* 31, 147–76.

(1994) 'Emergence, development and decline on Bronze Age Cyprus' in C. Mathers and S. Stoddart (eds.) *Development and Decline in the Mediterranean Bronze Age*, Sheffield Archaeological Monographs 8, Sheffield, 271–304.

(1996) *Near Eastern and Aegean Texts from the Third to the First Millennia BC*, vol. II of P. W. Wallace and A. G Orphanides (eds.) *Sources for the History of Cyprus*, Altamont.

(2001) 'Archaeology and ethnicity: A dangerous liaison', *Archaeologia Cypria* 4, 29–46.

(2008) *Prehistoric and Protohistoric Cyprus: Identity, Insularity, and Connectivity*, Oxford.

Knapp, A. B. and Cherry, J. F. (1994) *Provenience Studies and Bronze Age Cyprus: Production, Exchange and Politico-Economic Change*, Madison, WI.

Knapp, A. B. and Marchant, A. (1982) 'Cyprus, Cypro-Minoan and Hurrians', *Report of the Department of Antiquities, Cyprus*, 15–30.

Kozal, E. (2005) 'Unpublished Middle and Late Cypriot pottery from Tarsus-Gözlükule' in A. Ozyar (ed.) *Field Seasons 2001–2003 of the Tarsus-Gözlükule Interdisciplinary Research Project*, Istanbul, 135–44.

Kraay, C. M. (1976) *Archaic and Classical Greek Coins*, London.

Krzyszkowska, O. (2005) *Aegean Seals: An Introduction*, London.

Kull, B. and Röllig, W. (1991) 'Kleinasien. Mittelbronzezeit', *Tübinger Atlas des vorderen Orients*, vol. II, Tübinger, 114.

Lejeune, M. (1972) *Phonétique historique du mycénien et du grec ancien*, Paris.

(1976) 'Pré-mycénien et proto-mycénien', *BSL* 71, 199–206.

Liebhart, R.F. and Brixhe. C. (2009) 'The Recently Discovered Inscriptions from Tumulus MM at Gordion. A Preliminary Report', *Kadmos* 48, 141–56.

Lindblom, M. (2001) *Marks and Makers: Appearance, Distribution and Function of Middle and Late Helladic Manufacturers' Marks on Aeginetan Pottery*, Studies in Mediterranean Archaeology 128, Jonsered.

Lipiński, E. (1991) 'The Cypriot Vassals of Esarhaddon' in M. Cogan. and I. Eph'al (eds.) *Ah, Assyria . . . : Studies in Assyrian History and Ancient Near Eastern Historiography Presented to Hayim Tadmor, Scripta Hierosolymitana 33*, Jerusalem, 58–64.

(2004) *Itineraria Phoenicia, Studia Phoenicia* 18, Louvain.

Lloyd, S. (1967) *Early Highland Peoples of Anatolia*, London.

Loprieno, A. (1997) 'Hieroglyphs' in E. M. Meyers (ed.) *The Oxford Encyclopedia of Archaeology in the Near East*, vol. III, Oxford, 22–6.

Luckenbill, D. D. (1927) *Ancient Records of Assyria and Babylonia*, vol. II, Chicago.

Luraghi, N. (2010) 'The local scripts from nature to culture', *ClAnt* 29, 68–91.

MacGillivray, J. A. (2003) 'A Middle Minoan cup from Sidon', *Archaeology and History in Lebanon* 18, 20–4.

Mackay, A. (1965) 'On the type-fount of the Phaistos disc', *Statistical Methods in Linguistics* 4, 15–25.

Maguire, L. (2009) *The Cypriot Pottery and its Circulation in the Levant*, Tell el-Dab'a 21, Vienna.

Maier, F.-G. (1989) 'Priest kings in Cyprus' in E. Peltenburg (ed.) *Early Society in Cyprus*, Edinburgh, 76–391.

Marcoe, G. E. (1985) *Phoenician Bronze and Silver Bowls from Cyprus and the Mediterranean*, Berkeley.

Masson, E. (1970) 'Remarques sur le petit fragment de tablette chypro-minoenne trouvé à Enkomi en 1952', *SMEA* 11, 96–102.

(1971a) 'Rouleau inscrit chypro-minoen trouvé à Enkomi en 1967' in C. F. A. Schaeffer (ed.) *Alasia I, publié à l'occasion de la XXe campagne de fouilles à Enkomi-Alasia (1969), Missions archéologiques d'Alasia IV*, Paris, 457–77.

(1971b) 'Les boules d'argile inscrites d'Enkomi' in C. F. A. Schaeffer (ed.) *Alasia I, publié à l'occasion de la XXe campagne de fouilles à Enkomi-Alasia (1969), Missions archéologiques d'Alasia IV*, Paris, 479–504.

(1972) 'Les répertoires graphiques chypro-minoens' in M. S. Ruipérez (ed.) *Acta Mycenaea. Proceedings of the Fifth International Colloquium on Mycenaean Studies, Held in Salamanca, 30 March–3 April 1970, Minos* 11–12, Salamanca, 99–111.

(1973) 'A propos du grand cylindre inscrit d'Enkomi', *Kadmos* 12, 76–82.

(1974) *Cyprominoica. Répertoires. Documents de Ras Shamra. Essais d'interprétation*, Studies in Mediterranean Archaeology 31:2, Gothenburg.

(1975) 'Présence éventuelle de la langue hourrite sur les tablettes chypro-minoennes d'Enkomi', *Journal of the Royal Anthropological Society*, 159–63.

(1976) 'A la recherche des vestiges proche-orientaux à Chypre', *Archäologischer Anzeiger*, 139–65.

(1978) 'Deux fragments de tablettes chypro-minoennes trouvés à Enkomi en 1953 et 1969', *Journal des Savants*, 49–86.

(1979a) 'L'apparition de l'écriture à Chypre: témoignage probable des contacts entre l'île de Crète et l'île de Chypre au cours de la première moitié du deuxième millénaire' in V. Karageorghis (ed.) *Acts of the International Archaeological Symposium 'The Relations Between Cyprus and Crete*, c. 2000–500 BC', *Nicosia, 16–22 April 1978*, Nicosia, 134–8.

(1979b) 'Le chypro-minoen I: comparaisons possibles avec les syllabaires du Ier millénaire et l'étéochypriote' in E. Risch and H. Mühlestein (eds.) *Colloquium Mycenaeum*, Neuchâtel, 397–409.

(1983) 'Premiers documents chypro-minoens du site Kalavassos-*Ayios Dhimitrios*', *Report of the Department of Antiquities, Cyprus*, 131–41.

(1985) 'Les syllabaires chypro-minoens: mises au point, compléments et définitions à la lumière des documents nouveaux', *Report of the Department of Antiquities, Cyprus*, 146–54.

Masson, E. and Masson, O. (1983) 'Les objets inscrits de Palaepaphos-Skales' in V. Karageorghis (ed.) *Palaepaphos-Skales: An Iron Age Cemetery in Cyprus*, Constance, 411–15.

Masson, O. (1952) 'Deux petits lingots de cuivre inscrits d'Enkomi' in C. F. A. Schaeffer (ed.) *Alasia I*, Paris.

(1956a) 'Documents chypro-minoens de Ras Shamra' in C. F. A. Schaeffer (ed.) *Ugaritica III*, Paris, 233–50.

(1956b) 'Les écritures chypro-minoennes et les possibilités de déchiffrement' in M. Lejeune (ed.) *Etudes mycéniennes*, Paris, 199–206.

(1957a) 'Cylindres et cachets chypriotes portant des caractères chypro-minoens', *BCH* 81, 6–37.

(1957b) 'Les inscriptions étéochypriotes II. IV: Le texte des inscriptions d'Amathonte', *Syria* 34, 61–80.

(1957c) 'Répertoire des inscriptions chypro-minoennes', *Minos* 5, 9–27.

(1968) 'Ecritures et langues de la Chypre antique', *Archäologischer Anzeiger*, 615–19.

(1971) 'À propos de la découverte d'une inscription chypriote syllabique à Kition en 1970', *Report of the Department of Antiquitics, Cyprus*, 49–52.

(1984) 'Kypriaka, XV–XVII', *BCH* 108, 71–89.

(1985) 'La dédicace à Ba'al du Liban (CIS, I,5) et sa provenance probable de la région de Limassol', *Semitica* 35, 33–46.

(1992) 'Encore les royaumes chypriotes de la liste d'Esarhaddon', *Cahier du centre d'études chypriotes* 18, 27–9.

(1994) 'La plus ancienne inscription chypriote syllabique', *Cahiers du centre d'études chypriotes* 22, 33–6.

Masson, O. and Mitford, T. B. (1986) *Les inscriptions syllabiques de Kouklia-Paphos*, Constance.

Masson, O. and Sznycer, M. (1972) *Recherches sur les Phéniciens à Chypre*, Paris.

Matthäus, H. (2009) 'Max Ohnefalsch-Richter und die Anfänge wissenschaft-licher Archäologie auf der Insel Zypern' in S. Rogge (ed.) *Zypern und der Vortere Orient im 19. Jahrhundert*, Münster, 118–51.

Mellink, M. (1989) 'Anatolian and foreign relations of Tarsus in the Early Bronze Age' in K. Emre, B. Hrouda, M. Mellink and N. Ozgüç (eds.) *Anatolia and the Ancient Near East. Studies in Honor of Tahsin Ozgüç*, Ankara, 319–31.

Merrillees, R. S. (1993) 'The languages of Cyprus', *Cahiers du centre d'études chypriotes* 20, 3–17.

Merrillees, R. S. and Tubb, J. N. (1979) 'A Syro-Cilician jug from Middle Bronze Age Cyprus', *Report of the Department of Antiquities, Cyprus*, 223–9.

Michaelidou-Nicolaou, I. (1976) 'Literary, epigraphic and numismatic evidence on Nikokles, king of Paphos', *Kypriakai Spoudai* 40, 15–28.

(1980) 'Regroupement de deux fragments de tablettes d'Enkomi avec écriture chypro-minoenne', *SMEA* 21, 7–16.

(1993) 'Nouveaux documents pour le syllabaire chypriote', *BCH* 117, 346–47.

Michailidou, A. (2001) 'Script and metrology: Practical processes and cognitive inventions' in A. Michailidou (ed.) *Manufacture and Measurement: Counting, Measuring and Recording Craft Items in Early Aegean Societies*, Athens, 53–82.

Mitford, T. B. (1961) *Studies in the signaries of south-western Cyprus* (= University of London, Bulletin suppl. 10), London.

(1971) *The Inscriptions of Kourion*, Philadelphia.

(1980) *The Nymphaeum of Kafizin: The Inscribed Pottery*, Berlin/New York.

Moran, W. L. (1996) 'Akkadian documents from Amarna' in A. B. Knapp (ed.) *Sources for the History of Cyprus*, vol. II: *Near Eastern and Aegean Texts from the Third to the First Millennia* BC, Altamont, NY, 21–5.

Morpurgo Davies, A. (1992) 'Mycenaean, Arcadian, Cyprian and some questions of method in dialectology' in J.-P. Olivier (ed.) *Mykenaïka*, Ecole française d'Athènes, BCH suppl. 25, 415–32.

Muhly, J. D. (1998) 'Copper, tin, silver and iron: The search for metallic ores as an incentive for foreign expansion' in S. Gitin, A. Mazar and E. Stern (eds.) *Mediterranean Peoples in Transition: Thirteenth to Early Tenth Centuries BCE*, Jerusalem, 314–29.

(2003a) 'Greece and Anatolia in the Early Iron Age: The archaeological evidence and the literary tradition' in W. Dever and S. Gitin (eds.) *Symbiosis, Symbolism, and the Power of the Past*, Indiana, 23–35.

(2003b) 'Trade in metals in the Late Bronze Age and the Iron Age': in N. C. Stampolidis and V. Karageorghis (eds.) *Sea Routes: Interconnections in the Mediterranean 16th–6th c. BC*, Athens, 141–50.

Muhly, P. and Olivier, J.-P. (2008) 'Linear A inscriptions from the Syme sanctuary, Crete', *AE*, 197–223.

Myres, J. L. (1910) 'A tomb of the Early Iron Age from Kition', *Liverpool Annals in Archaeology and Anthropology* 3, 107–17.

Nahm, W. (1981) 'Studien zur kypro-minoischen Schrift', *Kadmos* 20, 52–63.

Nakou, G. (2007) 'Absent presences: Metal vessels in the Aegean at the end of the third millennium' in P. M. Day and R. C. P. Doonan (eds.) *Metallurgy in the Early Bronze Age Aegean*, Oxford, 224–44.

Obrink, U. (1979) *Hala Sultan Tekke: Excavations in Area 22 1971–3 and 1975–8, SIMA* 45, Gothenburg.

Olivier, J.-P. (2008) 'Les syllabaires chypriotes des deuxième et premier millénaires avant notre ère. Etat des questions' in A. Sacconi, M. Del Freo, L. Godart and M. Negri (eds.) *Colloquium Romanum. Atti del XII Colloquio Internazionale di Micenologia, Roma, 20–5 febbraio 2006*, Pisa/Rome, 605–19.

(in press) 'Writing in the Aegean' in J. T. Killen and A. Morpurgo Davies (eds.) *Documents in Mycenaean Greek*³, Cambridge.

Olivier, J.-P. and Godart L. (1995) *Corpus Hieroglyphicarum Inscriptionum Cretae*, Paris.

Oren, E. D., Olivier, J.-P., Goren, Y., Betancourt, P. P., Myer, G. H. and Yellin, J. (1996) 'A Minoan graffito from Tel Haror (Negev, Israel)', *Cretan Studies* 5, 91–117.

Palaima, T. G. (1989a) 'Cypro-Minoan scripts: problems of historical context' in Y. Duhoux, T. G. Palaima and J. Bennet (eds.) *Problems in Decipherment*, Louvain-la-Neuve, 121–87.

(1989b) 'Ideograms and supplementals and regional interaction among Aegean and Cypriot scripts', *Minos* 24, 29–54.

(1991) 'The advent of the Greek alphabet on Cyprus: A competition of scripts' in C. Baurain, C. Bonnet and V. Krings (eds.) *Phoinikeia Grammata. Lire et écrire en Méditerranée*, Studia Phoenicia, *Collection d'études classiques 6*, Namur/Liège, 449–71.

(2005) *The Triple Invention of Writing in Cyprus and Written Sources for Cypriote History*, Nicosia.

(2006) 'Wanaks and related power terms in Mycenaean and later Greek' in S. Deger-Jalkotzy and I. Lemos (eds.) *Ancient Greece from the Mycenaean Palaces to the Age of Homer*, Edinburgh, 53–71.

Palaima, T. G. and Sikkenga, E. (1999) 'Linear A > Linear B' in P. P. Betancourt, V. Karageorgis, R. Laffineur and W.-D. Niemeier (eds.) *MELETEMATA. Studies in Aegean Archaeology Presented to Malcolm H. Wiener as he Enters his 65th Year* (= Aegaeum 20), vol. III, Liège/Austin, 599–608.

Palma di Cesnola A. (1887) *Salaminia: Storia, tesori e antichità di Salamina nell'isola di Cipro*, Turin.

Palmer, L. R. (1958) 'Luvian and Linear A', *Transactions of the Philological Society* 1958, 75–100.

Panayotou-Triantaphyllopoulou, A. (2006) 'Languages and scripts in ancient Cyprus' in J. Chrysostomides and C. Dendrinos (eds.) *'Sweet Land...' Lectures on the History and Culture of Cyprus*, Camberley, 61–75.

Pardee, D. (1997a) 'Alphabet' in E. M. Meyers (ed.) *The Oxford Encyclopedia of Archaeology in the Near East*, vol. I, Oxford, 75–9.

(1997b) 'Ugaritic' in E. M. Meyers (ed.) *The Oxford Encyclopedia of Archaeology in the Near East*, vol. V, Oxford, 262–4.

Payton, R. (1991) 'The Ulu Burun writing-board set', *Anatolian Studies* 41, 99–106.

Peltenburg, E. (2007) 'East Mediterranean interactions in the 3rd millennium BC' in S. Antoniadou and A. Pace (eds.) *Mediterranean Crossroads*, Athens, 141–61.

(2008) 'Nitovikla and Tell el-Burak: Cypriot mid-second-millennium BC forts in a Levantine context', *Report of the Department of Antiquities, Cyprus*, 145–57.

(2012) 'King Kušmešuša and the decentralised political structure of Late Bronze Age Cyprus' in G. Cadogan, M. Iacovou, K. Kopaka and J. Whitley (eds.) *Parallel Lives: Ancient Island Societies in Crete and Cyprus*, British School in Athens Studies 20, London, 345–51.

Perna M. (2010) 'Nuove ricerche nel campo delle scritture sillabiche cipriote del secondo e primo millennio a.C.' in A. M. Jasink and L. Bombardieri (eds.) *Researches in Cypriote History and Archaeology. Proceedings of the Conference Held in Florence, 29–30 April 2009*, Florence, 147–54.

Petit, T. (1991) 'Syllabaire et alphabet au "palais" d'Amathonte de Chypre vers 300 avant notre ère' in Cl. Baurain, C. Bonnet and V. Krings (eds.) *Phoinikeia Grammata, Lire et écrire en Méditerranée. Actes du Colloque de Liège, 15–18 novembre 1989*, Namur, 481–95.

Pickles, S. and Peltenburg, E. (1998) 'Metallurgy, society and the bronze/iron transition in the East Mediterranean and the Near East', *Report of the Department of Antiquities, Cyprus*, 67–100.

Pilides, D. and Destrooper-Georgiades, A. (2008) 'A hoard of silver coins from the plot on the corner of Nikokreontos and Hadjopoullou streets', *Report of the Department of Antiquities, Cyprus*, 307–35.

Poncy, H., Casabonne, O., De Vos, J., Egetmeyer, M., Lebrun, R. and Lemaire, A. (2001) 'Sceaux du musée d'Adana', *Anatolia Antiqua* 9, 9–37.

Pope, M. (2008) 'The decipherment of Linear B' in Y. Duhoux and A. Morpurgo Davies (eds.) *A Companion to Linear B: Mycenaean Greek Texts and their World*, vol. I, Louvain-la-Neuve, 1–23.

Pope, M. and Raison, J. (1978) 'Linear A: Changing perspectives', *Etudes minoennes I. Le linéaire A*, Louvain, 5–64.

Quinn, P. S. and Day, P. M. (2007) 'Calcareous microfossils in Bronze Age Aegean ceramics: Illuminating technology and provenance', *Archaeometry* 49, 775–93.

Rahmstorf, L. (2003) 'The identification of Early Helladic weights and their wider implications' in K. P. Foster and R. Laffineur (eds.) *METRON: Measuring the Aegean Bronze Age. Proceedings of the 9th International Aegean Conference/9ᵉ Rencontre égéenne internationale, New Haven, Yale University, 18–21 April 2002*, Aegaeum 24, Liège/Austin, 293–9.

(2006) 'In search of the earliest balance weights, scales and weighing systems from the East Mediterranean, the Near and Middle East' in M. E. Alberti E. Ascalone and L. Peyronel (eds.) *Weights in Context: Bronze Age Weighing Systems of the Eastern Mediterranean: Chronology, Typology, Material and Archaeological Contexts. Proceedings of the International Colloquium, Rome 22–4 November 2004*, Rome, 9–45.

Rijksmuseum van Oudheden Leiden (1986) *Schatten uit Turkije. Gelegenheid van de tentoonstelling, Leiden, Rijksmuseum van Oudheden, 22 juni–22 september 1986*, Leiden.

Roller, L. E. (1987) *Nonverbal Graffiti, Dipinti, and Stamps*, Philadelphia.

Rupp, D. W. (1987) 'Vive le roi: The emergence of the state in Iron Age Cyprus' in D. W. Rupp (ed.) *Western Cyprus Connections, SIMA* 77, Gothenburg, 147–61.

Rutter, J. B., and Van de Moortel, A. (2006) 'Minoan pottery from the Southern Area' in J. W. Shaw and M. C. Shaw (eds.) *Kommos V: The Monumental Minoan Buildings at Kommos*, Princeton, 261–715.

Said, E. W. (1978) *Orientalism*, New York.

Saporetti, C. (1976) 'Cipro nei testi neoassiri', *Studi Ciprioti e Rapporti di Scavo*, vol. II, Rome, 83–8.

Sayce, A. H. (1905) 'The Hittite inscriptions translated and annotated', *Proceedings of the Society of Biblical Archaeology* 27, 191–254.

Schaeffer, C. F. A. (1930) 'The French excavations at Minet el Beida and Ras Shamra in Syria', *Antiquity* 4, 460–6.

(1939) *Ugaritica: Etudes relatives aux découvertes de Ras Shamra*, Paris.

Schaeffer, C. F. A., Courtois, J.-C. and Lagarce, J. (1968) 'Fouilles d'Enkomi-Alasia dans l'île de Chypre, campagne de 1967: Rapport préliminaire', *Syria* 45, 263–74.

Schniedewind, W. M. (2005) 'Problems in the paleographic dating of inscriptions' in T. E. Levy and T. Higham (eds.) *The Bible and Radiocarbon Dating: Archaeology, Text and Science*, London, 405–12.

Seeher, J. (2002) *Hattusha Guide: A Day in the Hittite Capital*, 2nd rev. edn, Istanbul.

Seton-Williams, M. V. (1954) 'Cilician survey', *Anatolian Studies* 4, 121–74.

Shaw, J. W. (1998) 'Kommos in southern Crete: An Aegean barometer for east–west interconnections' in V. Karageorghis and N. Stampolidis (eds.) *Proceedings of the International Symposium 'Eastern Mediterranean: Cyprus-Dodecanese-Crete, 16th–6th cent. BC', Organized by the University of Crete, Rethymnon and the Anastasios G. Leventis Foundation, Nicosia, Rethymnon 13–16 May 1997*, Athens, 2–17.

Shea, W. H. (1989) 'The inscribed tablets from Tell Deir Alla, part 1', *Andrews University Seminary Studies* 27, 21–37.

Sherratt, E. S. (1994) 'Commerce, iron and ideology: Metallurgical innovation in 12th–11th Century Cyprus' in V. Karageorghis (ed.) *Cyprus in the 11th century BC*, Nicosia, 59–107.

(1998) 'Sea Peoples and the economic structure of the late second millennium in the eastern Mediterranean' in S. Gitin, A. Mazar and E. Stern (eds.) *Mediterranean Peoples in Transition: Thirteenth to Early Tenth Centuries BCE*, Jerusalem, 292–313.

Sherratt, S. (1999) '*E pur si muove*: Pots, markets and values in the second-millennium Mediterranean' in J. P. Crielaard, V. Stissi. and G. J. van Wijngaarden (eds.) *The Complex Past of Pottery Production, Circulation and Consumption of Mycenaean and Greek Pottery (Sixteenth to Early Fifth Centuries BC)*, Amsterdam, 163–211.

(2000) *Catalogue of Cycladic Antiquities in the Ashmolean Museum: The Captive Spirit*, Oxford.

(n.d.) 'Pondering potmarks'. Paper presented to the Aegean Round Table on Writing and Non-Writing in the Aegean Bronze Age, Sheffield, 16–18 January 2009.

Sibella, P. (1996) 'The copper oxhide and bun ingots', *Institute of Nautical Archaeology Quarterly* 23:1, 9–11.

Smith, J. S. (2002a) 'Problems and prospects in the study of script and seal use on Cyprus in the Bronze and Iron Ages' in J. S. Smith (ed.) *Script and Seal Use on Cyprus in the Bronze and Iron Ages*, Boston, MA, 1–47.

Smith, J. S. (ed.) (2002b) *Script and Seal Use on Cyprus in the Bronze and Iron Ages*, Boston, MA.

Smith, J.S. (2003) 'Writing styles in clay of the eastern Mediterranean Late Bronze Age' in N. Stampolides and V. Karageorghis (eds.) Πλόες ... *Sea Routes ...: Interconnections in the Mediterranean 16th–6th c. BC. Proceedings of the International Symposium Held at Rethymnon, Crete, 29 September–2 October 2002*, Athens, 277–304.

Snodgrass, A. M. (1994) 'Gains, losses and survivals: What we infer for the 11th century BC' in V. Karageorghis (ed.) *Cyprus in the 11th century BC*, Nicosia, 167–73.

South, A. K. (1996) 'Kalavassos-*Ayios Dhimitrios* and the organisation of Late Bronze Age Cyprus' in P. Aström and E. Herscher (eds.) *Late Bronze Age Settlement in Cyprus: Function and Relationship, SIMA-PB* 126, Jonsered, 39–49.

(2002) 'Late Bronze Age Settlement Patterns in Southern Cyprus', *Cahiers du centre d'études chypriotes* 32, 59–72.

Steele, P. M. (2011) 'Eteocypriot: Linguistic and archaeological evidence' in A. Georgiou (ed.) *Cyprus: An Island Culture. Society and Social Relations from the Bronze Age to the Venetian Period*, Oxford, 122–32.

(in press) *A Linguistic History of Cyprus: The Non-Greek Languages, and their Relations with Greek, c. 1600–300 BC*, Cambridge.

Stewart, J. R. (1962) 'The Early Cypriote Bronze Age' in P. Dikaios and J. R. Stewart *The Swedish Cyprus Expedition*, vol. IV. part IA: The Stone Age and the Early Bronze Age in Cyprus, Lund, 205–394.

Stubbings, F. H. (1951) *Mycenaean Pottery from the Levant*, Cambridge.

(1975) 'The expansion of the Mycenaean civilization' in I. E. S. Edwards, C. J. Gadd, N. G. L. Hammond and E. Sollberger (eds.) *The Cambridge Ancient History*, 3rd edn, vol. II, part II: History of the Middle East and the Aegean Region c. 1380–1000 BC, Cambridge, 165–87.

Stylianou, P. J. (1989) *The Age of the Kingdoms: A Political History of Cyprus in the Archaic and Classical periods. Meletai kai Ypomnemata* II, Nicosia.

Swiny, S. (1986) 'The Philia culture and its foreign relations' in V. Karageorghis (ed.) *Acts of the International Archaeological Symposium 'Cyprus between the Orient and the Occident', Nicosia, 8–14 September 1985*, Nicosia, 29–44.

Symington, D. (1991) 'Late Bronze Age writing-boards and their uses: Textual evidence from Anatolia and Syria', *Anatolian Studies* 41, 111–23.

Theurillat, T. (2007) 'Early Iron Age graffiti: from the sanctuary of Apollo at Eretria' in A. Mazarakis Ainian (ed.) *Oropos and Euboea in the Early Iron Age, Acts of an International Round Table, University of Thessaly June 18–20, 2004*, Volos, 33–44.

Tsountas, C. and Manatt, J. I. (1897) *The Mycenaean Age: A Study of the Monuments and Culture of Pre-Homeric Greece*, London.

Valerio, M. (2008) 'Linear A *du* and Cypriot *su*: A case of diachronic acrophony?', *Kadmos* 47, 57–66.

Vandenabeele, F. (2007) 'Chronologie', in *HoChyMin*: 33–8.

Vermeule, E. T. and Wolsky, F. Z. (1978) 'New Aegean relations with Cyprus: The Minoan and Mycenaean pottery from Toumba tou Skourou, Morphou', *Proceedings of the American Philosophical Society* 122, 294–317.

(1990) *Toumba tou Skourou: A Bronze Age Potters' Quarter on Morphou Bay in Cyprus*, Boston, MA.

Vokotopoulou, I. and Christidis, A.-P. (1995) 'A Cypriot graffito on a SOS amphora from Mende, Chalcidice', *Kadmos* 34, 5–12.

Voskos, I. and Knapp, A. B. (2008) 'Cyprus at the end of the Late Bronze Age: Crisis and colonization or continuity and hybridization?', *American Journal of Archaeology* 112, 659–84.

Wachter, R. (1989) 'Zur Vorgeschichte des griechischen Alphabets', *Kadmos* 28, 19–78.

(1996) 'Alphabet. II Das griechische Alphabet' in H. Cancik and H. Schneider (eds.) *Der Neue Pauly: Enzyklopädie der Antike*, vol. I, Stuttgart/Weimas 537–47.

Walters, H. B. (1897–8) *Excavations in Cyprus*, London.

Ward, W. A. and Joukowsky, M. S. (eds.) (1992) *The Crisis Years: The 12th century BC*, Dubuque, IA.

Webb, J. M. (1999) *Ritual Architecture, Iconography and Practice in the Late Cypriot Bronze Age. SIMA-PB* 75, Jonsered.

(2002) 'Device, image and coercion: The role of glyptic in the political economy of Late Bronze Age Cyprus' in J. S. Smith (ed.) *Script and Seal Use on Cyprus in the Bronze and Iron Ages*, Boston, MA, 111–54.

Webb, J. M. and Frankel, D. (1999) 'Characterizing the Philia facies: Material culture, chronology, and the origin of the Bronze Age in Cyprus', *American Journal of Archaeology* 103, 3–43.

(2007) 'Identifying population movements by everyday practice: The case of 3rd millennium Cyprus' in S. Antoniadou and A. Pace (eds.) *Mediterranean Crossroads*, Athens, 189–216.

Webb, J. M., Frankel, D., Stos, Z. A. and Gale, N. (2006) 'Early Bronze Age metal trade in the eastern Mediterranean: New compositional and lead isotope evidence from Cyprus', *Oxford Journal of Archaeology* 25, 261–88.

Wengrow, D. (2010) 'The voyages of Europa: Ritual and trade in the Eastern Mediterranean, *c.* 2300–1850 BC' in W. A. Parkinson and M. L. Galaty (eds.) *Archaic State Interaction: The Eastern Mediterranean in the Bronze Age*, Santa Fe, 141–60.

Woolley, C. L. (1938) 'Excavations at Al Mina, Sueidia. I: The archaeological report', *JHS* 58, 1–30.

(1953) *A Forgotten Kingdom, being a Record of the Results Obtained from the Excavation of two Mounds, Atchana and Al Mina, in the Turkish Hatay*, London.

Yakubovich, I. (2008) 'Hittite-Luvian bilingualism and the development of Anatolian hieroglyphs' in N. N. Kazansky (ed.) *Acta Linguistica Petropolitana*, IV-I, Saint Petersburg, 9–36.

Yon, M. (1989) 'Sur l'administration de Kition à l'époque classique' in E. Peltenburg (ed.) *Early Society in Cyprus*, Edinburgh, 363–75.

(1992) 'Le royaume de Kition' in T. Hackens and G. Moucharte (eds.) *Numismatique et histoire économique phéniciennes et puniques, Studia Phoenicia* 9, Louvain, 243–60.

(1993) 'La ville de Salamine' in M. Yon (ed.) *Kinyras: L'archéologie française à Chypre, Travaux de la Maison de l'Orient*, Paris, 139–58.

(1995) 'La maison d'Ourtenou dans le quartier sud d'Ougarit (fouilles 1994)', *Comptes rendus de l'Académie des Inscriptions et Belles-lettres* 139, 427–49.

(1999) 'Chypre et Ougarit à la fin du Bronze Récent', *Report of the Department of Antiquities, Cyprus*, 113–18.

(2004) *Kition dans les textes: Testimonia littéraires et épigraphiques et Corpus des inscriptions. Kition-Bamboula V*, Paris.

(2006) *The City of Ugarit at Tell Ras Shamra*, Winona Lake.

Yon M. and Malbran-Labat, F. (1995) 'La stèle de Sargon II à Chypre' in A. Caubet (ed.) *Khorsabad, le palais de Sargon II, roi d'Assyrie*, Paris, 159–79.

INDEX OF INSCRIPTIONS CITED

Cypro-Minoan (second-millennium syllabaries / Bronze Age Cypriot script) inscriptions

All inscriptions are listed by their *HoChyMin* number.

Cypriot Syllabic (first-millennium syllabaries / nCMCs / Cypro-Greek) inscriptions

Linear A inscriptions

INDEX OF SYLLABIC SIGNS DISCUSSED

Cypro-Minoan (second-millennium syllabaries / Bronze Age Cypriot script)

001 42, 112
002 38
004 16–17, 28, 30, 41, 42, 113
005 30, 34, 42
006 28, 31, 34, 35, 37, 42, 115
007 38, 39
008 30, 34, 35, 42
009 118
011 16–17, 35, 42, 111–13, 120, 123
012 16–17, 42, 113, 123
013 31, 64
015 125
017 31, 114
019 17, 38, 64, 65
021 89
023 30, 34, 35, 36, 42, 64, 89, 116
024 16–17, 42, 64, 111, 113
025 28, 31, 37
027 31, 119
030 31, 64
033 42, 113
035 42
036 112
037 114, 123
038 114
039 64
040 38
041 28, 64
044 17, 30, 34, 42, 64
047 31
050 38
051 38, 40, 116
053 38, 65
055 38, 64

057 64
058 38
059 31
061 28
064 16–17, 28, 36, 42, 113, 119–20, 123
067 117–18
069 30, 65, 113
071 38
073 38, 39
074 38
075 31, 64
078 28
082 31, 64, 117
084 28
087 17, 28, 31, 37, 157
088 117
091 64
094 38
095 42–4
096 42–4
097 31, 119, 120
098 38
099 38, 65
100 38
102 30, 34, 42, 114, 115, 116, 119, 123
103 38
104 30, 117, 123
105 38
107 116, 118
108 120
109 115–16
112 115
& 28, 113

GENERAL INDEX

abjad, Phoenician 16, 70, 81, 92, 95, 126, 133, 141–2, 148, 149
Abydos, Egypt 84
Achaeans 79
Admatus (?), king of Tamassos 145
administrative use of writing 52–3, 74, 103
Aegean document types 14
Aegean relations with Cyprus 79–85, 105
Aegean scripts 49–50, 62, 78, 95, 123, 127
  see also Cretan Hieroglyphic, Cretan scripts, Linear A, Linear B
Aegean thalassocracy 79
Akestor, king of Idalion 145
Akestor, king of Paphos 140, 142
Akkadian 58, 71, 92, 94, 142
Alashiya 94, 140
Alassa, Cyprus 136
alphabets
  Anatolian alphabets 78, 91–2, 107, 127
  Carian alphabet 78, 92, 107
  Greek alphabet 16, 107, 120, 122, 126, 127, 128, 133, 141, 150–1, 154–6
  Lycian alphabet 78, 92
  Lydian alphabet 78
  Musteralphabet 127
  Phrygian alphabet 78, 107, 127
  Roman alphabet 68
  Sidetic alphabet 127
  Ugaritic alphabet 71–2, 94
Amarna letters 69, 94
Amathous, Cyprus 19–20, 141, 143, 144, 145–6, 150–1, 159
Anatolia 78, 88–93, 99–101, 104–5, 122
  relations with Cyprus 88–90, 98–9
Androkles, king of Amathous 150
Aphrodite 150
Apollo Amyklos 149

Arcadian dialect 128, 129
Arcado-Cypriot dialect 16, 26, 133, 138, 151–2
  see also Arcadian dialect, Cypriot dialect
archaeological context
  of CM 2 60–1
  of Cypriot multilingualism 69, 70, 73, 134–5
Archanes script 95
Argos 139
Assyrian administration 142–3, 144
Assyrian trade 92
Astarte 147
Athenaios 145
Ayia Irini, Cyprus 83
Ayia Irini, Kea 86
Ayia Paraskevi, Cyprus 81
Ayia Triada, Crete 80

Baalmilk, king of Kition 148
Baalrom, prince of Kition 149
Babylonian 11
Babylonian temple prostitution 79
bilingual/digraphic inscriptions 129, 149–50
Boğazköy *see* Hattusa
Byblos, Lebanon 84–5, 99, 146
Byblos script 94

Canaanite 81, 95, 105
Carian alphabet 78, 92, 107
Chalcidice, Greece 21
chronology 5–6, 29
  dating by sign forms 120
Chytroi, Cyprus 143, 145
Cilicia 21, 23, 89, 92, 100, 104, 119
clay balls 7, 12, 18, 28, 34, 52, 54, 59–60, 62, 63, 66, 67, 74, 77, 81

Sumerian 92
Syria 24, 38, 93, 94

Tamassos, Cyprus 143, 145–6
Tarsus, Turkey 88, 91
Tel Haror inscription 95
terminology 4–6
 chronological 5–6, 29
 epigraphic, general 27
 of the languages of ancient Cyprus 19–20
 of the scripts of ancient Cyprus 4–5, 19, 47, 82, 105, 108
Toumba tou Skourou, Cyprus 83

Tyre, Lebanon 146

Ugarit 11, 15, 38, 39, 55, 57–8, 69, 71–3, 82, 84–5, 94, 99, 105, 111
Ugaritic 11, 13, 18, 58, 71–3
Ugaritic alphabet 71–2, 94
Uluburun shipwreck 93
'unicity distance' 29, 32, 40

word-dividers 14, 15, 28, 30, 31, 32, 34, 40

Zotimos, king of Amathous 141

CPSIA information can be obtained
at www.ICGtesting.com
Printed in the USA
LVOW03s1725211117
557197LV00018B/317/P